GOODNESS and the Literary Imagination

GOODNESS
and the Literary Imagination

TONI MORRISON

Harvard Divinity School's 95th Ingersoll Lecture

WITH ESSAYS ON MORRISON'S MORAL AND RELIGIOUS VISION
edited by
DAVÍD CARRASCO, STEPHANIE PAULSELL, AND MARA WILLARD

UNIVERSITY OF VIRGINIA PRESS
Charlottesville and London

The Ingersoll Lecture 2012 "Goodness: Altruism and the Literary Imagination"
and "Writing Goodness and Mercy: A 2017 Interview with Toni Morrison"
© 2019 Toni Morrison

University of Virginia Press
Volume introduction and essays © 2019 by the Rector and Visitors of the
University of Virginia
Printed in the United States of America on acid-free paper

First published 2019

ISBN 978-0-8139-4362-6 (cloth)
ISBN 978-0-8139-4363-3 (ebook)

9 8 7 6 5 4 3 2 1

Library of Congress Cataloging-in-Publication Data is available from the
Library of Congress.

Frontispiece: Justin Knight, *Morrison Rethinking.* (Courtesy of Harvard University)

Cover photograph: Justin Knight, *Toni Morrison.* (Courtesy of Harvard University)

CONTENTS

III   Giving Goodness a Voice

ACKNOWLEDGMENTS

The editors of this volume would like to thank Toni Morrison for her unforgettable visit to Harvard Divinity School (HDS) in 2012, for the wisdom and warmth she shared with our community, and for the ongoing challenge of her work. Toni advised us on several aspects of the book including the important role of photographs in illustrating the interpretive work of the authors.

Many people contributed to making her visit a success. Foremost was Charlene Higbe, who worked closely with Divinity School administrators and technicians to ensure our six-week seminar on Morrison's writings was both effective and inclusive of students, faculty, staff, and visitors. Charlene coordinated with Toni Morrison's very able assistant Rene Boatman to make Morrison's visit to Harvard comfortable and engaging. At HDS, Morrison was warmly welcomed by Harvard Divinity School Dean David Hempton and Associate Dean Kevin Madigan. We appreciate the entire staff of the Office of the Dean including Suzanne Rom, Gina Lee, Bob Deveau, Karin Grundler-Whitacre, and Matthew Turner for their support. On campus, Toni Morrison was escorted by HDS student Pedro Morales, whom she dubbed her "charioteer."

Other valued members of our community helped prepare to welcome Toni Morrison to campus. We thank all the participants of our workshops — staff, faculty, students, and community members — and the speakers who helped guide our conversation. We are grateful to Harvey Cox for his rich, insightful presentation on *Jazz* and to Amy Hollywood for her good counsel and for introducing us to Biko Mandela Gray. We also thank Walter Johnson for introducing us to Tiya Miles.

At the University of Virginia Press, we thank Eric Brandt, Helen Chandler, Mark Mones, and the other editors and staff who produced this book under an exceptional timeline. We are grateful to Susan Murray for her careful copyediting. We also want to express our deep appreciation to Donald Cutler, who advocated for this book and made the connection with the team at UVP. We are grateful for the two anonymous readers who read the manuscript closely and offered crucial suggestions for improvement. The writers who have shared their work in these pages have been the best of travel companions, and we are honored by each of their contributions.

Kelly Dalke was a ready partner in preparing the manuscript for submission to the press.

We are grateful for the volume's photography editor, Ryan Christopher Jones, for finding and skillfully editing the images that accompany the essays. Other contributors of art and photography include Fabrizio Leon, Janet McKenzie, Sandra Hansen, Ronny Salerno, Milt Hinton, and The Milton J. Hinton Photographic Collection. Their genius, honesty, and creativity, together with the event photos taken in 2012 by Justin Knight, allowed us to produce a work that participates in the tradition that Toni Morrison began with her 1974 *Black Book*. The diligent work in Mexico of Mauricio Chavez enabled us to get access to the special photo of Toni Morrison, Gabriel García Márquez, and Carlos Fuentes.

Stephanie Paulsell would like to thank her mother, Sally Paulsell, who pressed *Beloved* into her hands in 1987 and said, "You must read this."

Davíd Carrasco thanks his mentor Charles H. Long for helping him think through the design of the seminar and Toni Morrison's visit to Harvard.

Mara Willard would like to thank Davíd Carrasco for trusting her enough to undertake the creation of this volume for a cherished friend and colleague and Stephanie Paulsell for officiating at her wedding, with the final pages of *Jazz* providing a benediction. Thank you also to Philip Weinstein, another important teacher. And to family.

GOODNESS and the Literary Imagination

Introduction

Toni Morrison's Religion

DAVÍD CARRASCO, STEPHANIE PAULSELL,
AND MARA WILLARD

Toni Morrison illuminates the history of this nation as few other writers have. Her richly imagined characters, living in the maw of slavery or its violent wake, are among the most memorable in American literature. Morrison examines black life in America through the lenses of slavery, gender, family, war, art making, home, and many others. Crucial among these is religion. "The history of African Americans that narrows or dismisses religion in both their collective and individual life, in their political and aesthetic activity," Morrison writes, "is more than incomplete — it may be fraudulent."[1] The religious traditions her characters inhabit and the religious practices by which they navigate a brutal world consistently structure her literary work. Rachel Kaadzi Ghansah puts it well when she says that Morrison's attention to the condition of being black in America is more than history — it is a "liturgy" that illuminates the religious dimensions of that history: "This is how we pray, this is how we escape, this is how we hurt, this is how we repent, this is how we move on."[2] The religious vision that animates Morrison's work and the religious quality of her writing have led some readers to regard it, as Gerald "Jay" Williams notes in his essay in this volume, as a kind of "holy writ."

Today Morrison's liturgy is more important than ever. With human dignity daily under attack in this country, racist ideologies finding voice in the halls of power, and racist violence turned upon people in their churches, synagogues, gurdwaras, and mosques, Morrison's liturgy of black life both narrates a history our nation must confront in order to survive and suggests a path forward. Her attention to the ways in which her characters create, in even the most desperate circumstances, rituals with the power to heal what has been broken, holy places in the space at hand, and genuine encounters with both the living and the dead invites us to imagine new forms of community marked by creativity and resistance, goodness and mercy.

These themes marked Toni Morrison's visit to Harvard Divinity School in 2012 to give the Ingersoll Lecture on Immortality. Held annually since 1896, the Ingersoll Lecture has been given by such luminaries as William James, Howard Thurman, Paul Tillich, and James Cone. To prepare for her visit, we invited interested students, staff, faculty, and members of the surrounding community to join us in a working group on the religious dimensions of Morrison's fiction and literary criticism. In the months leading up to her arrival on campus, we met regularly to read and discuss her work. Our discussions focused on the history of slavery and its continuing effects, the creativity Morrison's characters employ to survive, and the intersections between Morrison's literary art and the study of religion. Along the way, we explored Morrison's engagement with African religious traditions, Candomblé shamanism, and Christianity in her novels as well as the hymns, prayers, scripture, and sermons through which many of her characters express their fiercest hopes and griefs. We discussed Morrison's refusal to sentimentalize religion and how the presence of religion — in Morrison's novels as in life — was no guarantee of goodness. And we struggled to find language for the religious quality of Morrison's work itself.

The name of this ongoing seminar was "Have Mercy: The Religious Dimensions of the Work of Toni Morrison." In the eulogy she offered for James Baldwin in the Cathedral of St. John the Divine in 1987, Morrison said that Baldwin challenged her as a writer not only to "stand on moral ground but know that ground must be shored up by mercy."[3] The plea to "have mercy" is found often in Morrison's novels, but we meant to reference in particular a moment in her 2012 novel, *Home.* When Frank Money rescues his sister, Cee, from a doctor who has been using her body for medical experiments and brings her home to Lotus, Georgia, to heal, Miss Ethel Fordham examines her. When she sees what the doctor has done to Cee, she whispers, simply: "have mercy."[4]

The phrase "have mercy" belongs to the southern vernacular that many of Morrison's characters share. But Morrison helps us hear something more in the phrase. Certainly it is a prayer — to God, to the universe — that critiques the ways things are. But it is also a sentence of direct address in the imperative mood. While it exhorts God to have mercy, it also exhorts us, Morrison's readers. In Miss Ethel Fordham's quiet exclamation, we hear how appalled she is at the damage the doctor has inflicted on Cee's body and the evil one person can visit on another. But we also hear the claim

Morrison makes on us, her insistence that we not only witness the sin that has been committed against Cee but that we live differently because of it. Have mercy, reader, Morrison seems to say. For us, that phrase crystallizes the religious dimension of Morrison's work: a call not to a particular doctrine but to a way of receiving and responding to the world. It is a call to cultivate forms of community distinguished by acts of mercy. It calls us to follow the example of Ethel Fordham, who, after she prays for mercy for Cee, tells Cee's brother, Frank Money, "I got work to do."[5]

When Toni Morrison arrived on our campus, she gathered up the theme of mercy and intensified it in a lecture on goodness that asked difficult questions about where goodness comes from and what sustains it in the face of evil's glamour and seductiveness. Before the university community, she weighed her ideas in relation to the works of authors with whom she has been in conversation over a lifetime — Dostoevsky, Faulkner, Melville, and others — and also, wonderfully, in relation to her own work. "Expressions of goodness are never trivial or incidental in my writing," she insisted in her lecture, which appears for the first time in this volume. "In fact, I want them to have life-changing properties." The essays collected here attempt to explore those properties, as Biko Mandela Gray does in his essay about the process of reorientation that even the smallest gestures of goodness in Morrison's work can initiate.

In her lecture, Morrison says what she shows in her novels: that while encountering expressions of goodness in literature can help to change us, those encounters are never wholly sufficient. Morrison refuses any sentimental talk of goodness "winning." Goodness doesn't "win," she insists; it's too late for that. She recalls for us Claudia's words at the end of *The Bluest Eye:* "At least on the edge of my town, among the garbage and sunflowers of my town, it's much, much, much too late."[6] Claudia knows that the violence done to Pecola cannot be undone. Giving goodness a voice, Morrison suggests, will not redeem the suffering of the past or guarantee a future in which goodness overcomes evil, but it can cultivate the knowledge and moral clarity needed to move forward. Giving goodness a voice is a mercy.

One of the ways Morrison gives goodness a voice is to explore the lives of her characters from every angle: materially, spiritually, morally, religiously. In the religious dimensions of her work, we find the intertwined themes of goodness and mercy explored in rich complexity. In *Home,* Morrison points to the "devotion to Jesus and one another"[7] of

Ethel Fordham and the other women who nurse Cee as motivating the goodness they offer to this young woman who had once despised them. They heal Cee not only because they want to have something to say when God asks, "What have you done?"[8] but also because their commitment to their community, to one another, demands it. Miss Ethel offers her compassionate attention to Cee and also passes down the sense of responsibility that led her to offer it: "Somewhere inside you is that free person," she tells Cee. "Locate her and let her do some good in the world."[9] The many ways Morrison's characters engage with religion help them to locate their free selves and shape their choices about the actions they will take in the world in which they find themselves.

Goodness and mercy meet in acts of creation in Morrison's novels. She has said about the catastrophe of American slavery that "the story is that the people who were treated like beasts did not become beastly."[10] They chose creation instead, as Morrison emphasizes in her interview with David Carrasco, creating "jazz, the blues, schools, ideas" and shaping "a culture that this country could not do without." The religious expressions of the descendants of enslaved people are a crucial part of that culture. In her attention to those expressions in her novels, Morrison echoes Howard Thurman's 1947 Ingersoll Lecture at Harvard Divinity School, "The Negro Spiritual Speaks of Life and Death." Thurman wrote that the enslaved people who created the spirituals are among "the great creative religious thinkers of the human race."[11] In Morrison's work, the religious communities of their descendants are places where the practices necessary for survival are cultivated and where the habits of goodness — helping strangers, recognizing evil, taking risks for others — are, as Morrison says in her lecture, "taught and learned."

Morrison's own religious background reflects the diversity of religious experience she explores in her novels. Her mother was a member of the African Methodist Episcopal (AME) Church, a denomination founded before the Civil War by black Christians who, after being repeatedly mistreated by the white Christians with whom they worshiped, founded a church of their own. Morrison herself converted to Roman Catholicism when she was twelve years old. In honor of St. Anthony, she took Anthony as her baptismal name, transformed by her friends into Toni.

Morrison writes about religious practice with power and authenticity. Her descriptions of Baby Suggs preaching in the clearing in *Beloved* and the sermons of Reverend Misner and Reverend Pulliam in *Paradise* are among the most vivid and profound accounts of preaching in American literature. Her accounts of the hospitality of the AME Zion pastor who rescues Frank Money and of Miss Ethel's unsentimental nursing of Cee in *Home* offer detailed descriptions of pastoral care. From *The Bluest Eye* to *God Bless the Child,* Morrison has explored religion as an integral part of human life. Sometimes it is visible in exacting detail, sometimes hovering in nearly invisible traces. But it is always present, part of the richness of the human experience to which Morrison has given her lifelong attention.

Religion is present in Morrison's work not only in explicit descriptions of religious practices. It is also present in the way meaning spills over in her work, the way her characters discover that they are more than they knew themselves to be. Her interest in this kind of excess is reflected in the opening story of her Ingersoll Lecture, the story of the 2006 West Nickel Mines shooting. Morrison is fascinated by how, after their children were slaughtered in their schoolhouse, the Amish community attended the killer's funeral and raised money for the killer's widow and his children. Those acts of grace, Morrison notes, seemed "as shocking as the killings." So was the silence kept by the Amish community — "that refusal to be lionized, televised." Even more than the excessive violence in this story, the excessive goodness arrested her.

The human capacity for acts that exceed what we believe ourselves to be capable of is one of Toni Morrison's great preoccupations. It is the excess of Sethe, who kills her baby rather than see her enslaved in *Beloved;* of Florens's mother in *A Mercy,* who gives her daughter up to the white landowner Jacob Vaark because she believes her daughter won't be raped in his household; of Frank Money's painstaking turn toward redemption in the face of a terrible crime in *Home.* Goodness itself is excessive and disruptive for Morrison. Difficult to account for, goodness turns our attention toward the questions that religions have long posed: What is the significance of our lives? What do we owe one another? What are we capable of? Where is God in the midst of brutality and pain and injustice? How do people endure in the face of it?

The beauty of Morrison's writing and her complex integration of form and content also possess a religious quality. Morrison says in her interview at the end of this volume that, because she grew up with her mother singing both at home and in church, she listens for the music of words as she writes. "I know how I feel when I get something right in my writing," she says, "and now I wonder if my interior feeling is like hers when she sang in very satisfying ways, in ways that lifted her and us up in our little lower-middle-class lives." Listening to her mother sing taught Morrison to hear what was underneath the words, to listen for the meanings that the words couldn't express on their own. She often endows this excess meaning with a holy, sacred quality — giving it room to move in the spaces between her characters, in the moments when language cannot capture all that is happening. "In the beginning there were no words," she writes in *Beloved* as she describes the prayer of women seeking to save Sethe. "In the beginning was the sound, and they all knew what that sound sounded like."[12] In her writing, Morrison makes space for the meaning that exceeds what language can say.

For historian of religion Charles H. Long, a contributor to this volume, religion itself is excessive. Encompassing "how one comes to terms with the ultimate significance of one's place in the world," religion can be expressed through religious practices and particular faiths but not contained by them. For Americans of African descent, Long writes, Christian faith could provide a language for the meaning of religion but "not all the religious meanings of the black communities were encompassed by the Christian forms of religion." The "great critical and creative power" of what he calls the "extra-church orientations" of "folklore, music, style of life" are themselves expressions of the black religious imagination.[13] Morrison explores all of these expressions in her novels, and more.

Morrison expressed her broader approach to religion in a conversation with David Carrasco in the early 1990s, when they taught together at Princeton University. Morrison was in the early stages of writing her novel *Paradise* and invited Carrasco, a historian of religions, to collaborate with her on the research for the book. As they discussed Afro-Brazilian religions and the concept of paradise, Carrasco told her that he was interested in working on a book about the religious dimensions of her writings. He was fascinated with the way she drew upon both African American forms of Christianity and African myths and symbols in her novels. "Yes, you're right that I draw on those sources," she said, "but you left out the other part. Religion for me also includes all the strange stuff." We have tried in this volume to do justice both to the religious traditions and practices Morrison engages in her work and to the strange stuff that suffuses it all.

Morrison's engagement with religion in her work has been influenced, in part, by her many years working on college campuses where she enjoyed interdisciplinary engagement with colleagues from the fields of history, dance, music, religion, and others. She has relished working with students. During her years at Princeton (1989–2007) and especially through the Princeton Atelier she established in 1994, she explored the intersections between art, religion, and education. The Princeton Atelier was a yearly workshop in which writers, artists, and performers representing several genres and methodologies helped students create original works in various artistic fields. "No human being can live without art," Morrison insists. For her, "the idea of art is everywhere: music, theatre, dance, costume, painting your face, dancing in the sand."[14]

As we learned in the "Have Mercy" seminar, the same can be said of the presence and power of religion in her writings. Her novels explore religion's depths and excesses in the numinous of the everyday. Her appreciation of religion's ability to capture the excess moments in human experience is reflected as well in her hopes for the Atelier: that students would experience the "edge" of life, the "bloodletting" involved in making art, and come "to know the ferocity of what I think creative life is."[15]

Through its attention to these edges, Morrison's work has become a kind of sacred text, and reading her a spiritual practice for many. We read Morrison to have our usual ways of seeing the world—and our shared history—disrupted and revitalized. We read her to participate in her liturgy, to make ourselves vulnerable to the transformative quality of her writing, and to catch a glimpse of a goodness that so often eludes us and the world in which we live. Morrison notes in her Ingersoll Lecture that in our culture, "Evil has a blockbuster audience; Goodness lurks backstage." One of James Baldwin's gifts, she notes in her eulogy, was "to recognize and identify evil but never fear or stand in awe of it."[16] As in Baldwin's work, evil is observed, described, and given its due in Morrison's novels, but never glamourized. She does not stand in awe of evil; she reserves her awe for goodness. And so not only does her work challenge us politically, ethically, and spiritually, but it makes us want to risk putting ourselves in the path of the "life-changing properties" that expressions of goodness contain.

Carrasco first witnessed the powerful response of Morrison's readers to her work in 1992, when she came to the University of Colorado as part of the "Novel of the Americas" conference. After her keynote lecture in the largest auditorium on campus, filled to overflowing, a line of students—mostly women—asked her to sign their books. The line stretched across the stage, down the steps, and up to the end of the walkway. One after another they told her that she had led them to think about their lives differently and in more insightful ways. They said things like, "Reading your novel changed my life . . . saved my life . . . helped my sister out of a dark place . . . gave me hope . . . taught me about my soul . . . helped my mother and me reconnect . . . I saw my struggle in your story . . ." In these responses from students from diverse cultural backgrounds, Carrasco heard a widely shared religious response to Morrison's writings.

The essays in this volume are also offered by readers who have felt profoundly addressed by the work of Toni Morrison. The authors of these essays are not Morrison specialists but rather scholars of religion, history, theology, and ethics; four are both scholars and ministers. All of us have had our understanding of American history shaped by Morrison's work. All of us have felt the religious power of her writing, a power that has political resonance as well. We have sought in our contributions to this volume both to illuminate the religious dimensions of Morrison's writing and to seek in it some wisdom for living in these days.

The essays are divided into three sections: "Significant Landscapes and Sacred Places"; "Putting Goodness Onstage"; and "Giving Goodness a Voice." In the first section, historian Walter Johnson explores the history of slavery in the United States as the necessary background to Morrison's work. Critiquing accounts of the rise of capitalism that erase the lived experience of the enslaved people from whose unpaid labor it was born, Johnson argues for histories that make that experience visible, a project to which Morrison has made crucial contributions. His account of the way even the natural world was manipulated by the system of slavery to enhance surveillance of enslaved peoples' every move helps to illuminate the spiritual genius of those who survived and brought forward into the future the rich culture Morrison describes in the interview that closes this volume. As a scholar of the religions of Africa and the African diaspora, Jacob K. Olupona extends the context within which this volume considers Morrison's work by placing her within the tradition of the griots, the West African storytellers who travel from place to place, gathering up stories and songs and traditions and sharing them with their listeners. Olupona explores the presence of African cosmology, spirituality, culture, and worldview in Morrison's work as well as the ways in which she has brought African spirituality into conversation with African American aesthetics both to subvert and reimagine the popular global idea of blackness and black religiosity. Historian and novelist Tiya Miles offers further insight into the context of Morrison's work by exploring the "spirited landscape" inhabited by both enslaved black people and Native Americans. Through examining the hidden sacred places in the landscape of *Beloved,* Miles's essay shows how Morrison draws on Native American religious approaches to spiritual allyship, Afro-diasporic understandings of ghost and spirit forces, and Christian beliefs and practices.

In her lecture, Morrison says that too often goodness "lurks backstage" while evil gets the spotlight. The second section of this volume, "Putting Goodness Onstage," explores how Morrison does just that through her engagement with religious themes, practices, and traditions. Historian of religion Charles H. Long reads *Home* as a bildungsroman of geography and spirit, body and soul. Showing how Morrison draws on rituals of initiation and pilgrimage in the novel, Long illuminates the stages of Frank Money's transformative journey. Scholar of religion and ethics Mara Willard considers how the image of a grieving mother cradling her dead child in *Song of Solomon, Paradise,* and *Sula* reflects the image of the pietà from Morrison's Roman Catholic tradition. Through her several iterations of this image, shaped by experiences of violence and marked by legacies of enslavement and colonialism, Morrison invites the reader, Willard argues, to participate in the affective work of embodied love. Historian of religion Davíd Carrasco turns his attention to Morrison's 2003 novel, *Love,* unspooling the moral vision of love and goodness within its complex plot. He argues that Morrison places a ghostly narrator inside and outside history in order to accompany both the novel's characters and us, Morrison's readers, as a spiritual ally. Theologian Matthew Potts's reading of Morrison's 2008 novel, *A Mercy,* argues that "not all sacrifice is the same, and not all risk is reckless." Drawing on Christian ideas of sacrifice and freedom as well as the literary theory of Jacques Derrida, Potts illuminates the ties between social demonizing and gender dehumanization in the novel and argues that the sacrifice Florens's mother made to save her daughter from sexual violence was not a miracle but rather a mercy offered by one human being to another.

In the final section of the volume, "Giving Goodness a Voice," the authors listen closely for the voice of goodness in the words, whispers, and silences of Morrison's characters. Scholar of religion and literature Stephanie Paulsell examines the sermons preached in *Paradise,* the history that shapes them, and the claim they make on the reader. Jonathan L. Walton, ethicist and Pusey Minister of the Memorial Church at Harvard, explores the theological force of Morrison's analysis of the Africanist presence haunting ideas of freedom in literature by white American writers and returns to *Beloved* to find visions of holiness and goodness that escape the binaries upon which that literature relies. Scholar of American religion Biko Mandela Gray explores the silent and silenced reality of goodness in Morrison's first novel, *The Bluest Eye.* Morrison is teaching us, he argues, to listen for goodness in small gestures and "whispered conversations" that reveal "the reality, humanity, and complexity of goodness" and draw us into an ongoing process of moral reorientation.

The final two essays in this collection hew closely to the homiletic tradition reflected in scenes of preaching in Morrison's novels, a tradition from which Morrison draws deeply. Jay Williams, scholar of religion and pastor of Boston's historic Union Church, turns his attention to Pilate's eulogy for her daughter Hagar in *Song of Solomon,* taking Hagar's words as a text for Williams's own stirring and illuminating sermon on mercy. Josslyn Luckett, scholar of Africana studies and a self-described "unchurched preacher," brings us into the clearing with Baby Suggs in *Beloved* not only to teach us to listen for goodness but to commit to nurturing the "listening and collaborative communities" that can protect the "great big hearts" of the visionaries that the world won't love. These essays, which integrate academic analysis with homiletic exhortation, reveal the power of Morrison's work in fresh ways by experimenting with the religious forms reflected in Morrison's work themselves. Without them, too much would have gone unsaid about the religious work Morrison's writing has done and continues to do.

Toward the end of her Ingersoll Lecture, Toni Morrison offers her own understanding of goodness: "Allowing goodness its own speech does not annihilate evil, but it does allow me to signify my own understanding of goodness: the acquisition of self-knowledge. A satisfactory or good ending for me is when the protagonist learns something vital and morally insightful that she or he did not know at the beginning." Through her art and her criticism, Morrison challenges us to seek goodness in the quest to understand ourselves in relation to others and to the world around us. This quest is at the heart of her novels and animates her religious vision. To read her is to confront the difficulty of giving goodness the upper hand in ourselves and in our world. But it is also to glimpse that goodness in the humanity of her characters, in the "strange stuff" that deepens the mystery of the world around them, and in the possibility toward which her work is always pointing — that the world can change, and so can we.

NOTES

1. Toni Morrison, *The Source of Self-Regard: Selected Essays, Speeches, and Meditations* (New York: Knopf, 2019), 248.

2. Rachel Kaadzi Ghansah, "The Radical Vision of Toni Morrison," *New York Times Magazine,* April 8, 2015.

3. Toni Morrison, *The Source of Self-Regard,* 229.

4. Toni Morrison, *Home* (New York: Knopf, 2012), 116.

5. Morrison, *Home,* 116.

6. Toni Morrison, *The Bluest Eye* (New York: Vintage, 2007), 206.

7. Morrison, *Home,* 128.

8. Morrison, *Home,* 123.

9. Morrison, *Home,* 126.

10. Toni Morrison to Davíd Carrasco, private conversation.

11. Qtd. in Howard Thurman, *With Head and Heart: The Autobiography of Howard Thurman* (San Diego: Harvest, 1979), 218.

12. Toni Morrison, *Beloved* (New York: Plume, 1987), 259.

13. Charles Long, *Significations: Signs, Symbols and Images in the Interpretation of Religion* (Philadelphia: Fortress, 1986), 7.

14. Toni Morrison at https://arts.princeton.edu/academics/atelier/history/.

15. Toni Morrison at https://arts.princeton.edu/academics/atelier/history/.

16. Morrison, *The Source of Self-Regard,* 231.

Goodness

Altruism and the Literary Imagination
Ingersoll Lecture 2012

TONI MORRISON

O n an October morning in 2006, a young man backed his truck into the driveway of a one-room schoolhouse. He walked into the school and after ordering the boy students, the teacher, and a few other adults to leave, he lined up ten girls, ages nine to thirteen, and shot them. The mindless horror of that attack drew intense and sustained press as well as, later on, books and film. Although there had been two other school shootings only a few days earlier, what made this massacre especially notable was the fact that its landscape was an Amish community — notoriously peaceful and therefore the most unlikely venue for such violence.

Before the narrative tracking the slaughter had been exhausted in the press, another rail surfaced, one that was regarded as bizarre and somehow as shocking as the killings. The Amish community forgave the killer, refused to seek justice, demand vengeance, or even to judge him. They visited and comforted the killer's widow and children (who were not Amish), just as they embraced the relatives of the slain. There appeared a number of explanations for their behavior — their historical aversion to killing anyone at all for any reason and their separatist convictions. More to the point, the Amish community had nothing or very little to say to outside inquiry except that it was God's place to judge, not theirs. And, as one cautioned, "Do not think evil of this man." They held no press conferences and submitted to no television interviews. They quietly buried the dead, attended the killer's funeral, then tore down the old schoolhouse and built a new one.

Their silence following the slaughter, along with their deep concern for the killer's family, seemed to me at the time characteristic of genuine "goodness." And I became fascinated with the term and its definition.

Thinkers, of whom none was as uninformed as I was, have long analyzed what constitutes goodness, what good is good, and what its origins

are or may be. The myriad theories I read overwhelmed me, and to re-
duce my confusion I thought I should just research the term "altruism."
I quickly found myself on a frustrating journey into a plethora of definitions and counterdefinitions. I began by thinking of altruism as a more
or less faithful rendition of its Latin root: alter/other; selfless compassion
for the "other." That route was not merely narrow; it led to a swamp of
interpretations, contrary analyses, and doubt. A few of these arguments
posited wildly different explanations: (1) Altruism is not an instinctive act
of selflessness, but a taught and learned one. (2) Altruism might actually
be narcissism, ego enhancement, even a mental disorder made manifest
in a desperate desire to think well of oneself to erase or diminish self-
loathing. (3) Some of the most thought-provoking theories came from
scholarship investigating the DNA, if you will, seeking evidence of an
embedded gene automatically firing to enable the sacrifice of oneself for
the benefit of others; a kind of brother or sister to Darwin's "survival of
the fittest." Examples of confirmation or contradiction of the Darwinian
theory came primarily from the animal and insect kingdoms: squirrels
deliberately attracting predators to themselves to warn the other squirrels;
birds as well and especially ants, bees, bats all in service to the colony, the
collective, the swarm. Such behavior is very common among humans. But
the question being put seemed to be whether such sacrifice for kin and/
or community is innate, built, as it were, into our genes just as individual
conquest of others is held to be a natural, instinctive drive that serves
evolution. Is there a "good" gene along with a "selfish" gene? The further
question for me was the competition between the gene and the mind.

I confess I was unable and ill-equipped to understand much of the
scholarship on altruism, but I did learn something about its weight, its
urgency, and its relevance and irrelevance in contemporary thought.

Keeping those Amish in mind, I wondered why the narrative of that
event, in the press and visual media, quickly ignored the killer and the
slaughtered children and began to focus almost exclusively on the shock
of forgiveness. As I noted earlier, mass shootings at schools were perhaps too ordinary; there had been two such shootings elsewhere during
that same time, but the Amish community's unwillingness to clamor for
justice/vengeance/retribution, or even to judge the killer was the compelling story. The shock was that the parents of the dead children took pains
to comfort the killer's widow, her family and her children, to raise funds
for them, not themselves. Of the victimized community's response to that

almost classic example of evil, in addition to their refusal to fix blame, the most extraordinary element was their silence. It was that silence (that refusal to be lionized, televised) that caused me to think differently about goodness.

Of course thinking about goodness implies, indeed requires, a view of its opposite.

I have never been interested in or impressed by evil itself, but I have been confounded by how attractive it is to others. I am stunned by the attention given to its every whisper and shout. Which is not to deny its existence and ravage, nor to suggest evil does not demand confrontation, but simply to wonder why it is so worshiped, especially in literature. Is it its theatricality, its costume, its blood spray, the emotional satisfaction that comes with its investigation more than with its collapse? (The ultimate detective story, the paradigm murder mystery.) Perhaps it is how it dances, the music it inspires, its clothing, its nakedness, its sexual disguise, its passionate howl, and its danger. The formula in which evil reigns is bad versus good, but the deck is stacked because goodness in contemporary literature seems to be equated with weakness, as pitiful (a girl running frightened and helpless through the woods while the pursuing villain gets more of our attention than her savior).

Evil has a blockbuster audience; Goodness lurks backstage. Evil has vivid speech; Goodness bites its tongue. It is Billy Budd, who can only stutter. It is Coetzee's Michael K, with a harelip that so limits his speech that communication with him is virtually impossible. It is Melville's Bartleby, confining language to repetition. It is Faulkner's Benjy, an idiot.

Rather than rummage through the exquisite and persuasive language of religions — all of which implore believers to rank goodness as the highest and holiest of human achievement, and many of which identify their saints and icons of worship as examples of pure altruism — I decided to focus on the role goodness plays in literature using my own line of work — fiction — as a test.

In nineteenth-century novels, regardless of what acts of wickedness or cruel indifference controlled the plot, the ending was almost always the triumph of goodness. Dickens, Hardy, and Austen all left their readers with a sense of the restoration of order and the triumph of virtue, even Dostoevsky. Note that Svidrigailov in *Crime and Punishment,* exhausted by his own evil and the language that supports it, becomes so bored by his terminal acts of charity, he commits suicide. He cannot live without the language of evil, nor within the silence of good deeds. There are famous exceptions to what could be called a nineteenth-century formula invested in identifying clearly who or what is good. Obviously *Don Quixote* and *Candide* both mock the search for pure goodness. Other exceptions to that formula remain puzzles in literary criticism: Melville's *Billy Budd* and *Moby Dick,* both of which support multiple interpretations regarding the rank, the power, the meaning that goodness is given in these texts. The consequence of Billy Budd's innocence is execution. Is Ishmael good? Is Ahab a template for goodness, fighting evil to the death? Or is he a wounded, vengeful force outfoxed by indifferent nature, which is neither good nor bad? Innocence represented by Pip we know is soon abandoned, swallowed by the sea without a murmur. Generally, however, in nineteenth-century literature, whatever the forces of malice the protagonist is faced with, redemption and the triumph of virtue was his or her reward.

Twentieth-century novelists were unimpressed. The movement away from happy endings or the enshrining of good over evil was rapid and stark after World War I. *That* catastrophe was too wide, too deep to ignore or to distort with a simplistic gesture of goodness. Many early modern novelists, especially Americans, concentrated on the irredeemable consequences of war — the harm it did to its warriors, to society, to human sensibility. In those texts, acts of sheer goodness, if not outright comical, are treated with irony at best or ladled with suspicion and fruitlessness at worst. One thinks of Faulkner's *A Fable* and the mixed reviews it received, most of which were disdainful of the deliberate armistice between soldiers in trench warfare against each other driven by a Christ-like character. The term "hero" seems to be limited these days to the sacrificing dead: first responders running into fiery buildings, mates throwing themselves on grenades to save the lives of others, rescuing the drowning, the wounded. Faulkner's character would never be seen or praised as a hero.

Evil grabs the intellectual platform and its energy; it demands careful examinations of its consequences, its techniques, its motives, its successes however short-lived or temporary. Grief, melancholy, missed chances for personal happiness often seem to be contemporary literature's concept of evil. It hogs the stage. Goodness sits in the audience and watches, assuming it even has a ticket to the show. A most compelling example of this obsession with evil is Umberto Eco's *The Prague Cemetery*. Brilliant as it is, never have I read a more deeply disturbing fascination with the nature of evil; disturbing precisely because it is treated as a thrilling intelligence scornful of the monotony and stupidity of good intentions.

Contemporary literature is not interested in goodness on a large or even limited scale. When it appears, it is with a note of apology in its hand and has trouble speaking its name.

For every *To Kill a Mockingbird,* there is a Flannery O'Connor's *Wise Blood* or "A Good Man Is Hard to Find," striking goodness down with a well-honed literary axe. Many of the late twentieth-, early twenty-first-century heavyweights — Philip Roth, Norman Mailer, Saul Bellow, and so on — are masters at exposing the frailty, the pointlessness, the comedy of goodness.

I thought it would be interesting and possibly informative to examine my thesis on the life and death of goodness in literature using my own work. I wanted to measure and clarify my understanding by employing the definitions of altruism that I gleaned from my tentative research. To this end, I selected three:

1. Goodness taught and learned (a habit of helping strangers and/or taking risks for them).
2. Goodness as a form of narcissism, ego enhancement, or even a mental disorder.
3. Goodness as instinct, as a result of genetics (protecting one's kin or one's group).

An example of the first: A learned habit of goodness can be found in *A Mercy.* There a priest, at some danger to himself, teaches female slaves to read and write. Lest this be understood as simple kindness, here is a sample of punishments levied on white people who risked promoting literacy among black people: "Any white person assembling with slaves or free Negroes for purpose of instructing them to read or write, or associating with them in any unlawful assembly, shall be confined in jail not exceeding six months and fined not exceeding $100.00." That text appeared in Virginia's criminal law as late as 1848.

Examples of the third: Instinctive kin protection is the most common representative of goodness — and I acknowledge several areas of failure to articulate them. From the deliberate sticking of one's leg under a train for insurance money to raise their family in *Sula,* to setting a son on fire to spare him and others the sight of his self-destruction. Note this is the same mother who throws herself out of a window to save a daughter from fire. These acts are far too theatrical and are accompanied by no compelling language. On the other hand, there is the giving away of one's child to a stranger in order to save her from certain molestation in *A Mercy.* The motive that impels Florens's mother, a *minha mae,* seems to me quite close to altruism, and most importantly is given language which I hoped would be a profound, a literal definition of freedom: "To be given dominion over another is a hard thing; to wrest dominion over another is a wrong thing; to give dominion of yourself to another is an evil thing."

Another example of the third: Unquestioning compassion in support of not just kin but of members of the group in general. In *Home,* for example, women provide unsolicited but necessary nursing care to a member of the collective who has spent a lifetime despising them; their "reason" being responsibility to God: "They did not want to meet their Maker and have nothing to say when He asked, 'What have you done?'" A further instance of innate group compassion is the healing of Cee, physically as well as mentally. It was important to me to give that compassion voice: "Look to yourself," Miss Ethel tells her. "You free. Nothing and nobody is obliged to save you but you. . . . You young and a woman and there is serious limitation in both but you a person, too. . . . Somewhere inside you is that free person. . . . Locate her and let her do some good in the world."

An example of the second: Goodness as a form of narcissism, perhaps mental disorder, occurs in the very first novel I wrote. Determined to erase his self-loathing, Soaphead Church, a character in *The Bluest Eye,* chooses to "give," or pretend to give, blue eyes to a little girl in psychotic need of them. In his letter to God, he imagines himself doing the good God refuses. Misunderstood as it is, it has language.

Over time, these last forty years, I have become more and more invested in making sure acts of goodness (however casual or deliberate or misapplied or, like the Amish community, blessed) produce language. But even when not articulated, like the teaching priest in *A Mercy,* such acts must have a strong impact on the novel's structure and on its meaning. Expressions of goodness are never trivial or incidental in my writing. In fact, I want them to have life-changing properties and to illuminate decisively the moral questions embedded in the narrative. It was important to me that none of these expressions be handled as comedy or irony. And they are seldom mute.

Allowing goodness its own speech does not annihilate evil, but it does allow me to signify my own understanding of goodness: the acquisition of self-knowledge. A satisfactory or good ending for me is when the protagonist learns something vital and morally insightful that she or he did not know at the beginning.

Claudia's words, at the end of *The Bluest Eye:* "I even think now that the land of the entire country was hostile to marigolds that year. This soil is bad for certain kinds of flowers. Certain seeds it will not nurture, certain fruit it will not bear, and when the land kills of its own volition, we acquiesce and say the victim had no right to live. We are wrong of course but it doesn't matter. It's too late. At least on the edge of my town, among the garbage and sunflowers of my town, it's much, much, much too late."

Such insight has nothing to do with winning, and everything to do with the acquisition of knowledge. Knowledge on display in the language of moral clarity — of goodness.

I Significant Landscapes and Sacred Places

Haunted by Slavery

WALTER JOHNSON

I
n *Playing in the Dark,* Toni Morrison reveals an American literature haunted by blackness: blackness present but pushed to the margin, invisibly orchestrating the texts. She illuminates the "evasion," the "studied indifference" that characterizes American literature's treatment of African America. Reading a novel by Willa Cather, Morrison observes that we "never arrive at a nodding mention, much less a satisfactory treatment, of the black woman."[1] The evasion is neither consciously intentional nor wholly accidental. It is, rather, the condition of possibility for the undertaking as a whole. The erasure steadies the story as it passes silently over the central dilemma of American literature and history: the incoherence of a history of freedom based upon slavery and imperial violence. Morrison wants readers to perceive how white writers summon an "Africanist presence," how a spectral, misshapen, incomplete humanity haunts the margins of these texts, how black history "lubricates the turn of the plot and becomes the agency of moral choice" in ways that are indispensable to the stories of white protagonists. "The contemplation of this black presence is central to any understanding of our national literature and should not be permitted to hover at the margins of the literary imagination," Morrison writes.[2]

This essay seeks simply to follow Morrison in naming some of the ghosts that have been too often consigned to the margins of our histories of capitalism. I will focus on the first volume of Marx's *Capital,* although the same sort of analysis could be applied to Adam Smith's *The Wealth of Nations,* another text that is haunted by slavery.

THE HAUNTING OF CAPITAL

One does not need to be intimately familiar with the text of *Capital* to have been exposed to the baseline idea that slavery was succeeded by capitalism. That familiar idea does not just emerge out of thin air. It emerges out of the tradition of Western political economy. It emerges out of the writings of Adam Smith and Karl Marx. Like Smith, Marx in *Capital* treated slavery as the past to capitalism's present.[3]

The two great traditions of Western political economy both share this narrative structure: slavery is succeeded by and, in fact, is ended by the emergence of capitalism. Capitalism and slavery are analytically distinct. They are two different things and temporally successive — one comes after the other. That there was slavery, and then, after slavery, perhaps through the Civil War, and through the historical progress of the British Empire, industrial capitalism came to triumph over slavery, to put an end to slavery. This account implies a historical concomitance between the dawn of capitalism and the advent of emancipation.[4]

In the first volume of *Capital*, Marx treats the history of slavery as part of the larger history of primitive accumulations: the accumulation of capital that provided the reservoir of investment capital that produced the Industrial Revolution. Slavery, in this telling, is analogous to the enclosure of the Commons in Great Britain: taking common land, planting hedges on it, privatizing it, thus making it into capital while simultaneously, and just as importantly, turning its peasant inhabitants off the land and rendering them available for conscription as labor.

So slavery in *Capital* is a ghost, a revenant. It existed in the past and remains present in a veiled fashion, within the fabric, within the dead-labor-made-capital, of industrial development. As Jacques Derrida has pointed out, *Capital* is a book full of ghostly metaphors.[5] The haunted-by-slavery ghost, however, is banished from most of the text. It is banished most brazenly in the first section of *Capital*, the brilliant critique of the commodity form in which Marx outlines the distinction between use value and exchange value. He gives his account of the difference between the singular way that one makes a particular thing and the fungibility of a commodity, which is to say its comparability to all other things in the marketplace. And it is where he outlines his theory of the labor theory of value — the idea that all value is produced by human labor, that even capital itself is composed of dead labor. And he does all that through a description of the history of a bolt of linen.

A skeptic might be forgiven for exclaiming: "A bolt of linen? At a time when English mill hands expended the few calories they derived from American sugar in the processing of American cotton? In a historical and material study of an economy in which British banks yearly shipped millions of pounds of credit across the Atlantic Ocean in return for millions of bales of cotton? In the shadow of a Civil War in which the foreign policy of the Confederate States of America had been premised upon the almost-true idea that the disruption of the cotton trade would cause such suffering in the manufacturing sector in Great Britain that the British would support secession? A bolt of linen?!"

By focusing on a bolt of linen made from flax, indigenous to Great Britain, Marx banishes the history of slavery from his history of the commodity form. Cotton was, in fact, the foundation of the existing capitalism of the nineteenth century and of the social conditions he set out to analyze. By banishing slavery from his account, he nationalizes and whitens the history of capitalism. It is in this way that the history of Western thinking about political economy should be seen as haunted, invisibly orchestrated by slavery, by a figure that has been banished to the margins.

Before continuing, I must make visible how the patterns of denial and silencing have reached even into this project of intellectual history. This black-banishing dark magic continues right up to the present day. If you are even marginally interested in middlebrow print culture in the United States, you have seen that there is a lot of ink being spilled about the question of "capitalism and slavery." And the disturbing thing about that is how little of that ink is shaped into the letters that spell out the names of Du Bois but also Eric Williams, Walter Rodney, Frantz Fanon, Cedric Robinson, Angela Davis, and Stuart Hall. Still less, Leslie Howard Owens, Norrece T. Jones Jr., Gerald Horne, and Stephanie Smallwood. A self-proclaimed "new" history of capitalism emerges with only decorative reference made to the work of the black scholars whose work it alternately ignores and misunderstands. An unholy alliance of Ortho-Marxists and neoclassical ideologues stage debates between "economic historians" and "historians of capitalism," who are mutually intelligible to one another because they have reached the conclusion that it is possible to write the history of slavery without being centrally concerned with the experience of enslaved people and the intellectual history of the Black Radical Tradition.[6] Here again, Morrison's analysis of American literature provides insight for American history when she urges us to read in a way that "invites re-reading" that "motions to future readings as well as contemporary ones," to imagine ourselves into scholarship in a spirit that is, at once, reverential, engaged, and hopeful.[7]

One might begin with a rereading of W. E. B. Du Bois's *Black Reconstruction,* which suggests the historical depth of Black Radical engagement with the question of capitalism and slavery, a more nuanced and searching account of that relationship than that found in all but the very best of the recent works and an insistence on naming the ancestors of our contemporary struggles.[8] Until we fully and forthrightly engage the old history of capitalism and slavery, we will only be telling half the story — not even that.

The history of American capitalism, according to Du Bois, was ineluctably racial and imperial. It began, as Morrison remembers in *A Mercy* but so many of the historians of capitalism and slavery, or even "slavery's capitalism," have forgotten, with "the slaughter of opposing tribes and running the[m] off their land."[9] It began with the creation of landed capital out of imperial warfare. The history of the Cotton Kingdom was made on the stolen land of the Choctaw, the Chickasaw, the Creek, the Seminole, and the Cherokee, defended on its boundaries and expanded in the Wars of 1812 and 1846 — land that is so tellingly, so misleadingly, so accidentally confessionally labeled "ghost" acreage in what is perhaps the most influential historical account of the global history of capitalism.[10] Capitalism in the United States was always and already based upon racial expropriation of this sort. In Cedric Robinson's phrase, it was "racial capitalism," memorialized in ghostly place-names like Tuscaloosa and Tombigbee.[11]

That stolen land was planted in cotton, the plant that knit the destinies of Mississippi and Manchester (not to mention Massachusetts) together in an annual cycle — the racial capitalist bedrock of the nineteenth-century Atlantic world. The hybrid strain of cotton that came to dominate the Cotton South was called Petit Gulf cotton, prized for its durability and its "pick-ability." It is on this hybrid strain that the neoclassical defenders of the notion of capitalism as prefreedom have founded their argument. For them, the unprecedented productivity of the Cotton South (and, hence, the unprecedented profitability of the cotton trade as a whole) was wholly explained through technological innovation (not slavery!): the invention of the cotton gin (1792) and the development of the hybrid strains. Missing from their argument, of course, pushed to the margins, are the hands that picked the cotton and cranked the gins, the telling fact that Petit Gulf was prized above all for its "pick-ability." What they meant was that the boll of the Petit Gulf plant opens very widely, and the fibers are attached to it so loosely that they can be pulled out easily. This technobiological hybrid was designed to the specifications of an enslaved person's hand ("a hand's hand," in the parlance of the day). It was itself an artifact of the very history of racial capitalism that the self-declared defenders of economic history seek to forget through their particular form of slanted remembering. It is this moment in the history of imperial-racial-agro-capitalism that frames Morrison's novel *Beloved*—the moment when the Indians were removed, the woodlands stripped of trees, and the Lower South put under the dominion of a single plant that had been tailored to exploit the capacities of a human hand. By emphasizing the "pick-ability" of Petit Gulf cotton, I want to try to reassert the connections of the world of *Beloved* to the world of *Capital* and the haunting of Marx's analysis of political economy with the spirit of the enslaved people.

With that in mind, let us turn to a rereading of Marx's bolt of linen— the one that stands in for the cotton-and-slavery economy that, silenced, haunts the margin of his analysis. The cotton market, hungry for cotton of purest whiteness, provided the actual bedrock of the global economy of the nineteenth century. The merchantability of cotton on the exchange in Liverpool depended upon this cotton not being dusty or stained, a market standard that was defined by grades: high-quality, fair, middling, ordinary, trash. All of those grades had different prices. The very things that made Petit Gulf "pick-able" also made it vulnerable. The fibers, so easily detached in the grip of a human hand, might also blow away in a strong wind. Cotton had to come out of the field extremely quickly after it bloomed to preserve its marketability. When it bloomed, it needed to be picked. If it was not, then that wide-opened boll was likely to get dust blown into it. Or it would rain, and a mud puddle would form at the bottom of the cotton plant. And then new drops of rain would come down and splash muddy water up onto the open cotton plant. When slaveholders drove people to pick more, faster, better, cleaner cotton, they were doing it for a reason. It's not simply that they were all psychotics or sadists, although many of them surely were. It was because they had a market standard in mind. The relationship between the resurgent history of slavery in the American South and industrial development in Great Britain is dialectical. By 1850, 85 percent of the cotton produced in the United States of America was sent to Great Britain. And 85 percent of the cotton that was processed in Great Britain was produced in the US South.

Already, you can understand how the racial capitalism of the nineteenth century would have had catastrophic effects on African American people — effects that might make it seem distasteful, if not just plain old immoral, to try to stage a debate about whether or not university-based historians need to pay more attention to university-based economists on the bloody ground of the Cotton Kingdom. Imperial wars and Indian removal cleared land that was repopulated by enslaved people stolen by the soul traders and sold through the slave trade — as many as a million people between 1820 and 1860, one of the largest forced migrations in human history.[12] So alongside the cotton gin and the seed hybrids, one might count the concentration camp, the human coffle, and the bill of sale as the foundational technological innovations of the nineteenth-century economic boom: the technologies of racial capitalism.

The landscape of the Cotton Kingdom was also a sort of technology, a technology of counterinsurgency. By cutting down all the trees and planting everything in rows of cotton, slaveholders created a landscape that facilitated visual surveillance — the world according to Agent Orange. In nineteenth-century narratives, one of the things that comes through is enslaved people's sense that they were always being watched. Indeed, the image of enslaved people working in cotton fields, working their way along rows that allowed their work rate to be compared to the work rate of others, is a sort of visual metonym for the whole of American slavery. To sustain the point, one need not look a whole lot further than the word "overseer." It's not an accidental word. Nor is it accidental that slaveholders referred to those people whom they thought were shirking their work as "providing eye service," as looking like they were serving without really doing so. Out of European literary genres of the "gothic" and the felt power of the "diabolic," Morrison presents her readers with the terrifying excesses of violence imposed upon enslaved people.

The landscape of the Cotton Kingdom was created by and for men like Morrison's schoolteacher, looking to their family Bibles to justify their work in the work, underlining the passages from Genesis on dominion and Romans on the divine justice of law and order, exerting their mastery over all the known world by stripping forests, planting cotton, and driving slaves.

But at the edge of their dominion lay different landscapes. A residual landscape, forests that had not yet been clear-cut, and swamps that had not yet been drained, yes, but, even more to the point, an emergent post-capitalist landscape — wasted fields returning to scrubby forest. After a planter planted cotton so many times that he had exhausted the soil, he would move on. Their mono-cropping wastefulness was one of the rea-

FIG. 1. *King Cotton and His Slaves,* Greenwood, Mississippi, ca. 1920. (Library of Congress, Prints and Photographs Collection)

sons that the southern slaveholding regime is so expansive, so imperial: it was an ecological dimension of nineteenth-century racial capitalism. Rather than rotating the landscape through the field by planting cotton, then beans, then cotton, then beans, slaveholders expanded the field across the landscape. In South Carolina, Georgia, Alabama, Mississippi, Louisiana, Texas, they planted cotton, cotton, cotton.[13] In their wake they left ruined land and scrubby pine. They called it "old field."

This dystopic landscape is ruined by mono-cropping, by erosion, by soil exhaustion, by the pestilence that comes with the narrowing of the genetic spectrum, by the floods that come with deforestation and levying of the rivers, and by starvation. Like the landscape of *Beloved,* this is a landscape haunted by slavery. The lives of those who labor in these lands are haunted by dread of the day when children would be stripped away from mothers: sold, raped. The haunting occurs in the bright sunlit fields, where the overseer stalked the daily lives of the slave communities. The image of the men of Sweet Home, unwilling to live within the narrowed lives allotted them, swinging dead from trees as emblems of white power's warning, terrorizing others in the slave community to adhere to lives narrowed to suit the purposes of plants. Sethe is haunted by her stolen milk. Her back holds the raised wounds of a chokecherry tree, blooming with roses of blood, lashed into her back while she lay on the ground, a hole dug for her pregnant belly. Frederick Douglass described slaves' lives, which haunt these linkages between production and consumption, between extraction and death, this way: "They are food for the cotton fields."[14]

Marx's *Capital* is haunted by the ghosts of these untold stories. Perhaps they might be described in Morrison's phrase: "unspeakable things, unspoken." And yet the ethics of Toni Morrison's historical imagination imagines the beauty and humor, the love and the laughter, the flourishing, even, of these people, whose lives were pushed to the margins, for Americans, and the world. Such imagination might unclench the denial of political economy and the blinders that its history has imposed on its own writing. Revisiting the landscapes not only of American literature but also the landscapes of the plantation, the countryside, and inner human lives, Morrison renders the absurdist, nihilistic history of the Cotton Boom tactile, assimilable, and understandable, if never quite familiar. In a starveling landscape, Morrison helps us imagine the way to moments of human fullness. Charles Ball, an enslaved man in Maryland, sold to South Carolina, described it this way, "*The people must expect to make acquaintance with hunger.*"[15] Morrison, in *Beloved,* imagines that hunger into meaning:

> Sixo experimented with night-cooked potatoes, trying to pin down exactly when to put smoking-hot rocks in a hole, potatoes on top, and cover the whole thing with twigs so that by the time they broke for the meal, hitched the animals, left the field and got to Brother, the potatoes would be at the peak of perfection. He might get up in the starlight; or he would make the stones less hot and put the next day's potatoes on them right after the meal. He never got it right, but they ate those undercooked, overcooked, dried-out raw potatoes anyway, laughing, spitting, and giving him advice.[16]

As important as any word in this beautiful, loving passage is the word "they." Food, Morrison, teaches us, could be the substance of human connection. There is a great deal of humanity in that observation but also a powerful insight about the character of the slave community. For the potatoes that Sixo cooks are at once an artifact of the power of slaveholders and the endurance — the self-care, the mutual succor, the love, the humor, the flourishing — of enslaved people. "They knew how to survive, teach each other love . . . and they also knew who the villains were," says Morrison.[17] Here we see a community cultivating humanity and recognition. The brief lines of her illustration give depth to the practices of laughter, daily renewed, that taught defiance of subjection to psychic or physical starvation.

Beloved is Morrison's revisiting of the landscapes, not as a calculus for sold pounds of cotton but as they were experienced by those who lived and worked on plantations. She describes how the density and the silence of the woods, the "old field," was tactical as well as spiritual. When Sethe's daughter imagines her mother running away from schoolteacher, she imagines her passing invisible and alert, and she feels the weight of responsibility she must have felt, thinking of "this 19-year-old slave girl — a year older than herself — walking through the dark woods to get her children who are far away. She is tired, scared maybe, maybe even lost. Most of all she is by herself and inside her is another baby she has to think about too." She imagines further the haunting dread that her mother must have experienced, running, for the woods are white dominion, haunted by slave catchers: "She's not so afraid at night because she is the color of it, but in the day everything is a shot or a tracker's quiet step."[18] Even after crossing the river from Kentucky to the free state of Ohio, her mother cannot rest from this dread. After the US Supreme Court *Dred Scott* decision in 1857, an escaped slave even in a free state was still chattel. Her mother ran knowing that her daughter, too, could be claimed as property by the ropes of law and bounty hunters who tracked escaped slaves across state lines for reward. The communal, intergenerational work of teaching "how to survive, how to love, to cultivate humanity and recognition" went on without respite from the haunting.

The metaphor of clear-cutting is apt for the paper trail of early capitalism as well. Political economy attempts to efface presence, to mark in quantitative terms an absence of humanity. But the possibility of revisiting the landscape to look again — to perceive humanity, ecology, contingency — is an ethical demand whose possibility is modeled by the likes of Du Bois and Morrison. It is given strength by a new generation that includes Yaa Gyasi's *Homegoing*, Colson Whitehead's *Underground*

Railroad, and the screen revivals of *Twelve Years a Slave* from the 1853 memoir by Solomon Northup.[19]

The received history of ledgers and numbers records a quantitative history of two million slave sales. The received ecosystem is the miles of scrubby pines through which the highways of the American South pass. We do not have a full historical record. The incomplete record functions to hide human and ecological realities that made the capitalist economy possible. The historian is challenged to accommodate the insight of the slave William Wells Brown that "slavery has never been represented, slavery never can be represented."[20] The ethics of how we revisit the landscapes of early capitalism, of American history, are complex and must remain accountable to Brown.

What Morrison teaches us in the Ingersoll Lecture, and also in her novels, is that although whites sought total control of slaves' lives on the southern plantations of the Cotton Boom, they never wholly realized this fantasy. We must learn from Morrison's ethics of reimagining the occasional moment of solitude or connection — small events of healing, a quick passage through a holy place. The dystopic landscape of the Cotton Boom can be shown to hold spaces that, like windows in an advent calendar, can be opened onto microhistories of places and moments kept beyond surveillance. We have an obligation to bear witness to the small, gentle, exhausting work of instilling and sustaining the habits of the beloved community against the history of racial capitalism. The work of revisiting the past and remembering the dead, those whose lives history's records elide and historians' arguments marginalize, requires historians (and even economists) to change our methods, to hold our categories accountable to the truths sustained in Morrison's fiction. This volume is a contribution to how we talk about what my colleagues in religious studies have termed "abundant histories."[21] Scholars of history and political economy must continue conversations about how we honor claims that are symbolic truths, even as they exceed the facts of events that entered the historical record.

NOTES

1. Toni Morrison, *Playing in the Dark* (Cambridge: Harvard University Press, 1992), 13.

2. Morrison, *Playing in the Dark,* 13.

3. Adam Smith, *The Wealth of Nations* (London: W. Strahan and T. Cadell, 1776).

4. For a rereading of the intellectual history of Western political economy through the lens of the history of slavery, see Cedric Robinson, *Black Marxism: The Making of the Black Radical Tradition* (Chapel Hill: University of North Carolina Press, 2005).

5. Jacques Derrida, *Specters of Marx: The State of the Debt, the Work of Mourning and the Law of the New International,* trans. Peggy Kamuf (London: Routledge, 1993).

6. You think I'm exaggerating? See https://s-usih.org/2018/08/asking-new-questions -of-the-new-history-of-capitalism/ or James Oakes's celebration of the technologically deterministic and economically rationalistic work of the scholars Paul Rhode and Richard Olmstead in the pages of the journal *International Labor and Working-Class History,* no less.

7. Morrison, *Playing in the Dark,* xii

8. W. E. B. Du Bois, *Black Reconstruction* (New York: Harcourt, Brace, 1935).

9. Toni Morrison, *A Mercy* (New York: Knopf, 2008), 10.

10. Adam Rothman, *Slave Country* (Cambridge: Harvard University Press, 2005); Kenneth Pomeratnz and Steven Topik, *The World That Trade Created: Society, Culture and the World Economy 1400 to the Present* (New York: M. E. Sharpe, 1999); Kenneth Pomerantz, *The Great Divergence: China, Europe, and the Making of the Modern World Economy* (Princeton: Princeton University Press, 2000).

11. Robinson, *Black Marxism,* 2.

12. Frederic Bancroft, *Slave Trading in the Old South* (Baltimore: J. H. Furst, 1931); Michael Tadman, *Speculators and Slaves: Masters, Traders, and Slaves in the Old South* (Madison: University of Wisconsin Press, 1989); Michael Tadman, "The Demographic Cost of Sugar: Debates on Slave Societies and Natural Increase in the Americas," *American Historical Review* 105, no. 5 (2000): 1534–75; Walter Johnson, *Soul by Soul: Life inside the Antebellum Slave Market* (Cambridge: Harvard University Press, 1999); Walter Johnson, "A Nettlesome Classic Turns Twenty-Five," *Common-Place* 1, no. 4 (2001), http://www.common-place.org/vol -01/no-04/reviews/johnson.shtml; Walter Johnson, ed., *The Chattel Principle: Internal Slave Trades in the Americas* (New Haven: Yale University Press, 2004); Johnson, *River of Dark Dreams: Slavery and Empire in the Cotton Kingdom* (Cambridge: Harvard University Press, 2013); Edward Baptist, "'Cuffy,' 'Fancy Maids,' and 'One-Eyed Men': Rape, Commodification, and the Domestic Slave Trade in the United States," *American Historical Review* 106, no. 5 (2001): 1619–50; Edward Baptist, "The Absent Subject: African-American Masculinity and Forced Migration to the Antebellum Plantation Frontier," in *Southern Manhood,* ed. C. Friend and L. Glover, 136–73 (Athens: University of Georgia Press, 2004); Daina Berry, "'In Pressing Need of Cash': Gender, Skill, and Family Persistence in

the Domestic Slave Trade," *Journal of African American History* 92, no. 1 (2007): 22–36; Daina Berry, "'Ter Show Yo'de Value of Slaves': The Pricing of Human Property," in *Creating Citizenship in the Nineteenth-Century South*, ed. W. Link et al., 21–40 (Gainesville: University Press of Florida, 2013); Daina Berry, *The Price for Their Pound of Flesh: The Value of Human Chattels, 1740–1864* (Boston: Beacon, 2017); Calvin Schermerhorn, *Money over Mastery, Family over Freedom: Slavery in the Antebellum Upper South* (Baltimore: Johns Hopkins University Press, 2011).

13. Steven Stoll, *Larding the Lean Earth: Soil and Society in Nineteenth-Century America* (2002) and *The Great Delusion: A Mad Inventor, Death in the Tropics, and the Utopian Origins of Economic Growth* (2008).

14. Frederick Douglass, "Oration," delivered in Corinthian Hall, Rochester, July 5, 1852 (Rochester, NY: printed by Lee, Mann & Co., 1852); published under the title, "What to the Slave Is the Fourth of July?," in *The Frederick Douglass Papers, Series One: Speeches Debates, and Interviews*, vol. 2, *1847–54*, ed. John W. Blassingame, 359–87 (New Haven: Yale University Press, 1982).

15. Charles Ball, *Fifty Years in Chains* (Mineola, NY: Dover, 1970), 2; italics in original.

16. Toni Morrison, *Beloved* (New York: Knopf, 1987), 21

17. Toni Morrison, interview by Davíd Carrasco, in this volume.

18. Morrison, *Beloved*, 77–78.

19. Yaa Gyasi, *Homegoing* (New York: Knopf, 2016); Colson Whitehead, *The Underground Railroad* (New York: Doubleday-Penguin Random House, 2016); Steve McQueen, dir., *12 Years a Slave*, 2014, based on Solomon Northup, *Twelve Years a Slave: Narrative of Solomon Northup, a Citizen of New-York, Kidnapped in Washington City in 1841, and Rescued in 1853, from a Cotton Plantation near the Red River in Louisiana* (New York: Miller, Orton & Mulligan, 1853).

20. William Wells Brown, *A Lecture Delivered before the Female Anti-Slavery Society of Salem, at Lyceum Hall, Nov. 14, 1847* (Boston: Massachusetts Anti-Slavery Society, 1847).

21. Robert A. Orsi, *History and Presence* (Cambridge: Harvard University Press, 2016); Amy Hollywood, *Acute Melancholia and Other Essays: Mysticism, History and the Study of Religion* (New York: Columbia University Press, 2016).

Ọmọ Òpìtàńdìran, an Africanist Griot

Toni Morrison and African Epistemology, Myths, and Literary Culture

JACOB K. OLUPONA

INTRODUCTION

There cannot be a better time for a conversation like this than now. Marvel Cinematic Universe's recently released film *Black Panther* (2018) has generated conversation relating to Africanity itself and how the mutual suspicions between Africans and African Americans are now coming into the open. Though contentious, these conversations are also grounded in continuity of tradition, similarities of culture, and the common dilemma facing black people's status in the world today; they hint at the progress that Pan-Africanism can provide. My reading of Toni Morrison will begin from that perspective, focusing on the hard and troubling questions raised by the portrayals of these tensions within literature and popular culture with the intention of exploring both the diversions and commonalities between the worldviews of Africans and African Americans.

A classic example of Pan-Africanism in contemporary African American culture is celebrated performance artist Beyoncé's most recent visual album, *Lemonade* (2016), which featured performances paying homage to the Yoruba goddess Ọsun, for whom fertility and motherhood are particularly important, as well as her subtle nod to the sacred art of the Ori as adorned on the faces and bodies featured in her elaborate visual fête. In her artistic visual performances, accompanied by her musical expressions for the album, Beyoncé saturates African indigenous spirituality into the contemporary African American moment by presenting herself as Ọsun (goddess of fertility and motherhood), as Mary the mother of Jesus, and as the Hindu goddess Kali (the destroyer). Most notable is Beyoncé's juxtaposition of Christian Mariology with various representations of Ọsun through both color and performance, which displays and catalyzes an ongoing conversation, one that brings African spirituality into direct contact with African American aesthetics to reimagine and reimage a sub-

35

version of the popular global idea of blackness and black religiosity. One might say that Beyoncé's work is revolutionary in that it makes a bold religiopolitical statement by infusing Africanness and African Americanness into the realm of popular culture and mainstream ideology.

It is with this background that we now engage Toni Morrison's contribution to this dialogical exchange and examine how her acclaimed works have inculcated Africanity and provided a platform for African worldview and sensibility. I must caution that while Morrison doesn't explicitly discuss Africa in the books we have selected for this essay, a careful reading of these novels reveals that the depth of her work is deeply imbued with African cosmology, spirituality, culture, and worldview. Several scholars have attended to how Morrison's understanding of African religious traditions has influenced her work. My role in this article, however, is to explore and expose a few of these themes from my own knowledge, experience, and understanding of African spirituality in order to highlight how they can be in conversation with each other.[1]

I argue that the "goodness" in Morrison's writing comes, in part, from building a bridge between fragments of an African heritage and the aesthetic and religious creations of African Americans. She is Ọmọ Ópìtàńdìran, the storyteller who helps create a new, hybrid cultural heritage for African Americans even as she acknowledges the tensions and commonalities between African and African American cultures. My goal is to show how she invokes African cosmology and African ritual practices to bring to life what she is writing about and who she is writing for. To this end, I will discuss to what extent Morrison's body of work has reflected and underscored the tensions and commonalities between African and African American culture. As I read her from that angle, I would also like to note that while she does not explicitly refer to Africa in depth, she knows and acknowledges that there is a distinct difference between African blacks and African American blacks. However, I am more interested in asking how Morrison invokes African cosmology, including African religious tradition, ritual, and practices, to bring to life what she is writing about and who she is writing for. How does she deploy African ways of being both as a source of epistemology and as a way of using them to describe the religious and the transcendent/sacred?

To this end, I will discuss a few of her novels under the following categories:

1. Ancestral spirituality and the idea of reincarnation.
2. The place and role of women's generative power and women's spirituality.[2]
3. Morrison's wielding of physical and natural sources as imagery that guides African orientations and views of life in her stories.
4. Africanist aesthetics as implemented in Morrison's storytelling.

One can even ask, "Who is an *Africanist?*"[3] in Toni Morrison's work? She seems to use the term in a somewhat universalizing way—that is, in a Pan-Africanist way to denote those of African and African American descent living in America. In that way, she differs from many African American authors who view blackness through a monolithic lens, which sometimes prioritizes the African American experience after their enslavement in America over the African immigrant one. I use the term "African immigrant communities" to refer to the millions of free Africans who have been coming to the shores of America since the end of slavery. As my work on immigrant religious communities has shown, these invisible Africans are filtered into the African American mosaic without being acknowledged as people holding legal African identities, like other migrants to the United States such as Asians and Latin Americans. Millions of Africans have laid claim to America and its melting pot.[4]

Morrison's work demonstrates an interstitial identity borne by the African American person, one that constantly seeks for its past but also pursues a future by building on the experiences of its present. The Africanness of this identity is also American, and its Americanness is also African. It lives in a liminal space where it must articulate itself by reaching out to both aspects and creating new ways to affirm its existence. This particular aspect of Morrison's work underscores her bridge-building efforts as is evident in many of her books but most notably in *Song of Solomon, The Bluest Eye, Paradise,* and *God Help the Child,* as well as in her books of literary criticism, *Playing in the Dark* and *The Origin of Others.* While I will periodically refer to other sources where Morrison has added nuance to the spirit of her work, such as interviews and lectures given, it is on these novels and two monographs that we shall focus our thoughts in this reflection.

FIG. 2. Aktuer, *Young Princess of the Babungo Kingdom with Her Baby.*
(Courtesy of Shutterstock.com)

ANCESTRAL SPIRITUALITY AND THE IDEA
OF REINCARNATION

African indigenous religions often give prominence to the presence, place, and participation of the ancestors in day-to-day living. The ancestors are perceived as the silent spectators to everyday life and often expected to intervene on behalf of their descendants if needed. In African spirituality, ancestral veneration is central to both the cosmology and the lived religious practices. For example, when my son, the fourth of four children, was born just after the transition of my father, he was named Babajídé (i.e., "Our father has come back") as a reminder of the Yoruba African belief in the reincarnation of a deceased father. It is also very interesting that when my grandfather died, my brother, the third of four surviving children, was named Babatúndé by my father, meaning that his father has come back. Both illustrate the ancestral hold over Yoruba African family systems and are two versions of the same phenomenon. I should hasten to add that a girl born after the transition of a grandmother will be named Iyabo or Yetunde, which mean the same thing, that is, "Our mother has returned." Such children are special and are usually pampered and truly believed to be the return of these loved ones.

I should also add that this phenomenon makes the annual celebration of Yoruba ancestors central to festivals and ritual practices. The Egungun festival, when the community collectively remembers its dead, is almost the equivalent of All Souls'/All Saints' Day. The community believes that the dead return to interact with the living, bestow blessings on them, and, in return, are given gifts to celebrate their reunion with the living.

In *Song of Solomon*, Morrison approaches the African cosmological idea of reincarnation and points to African ancestral heritage as a significant aspect of slave history. In one instance, the characters Macon and Milkman (Macon Jr.) engage in a conversation about Macon's parents' history, in which his father addresses his slave lineage to add nuance to their investigation of Milkman's family tree, a tree that lives in the United States with roots reaching to Africa. Macon addresses Milkman, saying: "I don't remember mother too well. She died when I was four. Light-skinned pretty. Looked like a white woman to me. Me and Pilate take nothing after her. If you ever have a doubt we from Africa, look at Pilate. She looks just like Papa and he looked like all them pictures you ever see of Africans. A Pennsylvania African. Acted like one too. Close his face up like a door" (*Song of Solomon,* 54). Macon's conversation with Milkman here is also reminiscent of conversations that sometimes take place in African homes, where children deliberate who resembles one of the relatives, or a father or mother. In African culture and social settings, children are often described in resembling form, that is, "she resembles so and so from her mother's side," or "she is a replica of so and so from her father's family." These connections are often also significant in tracing lineages and relatives who look alike and are a signifier of their relations to the outside world. In modern-day parlance, this would be similar to a tracing of DNA and heritage, which is common among African Americans. Morrison's use of this image is not peculiar, as it often happens in familial circumstances, but is distinctive in the way it is portrayed by Macon, seeming to identify a continuity with the skin color and African homeland of relations whom Milkman had never met.[5]

In another instance, Milkman visits the house of his cousin Susan Byrd, a local griot of sorts who kept the stories of the local people and, more importantly, Milkman's extended family. Susan Byrd makes reference to their grandfather Solomon and how he disappeared from their grandmother Heddy's life.

> "He was one of those flying African children. They must all be dead a long time now."
>
> "Flying African children?"
>
> "Um hmm, one of Solomon's children. Or Shalimar—I never knew which was right." . . .
>
> "Why did you call Solomon a flying African?"
>
> "Oh, that's just some old folks' lie they tell around here. Some of those Africans they brought over here as slaves could fly. A lot of them flew back to Africa. The one around here who did was this same Solomon, or Shalimar—I never knew which was right." (*Song of Solomon,* 321–22)

Solomon's flight "back to Africa" in this passage is a symbolic interpretation of death and transition into the afterlife. In African cosmology, death is not a removal of the person from this world; rather, it is a journey in which the person changes addresses, in this case from America to Africa. The enslaved Africans often conceived of the afterlife as an eschatological destination (a hereafter). The idea of the afterlife as "home" hinted at freedom from the body and therefore also freedom from slavery. The Vodou Haitian experience is very insightful in this instance. Vodou spirituality teaches us that death and transition means a departure to "Guinea" or the spirit world. When there is death, they will say, "He/She has gone on to Guinea"—a symbolic representation of the African homeland as "Guinea." This is confirmed again in a later passage when Macon relays to Sweet his great-grandfather's ability to "fly" away from slavery and obtain freedom by returning "home."

> "Where'd he go Macon?"
> "Back to Africa. Tell Guitar he went back to Africa."
> "Who'd he leave behind?"
> "Everybody! He left everybody down on the ground and he sailed off like a black eagle. 'O-o-o-o-o-o-o Solomon done fly, Solomon done gone / Solomon cut across the sky, Solomon gone home!'" (*Song of Solomon,* 328)

There is a distinct sense of Africanism in this passage that we can argue connects Solomon back to Africa. From the experience of Africans living in America, the desire to return home grows stronger. This home-return is often expressed as a return to a pristine secured home and an escape from the terror of American suffering and experience that has defined their entire career and lives in a foreign land. To them, the only escape from American racism and alienation is a return home. A Yoruba proverb illustrates this very vividly, *Ilé lábọ̀ ìsimi oko* (Native home is the final resting place from life's daily suffering and toils). To Macon, Solomon is an ancestor two generations past but one who concretely links Milkman back to his heritage, which lies in Africa. Thus, when Macon and Mrs. Byrd connect Milkman back to his long-lost heritage, they also connect him back to his African roots.

In *Playing in the Dark,* Morrison chides American literary scholarship and authors for not recognizing the humanity of the Africanist presence in literature.[6] The "Africanist presence," as a white-generated literary device, illustrates the American impulse to paint a national literature that includes a troubling and fearful reaction to the presence of black people. She suspects that the characteristics of American literary "individualism, masculinity, social engagement versus historical isolation; acute and ambiguous moral problematics; the thematics of innocence coupled with an obsession with figurations of death and hell-are . . . responses to a dark, abiding, signing Africanist presence."[7] As we shall see, Morrison, in her own writings, gives life to the Africanist presence by showing its ancestral heritage with its own norms, sources, and influences that is re-created in America as a new identity in a new place.

To the white imagination that Morrison is confronting, the African is visible only as a convenience for white manipulation and often made invisible in the service of white popular aesthetics. The Africanist presence is simultaneously visible and invisible — visible in the white imagination when it suits it and invisible in the real sense. It also speaks of the paths not taken, and people not noticed by American literature who are rendered invisible by American institutions and systems just as they are by its literature. Morrison rightly calls our attention to the neglect of authentic African American narratives and presence within mainstream American literature. These forced silences speak volumes about white racism in the United States.

Paradoxically, reading Morrison's novels in the context of contemporary America's immigration debate poses a serious dilemma.[8] Does the Africanist presence encompass millions of recent African immigrants, whose identity and history have been marginalized, erased, and queried by the very people who share their African blood with them? Africans in the United States are marginalized not only from the mainstream white majority but from their African American brothers and sisters, who often see them as intruders and the beloved of the white establishment.[9] As Morrison notes, the reliance on a negative portrayal of Africanism is also crucial to sustaining what scholar Emilie Townes refers to as the *fantastic hegemonic imagination:* "Through significant and underscored omissions, startling contradictions, heavily nuanced conflicts, through the way writers peopled their work with signs and bodies of this presence — one can see that a real or fabricated Africanist presence was crucial to their sense of Americanness. And it shows."[10]

In *The Bluest Eye,* Morrison brings forth the idea of this ancestry as a shunned identity, where a black girl abhors her brown eyes and longs for blue ones to erase her connection to Africa. In this novel, the "African" heritage is an unwanted inheritance, a mark of scorn and a reminder of slave history. Morrison's portrayal of Africanism is one that is torn between the acquisition of both the new Victorian identity of the slave master/oppressor and a yearning by "black people" for acceptance in their new home, America. The in-betweenness Morrison invokes uses literature as a lens to reflect on the debates on the place of physical features, colorism, and problematics of pigmentation and even possibly of diction and the accents on speech that are considered acceptable in America. In later years, as in the era of Michael Jackson, it is the preference for the pointed nose and patrician features obtained through plastic surgery or color bleaching that transforms black bodies into supposedly acceptable figures. The affirmation that black is beautiful is suddenly relegated to a goal that seems unattainable. Although Martin Luther King Jr. and other apostles of the civil rights movement preached about blacks not being judged "by the color of their skins but by the content of their character,"[11] the truth is that the color of one's skin can be a great burden on the self, so much so that from birth to the grave, blacks are constantly confronted by this issue. The dilemma of the desire to look like whites to assure one's survival in an inhospitable and racialized white society is actual.

Similarly, in *Paradise* the only mention of Africa is in reference to the African identity of African Americans. Outside of the utopian social construction of the all-black town of Ruby, a bunch of desolate social vagabonds, all women, live together in the Convent, a mansion several miles away. The Convent sometimes serves as a transitional rest stop where residents of Ruby can escape from the pressure of their town under the guidance of Consolata, an erstwhile spirit-guide. As Shirley Ann Stave has noted, colorism plays a major role in this novel, where both whites and light-skinned blacks are "equally antipathetic, a hostility stemming from the event [the Disallowing] that has frozen history for all time for these characters."[12] On one occasion, Morrison demonstrates the "twoness" of the African American identity, which W. E. B. Du Bois names as "double consciousness," in the following conversation between Patricia Best and the Reverend Misner, who seems to urge her to connect her students' Negro history to its roots, lest they fail to know it completely.

> "Of course it's good. It's just not enough. The world is big and we are part of that bigness. They want to know about Africa — "
> "Oh, please Reverend. Don't go sentimental on me."
> "If you cut yourself off from the roots, you'll wither."
> "Roots that ignore the branches turn into termite dust."
> "Pat," he said with mild surprise. "You despise Africa."
> "No, I don't. It just doesn't mean anything to me." (*Paradise,* 209)

Here, the need to be associated with the "bigness" of the world points to the yearning for an ancestral heritage, while the response from Patricia simultaneously depicts the discomfort with which some African Americans view their African heritage and its troubling past. Morrison's repetitive use of the metaphor of roots and branches is also significant here as reflective of the way Africans think about intergenerational contact in terms of how one era comes while another fades away into the past. As we can see from these examples, Morrison is critically aware of the dual identity of the African American and how it is perceived by its bearers. She is also analytically able to portray it in her writing with notes of the in-betweeness within the African American individual torn between the future and the past and yet rooted in the present.

THE PLACE AND ROLE OF WOMEN'S GENERATIVE POWER IN CULTURAL PRODUCTION

In recent scholarship, the place and role of women — who have often been denied the opportunity to feature as the protagonists of their own story — have been recalibrated to reflect their importance in social and cultural history. Morrison's work, however, has always centralized the role of women. Her novels have highlighted major female characters around whom the narratives are built and emphasized the strength of femaleness as well as its role in preserving the heritages and histories of cultural traditions. The references to Africa here are mostly related to the traditional heritage of African social systems, which are presented in terms of folk songs, oral narratives, metaphors, and symbolism. In *The Bluest Eye,* Morrison's underlying female stylistic impetus is depicted in the following passage: "The hands that fell trees also cut umbilical cords; the hands that wrung the necks of chickens and butchered hogs also nudged African violets into bloom; the arms that loaded sheaves, bales and sacks rocked babies to sleep" (138).

In this passage, Morrison infers the flexible nature of women's roles during the times of slavery. Black women of this time lived under "double jeopardy," which Frances Beal defined in her famous pamphlet of the same name. To be black and female in America meant that one was too black to be considered female and too female to be considered black.[13] Gender roles did not apply to them; they did what was required of their male counterparts, and they were still expected to tend to their families and homes. This depiction of black womanhood transcends the distance to touch back on cultural constructions of African womanhood as defined by African women scholars like Ifi Amadiume, Dorcas Akintunde,

and Musimbi Kanyoro. African constructions of womanhood prehistor-
ically transcended contemporary gender roles, as historian Cheikh Anta
Diop has pointed out in *The Cultural Unity of Black Africa*. In decrying
Western denials of matriarchal systems in precolonial Africa, Diop notes:
"Matriarchy [here in direct opposition to patriarchal structure] is not an
absolute and cynical triumph of woman over man; it is a harmonious
dualism, an association accepted by both sexes, the better to build a sed-
entary society, where each and every one could fully develop by following
the activity best suited to his/her physiological nature. A matriarchal regime, far from being imposed on a man by circumstances independent of
his will, is affected and defended by him."[14]

As Diop notes, prior to the colonial invasion of the African continent,
gender parity reflected the collectivity and union of social existence in
which roles were distributed according to ability and preference and were
not particularly contingent on gender. This is not to say that African
communities were not patriarchal or androcentric even then. However,
it demonstrates that gender disharmony came into being when maleness
was prioritized over femaleness. In a similar tone, Sojourner Truth's famous 1851 "Ain't I a Woman?" speech indicts the white feminist movement, addressing the nature of black femaleness under the conditions of
slavery as compared to its white counterpart. Truth rebuts the view that
the African American woman was less female than white women were.
Truth and Morrison's awareness of these underlying social formations are
to me a reflection of the Africanist presence carried to America and the
Caribbean by the slaves from their first home in Africa.

In a second passage, Morrison refers to the enigma of womanhood for
African American women when she points to black femaleness's reliance
on a Victorian exemplar as presented to her by the oppressor yet being
incommensurate with the reality of the African presence that cements her
womanhood in difference from her white female counterparts. Unlike the
previous quote, this one defines the performance of womanhood in the
African American's new home with reference to a white British noble-
man, Sir Whitcomb, who fathers a mulatto child with a woman of West
Indian heritage. Whitcomb's "mulatto bastard" trains his mulatto wife in
the ways of the white man to ensure that she could live up to the ideals of
what it meant to be a good wife and mother and later transferred these
to her children and grandchildren: "She, like a good Victorian parody,
learned from her husband all that was worth learning—to separate her-

self in body, mind, and spirit from all that suggested Africa; to cultivate the habits, tastes, preferences that her absent father-in-law and foolish mother-in-law would have approved" (*Bluest Eye*, 167–68).

Here, Morrison seems to point toward a reluctantly acquired identity—that of the Victorian ideal—often presumed by feminist authors as the cancer that not only engendered the patriarchal impulse but also the spirit that perpetrates it.[15] The strains of white blood mingled within African Americanness, many times a product of the rape of enslaved African women, are crucial in understanding what prompted Pecola's visit to Soaphead (a local *babaláwo* [diviner] of sorts) to ask him for blue eyes. There is a yearning for whiteness, white skin, and Caucasian physical features that emerges from a self-hatred within Pecola, a desire to imitate what the Victorian age (1837–1901), also known as the domestic age, saw as a superlative. The Victorian ideal was epitomized by the British queen, Victoria, who represented a kind of femininity that was (supposedly) centered on family, motherhood, and respectability, which then was filtered into the church and mainstream Christianity.[16] Slave women were forced to dress differently after conversion. They were expected to talk and act similar to their mistresses, who portrayed an ideal of womanhood that was to be studied, emulated, and desired.

In a recent book, *God Help the Child* (2015), Morrison turns to these themes explicitly. The novel begins: "It's not my fault. So you can't blame me. I didn't do it and have no idea how it happened. It didn't take more than an hour after they pulled her out from between my legs to realize something was wrong. Really wrong. She was so black she scared me. Midnight black. Sudanese black. I'm light-skinned with good hair, what we call high yellow and so is Lula Ann's father. Ain't nobody in my family anywhere near that color" (03).[17]

This syndrome has gone on to become a part of African life on the continent. Famed Nigerian musician Fela Kuti sarcastically referred to skin-lightening trends among black Africans as "Yellow Fever." The rise of harmful skin-lightening products in the global market is currently a medical concern that goes to show that perceptions of beauty and womanhood are still trained on Victorian ideals. Colorism and the preference for lighter skin to darker skin in media images and representation continue to draw attention to a deep-seated influence of perceptions of beauty in the world. Fela sang another satirical song about the change in representations of African femininity in 1972.[18] The song contains a dialogue between the words "woman" and "lady" as a way to assert the power of African women to define and speak for themselves. We are told that African women won't agree to what outsiders mean when through Western eyes they call them a "woman."

African woman no go 'gree . . .	An African woman will never agree to it . . .
She go say, "I no be woman"	She will say "I'm not a woman"
She go say, "Market woman na woman"	She will say "A market woman is a woman"
She go say, "I be lady"	She will say "I'm a lady"

The song "Lady" seems to exaggerate the Westernization of African women in postindependence Nigeria in the 1970s; it even goes on to speak of things the lady will not do that the African woman should do. Anyone who knows the life and times of the composer of these words, however, will understand the satirical undertones of its words and how it is a satiric portrayal of feminine "strength." Fela's own mother, Funmilayo Anikulapo-Kuti, was the embodiment of female strength and can arguably be named as one of the first African feminist-activists. When one listens closely, this song unexpectedly becomes a social commentary on the African woman's power to define herself. The song ceases to be a mockery of the thirst for an ephemeral idea of womanhood and beauty and becomes a challenge to African women to embrace their identity once again. What Fela does in these lyrics is similar to what Morrison captures in *The Bluest Eye*. It is a satirical look at the desire for something that will always be beyond the reach of black women and enfolded within, a call to the recollection of true womanhood. And what is this true womanhood? The African American femininity, which she affirms in this narrative as being beautiful, strong, and unique.

INTERPRETATION OF PHYSICAL AND NATURAL SOURCES

Morrison also uses imagery to break down stereotypes of contemporary conceptions of Africa. Literary devices common to African oral traditions — allegory, imagery, and repetition — are used in narratives and storytelling to give emphasis to a particular issue or problematic that the storyteller assumes deserves the audience's attention. Morrison seems to use these literary devices to exaggerate a perceived idea of Africa or to accentuate the idea of African Americans she aims to communicate to her audience. Her use of such African literary concepts and imagery refers to both the physical and the natural and points toward a social location familiar to both the "African" in the African American and the "American" in the African American. Morrison attempts to heal the disconnection between the dual identity and joins them together to guide them to a new beginning. The use of language to communicate what can be seen, touched, and experienced is important in griotism. As my title indicates, Morrison clearly plays the role of a storyteller or griot that is common in the West African tradition, and her biography clearly indicates her lineage as one of griotism; hence my allusion in the title to Morrison's inheritance of griotism. The work of the griot is to retell and recount history by painting a picture with their words and praise songs that carry the hearer into the moment being spoken about. The griot can add nuance to a name by deconstructing that name into places, events, and people associated with it, thereby telling a story.

In *Paradise,* for example, Morrison does this by using the word "African" to designate a cultural and racial location, thus evoking cultural memory through metaphor. In one passage, Soane Morgan muses about Royal's elaborate speech compelling the residents of Ruby to move the town into an era of progress. As Royal speaks, Soane contemplates:

> He wanted to give the Oven a name, to have meetings to talk about how handsome they were, while giving themselves ugly names. Like not American. Like African. All Soane knew about Africa was the 75 cents she gave to the missionary society collection. She had the same level of interest in Africans as they had in her: none. But Roy talked about them like they were neighbors or, worse, family. And he talked about white people as though he had just discovered them and seemed to think what he'd learned was news. (104)

Soane draws a history around the reason why Royal and his compadres needed to elevate the life and status of the Oven. Using imagery, she constructs and breaks down who the characters at the Oven were, the personality of Royal as one of their leaders, as well as what Soane, a visitor to the Oven, thought about Royal's leadership and ideas. The word "Africa" in this passage is used in reference to the past, the present, and the future. It becomes a locality that gathers the story together.

In yet another passage, Morrison uses imagery to portray the reduction of the cross to two intersecting lines:

> Even as children, they drew it with their fingers in snow, sand or mud; they laid it down as sticks in dirt; arranged it from bones on frozen tundra and broad savannas; as pebbles on riverbanks; scratched it on cave walls and outcroppings from Nome to South Africa. Algonquin and Lapland-ers, Zulu and Druids — all had a finger memory of this original mark. The circle was not first, nor was the parallel or the triangle. It was this mark, this, that lay underneath every other. This mark, rendered in the place-ment of facial features. This mark of a standing human figure poised to embrace. Remove it, as Pulliam had done, and Christianity was like any and every other religion in the world: a population of supplicants beg-ging respite from begrudging authority; harried believers ducking fate or dodging everyday evil; the weak negotiating a doomed trek through the wilderness; the sighted ripped of light and thrown into the perpetual dark of choicelessness. (*Paradise*, 145)

Here, there is a retelling of the forcible nature of Christian worship in a community, which had witnessed much pain and suffering. The inclu-sion of South Africa and Zulu is used to refer to the greater connection to humanity. It deliberately inserts blackness into all other populations of the world under the umbrella of Christianity and suffering. Morrison's intent here may not be to refer to Africa, or the Africans who hail from South Africa and Zululand; instead the use of these images identifies traces of her Africanity, in that considering a world without Africa would be impossible. They also point to a struggle shared by people of African descent. If one is to compare and contrast it in this way, then it behooves them to ignore the people from whom the African American characters in *Paradise* came. Here, the tension between Africa and African America is once again revealed. The inclination to think about "going back" as a backwardness or as a return to an uncivilized way has often been por-trayed thus in research and scholarship. However, here it is almost brought together as if to commiserate with one another, as an idea of shared mis-ery and accursedness both in slavery and colonialism that, regrettably, is also very closely related to Christianity and the hope for salvation.

AFRICANIST AESTHETICS AND THE
LITERARY IMAGINATION

In my book *African Religions: A Very Short Introduction,* I highlight the role of the sacred arts and ritual performances in African communities as a communal dictate on what the community honors or observes as being sacred for a certain season or time.[19] Here we must consider how the Africanist presence Morrison articulates in her work embodies the similarities that exist between Africans and African Americans, especially when it comes to the idea of the good and the beautiful. Oral literature and the passing on of stories from one generation to another has become a source of ritual and the arts for the African American community. Through art, music, dance, and film, African Americans express the struggle of living in a world where class repression and racial discrimination are the order of the day. These rituals are the aesthetic of the African American struggle. They have come to mark the language of their pain and struggle, and they are what Morrison attempts to capture in her writing about aesthetics in African American lives.

The perception of beauty and goodness is prefigured into the way her characters appear to the audience. In a recent interview with *The Late Show* TV host Stephen Colbert, Morrison explained that when writing a story, she is never fully aware of how the character will turn out. This means she could begin truly despising a character in the beginning and change her mind about her halfway through the book. In *The Bluest Eye,* for example, it is quite conceivable for the reader to judge Pecola for her desire to have blue eyes. It may seem irrational, selfish, and perhaps downright foolish for someone who all the characters in the book thought to be plain to look down further upon herself. However, reading Pecola's story reminds the reader to extend compassion when one is not fully aware of the trials the character is facing. Perhaps, like Morrison, they are compelled by the end of the book to sympathize deeply with Pecola rather than judge her. This stylistic use of imagery is also common to African oral narratives and traditions. Imagery and metaphor aim to institute moral wisdom and values by painting a picture that forces the audience of a given story to insert themselves into the narrative idea and make a moral judgment about the issue being presented. In African upbringing, children are exposed to such stories from an early age. This is considered as an informal kind of education of youth and children. Such narratives are loaded with moral wisdom and cautionary tales in which fable characters and animals are often depicted.

Playing in the Dark is part of Morrison's long-range twofold literary critical project about the aesthetics and humanity of African Americans. She identifies and defines an "African presence" in the imagination of white writers as constructors and upholders of what she calls "a disabling virus." She uses *Playing in the Dark* as a basis, in part, to counter this imagination through her critical writings and novels that resist the virus and redefine the African American. We see her twofold approach in the opening statement that *Playing in the Dark* is meant as a "critical geography and . . . map to open as much space for discovery, intellectual adventure and close exploration as did the original charting of the New World — without the mandate for conquest" (3). She is exposing dangers of one geography and mapping the way to an opening so that she and others can write a new world where the Africanist presence can survive and thrive.

Soon after these words of charting a new world, she notes: "My curiosity about the origins and literary use of this carefully observed and carefully invented Africanist presence has become an informal study of what I call American Africanism. It is an investigation into the ways in which a nonwhite, African-like (or Africanist) presence or persona was constructed in the United States, and the imaginative uses this fabricated presence served" (*Playing in the Dark*, 6).

Morrison's critical assault on this disabling virus and fabricated presence both accompanied her earlier novels and set the stage for further writings that pushed the Africanist presence into a new horizon in American literature, one that exists primarily in a new space in which identity is being newly discovered. What she strove to achieve, in part, earlier in *Song of Solomon* and *Beloved,* and later in *Paradise* and *God Help the Child,* was the narration of an Africanist presence that is both the preservation of an African American cultural memory and the construction of a new identity in America. The African-like persona not only is preserved by its heritage but is also self-constructed by its agents. African-like people living in America are therefore both carriers and crucibles of the Africanist presence, by which their existence is made known to non-Africanists. What Morrison draws out by illustrating this particular tension in the Africanist presence is a conflictual reality in which memory becomes a literary tool in the hands of modern-day griots, whose role is to preserve the remembrance of the past but also to usher the African-ist imagination into the new age. Morrison is aware that in African oral tradition, epics and hero stories were the capsules inside which tradition and heritage were hidden. The glory and achievements of heroes and her-oines of old are preserved in oral narratives that are told for inspiration or as cautionary tales to signify both what is good and to be desired in society.

Harvard had the recent honor of hosting Morrison for a series of lec-tures in which she presented a number of essays that I think embodied the underlying aesthetic of the Africanist presence. These essays have recently been published in a collection titled *The Origin of Others* (2017) and de-pict an idea of what we have been attempting to capture in this essay. The tension between who belongs and who is excluded is felt by African Americans in their daily lives; it is expressed in the rhythm of blues music, the undertones of spoken word and rap music, and colored by the beauty of African American culture and artifacts. A new wave of this aesthetic is featured in Afrofuturism, a budding genre in film, literature, and art that uses the black cultural lens to speculatively consider the world.[20] Morri-son's fourth essay in *The Origin of Others*, "Configurations of Blackness," while not explicitly self-named as a work of Afrofuturism, attempts to do the same in defining what blackness is. In it, Morrison traces the genesis of the definition of *blackness* as an identity marker, referring directly to its problematic nature and how self-definition restructures the idea of blackness altogether. She asks, "Once blackness is accepted as socially, politically and medically defined, how does that definition affect black people?"[21] Perception as an underlying factor in determining the episte-mology of aesthetics plays a pivotal role in the question Morrison asks. How are black people perceived? How is black art and black literature prefigured by the qualifier "black"? What emerges out of black culture that sets it apart from nonblack culture? In response to her own question, Morrison responds by pointing to *Paradise:*

> In *Paradise* I wanted to reconfigure blackness. I wanted to trace the purity requirement and the response by the townspeople when black purity was threatened by the lesser or the impure. In *Paradise* I played with these con-fused and confusing concepts of blackness. I began at the very opening, which signals race, purity, and violence: "They shoot the white girl first. With the rest they can take their time." Just as the "white girl" is never

identified, none of the killers is given a name in the initial onslaught. The men committing the murders are a son or nephew or brother, uncle, friend, brother-in-law—but no proper names. (*The Origin of Others,* 65)

The deliberate anonymity Morrison uses in *Paradise* tempers the audience's impulse to assume that the murderers are less than human. It is not automatically obvious to the reader who the murdering men in *Paradise* are. The tension in Morrison's work pushes against the prefigured compulsion to assume that black males are naturally violent and would be the most likely suspects in this kind of crime.

In the media today, we continue to see egregious imbalances in the portrayals and use of language related to whiteness and blackness. The tendency to stereotype and villainize blacks while sympathizing with whites and whiteness demonstrates the impact of the racial hierarchy on public perception and opinion.

A last implication of Toni Morrison's work is perhaps its inadvertent definition and identification of an internal other and an external other. Morrison has never been gun-shy about speaking on race. In several interviews, she refers to race as a "construct" of society, one that cannot have power on its own. In her essay "Being or Becoming the Stranger," she flips the notion of the other on its head by once again claiming a new definition for race. In this particular essay, she takes on what knowledge does to shape and invent what human beings eventually see and believe. She posits language and image as *godlings,* which "feed and form experience."[22] She goes on to speak of her creation of a character she had imagined and uses it to demonstrate how shaping the idea of an image can be easily destroyed by language and image. She laments: "I had forgotten the power of embedded images and stylish language to seduce, reveal, control. Forgot too their capacity to help us pursue the human project—which is to remain human and to block the dehumanization and estrangement of others. . . . Succumbing to the perversions of media can blur vision; resisting them can do the same."[23] In this quote, Morrison's dedication to her craft is evident. It is careful and does not randomly assign truth to an idea or an image. It is this literary caution that urges her to ask and admonish: "Why should we want to know a stranger when it is easier to estrange another? Why should we want to close the distance when we can close the gate? Appeals in art and religion for comity in the Common Wealth are faint."[24] This kind of self-awareness is rare. To recognize oneself in a character someone dreamed up is simple and obvious; to imagine one-self apart from it is a more difficult mission.

This is the work that Morrison aims to do with the Africanist instinct to imagine an identity outside of a definition that did not arise from it. We can argue that the earlier conversation on Africanism is really a conversation about the question of African identity and who can lay claim to it. Morrison responds to African philosopher Valentin Mudimbe, to whom Africanism is a body of knowledge and a methodological tool with which Africa can be studied, separating herself from his definition of Africanism. For Mudimbe, Africanism is a scientific method, wielded by early Western anthropologists to define blackness.[25] An Africanist is one who views Africanness from the outside looking in but also as an epistemological tool by which Africa came to be studied. Thus Africans who study Africa, the notion of Africanness, anyone who uses "Africanism" is in this sense Africanist. Mudimbe uses the word to depict those who are concerned with Africa in an investigative manner. Morrison eschews Mudimbe's definition, yet in her work still embraces it in a new dimension. African American origins are reminiscent of Africa; they are Africans in a non-African location.

Morrison's curiosity, examination, and discourse on Africanism reminds me of a Yoruba saying: *Kó sí ẹni tí ó mọèdè àyàn, àfi ẹnití ó mú ọpá ẹ lọwọ* (Only the drummer can understand the language of the talking drum). While one cannot go too deeply into this saying's mythology, it suggests that the language of the drum can be interpreted in multiple ways depending on who plays the drum. It is an important principle of hermeneutics that interpretation of a culture may traditionally involve the owner of the culture itself, who understands where the shoe pinches. Toni Morrison interprets Africanism in the same manner. It means, for her, those for whom African DNA runs in their blood can understand the nuances of Africanism. It excludes European and Anglo-American scholars, who in Mudimbe's definition constructed methods to study African culture and instituted them as the only epistemology, no matter how distinguished they are. Does this then mean that Morrison's definition involves an ethnic or racial categorization of who an Africanist is or ought to be?

Yes, it touches squarely on the notion of identity, which is very central to the categorization of Africanism but is more specifically prototypical of African Americans. While it may appear that she touches on a kind of kinship with Africa, she has also opened a Pandora's box because it addresses a live issue that also affects the Africans who have immigrated to America and are automatically categorized as black. Is it possible that while they don't share in the Africanist presence as Morrison portrays it, they must partake in it? Is Morrison's conversation helpful or harmful to this conversation?

Morrison's work encompasses critical, analytical, and fictional texts, and by and large they reflect quite a number of fascinating motives and issues and themes in African thought and praxis. However, we must caution that these references are not directly obvious in a general reading of her body of work. They will require more in-depth understanding and interpretation of Morrison because her literary style heavily depends on vernacular African American epistemology. Morrison's references particularly to epistemological, metaphysical, and moral motifs are considered to be germane to African worldview and experiences. So the question then is, From what perspective does she write? She wrote long before the concept of Africana studies became popular in the academy, and by Africana studies I refer to the body of knowledge that brings under the same umbrella discourse on Africa, African American and the African diaspora, and the Afro-Caribbean (although she may not situate herself as part of that genre).

Apparently, Morrison seems to have embraced a kind of Pan-Africanism or Africanist perspective that makes her equate her approach with blackness so that ontological blackness is concerned with the status, suffering, and state of being of all black people in America and perhaps throughout the world. She addresses human conditions as they speak to the status of the blacks in America. Though her ethnographic references and case studies are located in the United States, where she was born and raised, it seems to me that the stories she espoused speak to the conditions that affect the long-suffering of people of African descent all over the world. To some extent, we can classify it as a Pan-Africanist approach to literature that invoked past memories of the suffering of African Americans, particularly in the Middle Passage and the transatlantic slave trade and beyond, in their new home in America. *Song of Solomon* addresses the idea of the desire to return to Africa during slavery and shortly after, the nostalgia for a paradise lost and the idea of Africa as their ancestral home. Morrison's novels vividly capture a transitional era when the black church emerges as a dominant spiritual space for African American religious expression. Negro spirituals were born out of this memory, history, and the presence of suffering, and they embedded in their rhythm the hope to return to their homeland.

This cultural evolution came together with the processes involved in enslaved Africans transitioning into African Americans in the new land but nevertheless forcing them to reflect back on the old tradition they brought with them from the motherland. Examples are stories of children who still play the old African games. Morrison's work in *Song of Solomon*, for example, is a fictional equivalent of the classical historical work such as what we refer to in Yoruba, *Ẹkún ìyáwó,* meaning "songs of lamentation" rendered by maidens who are confronted with the dilemma of leaving their ancestral homes to pursue a new life in marriage. It is obvious to most readers of Toni Morrison that she comes from a background, heritage, and formation that is in tune with oral literary narrative. Both her grandmother and her great-grandmother were probably griots, too, in the sense that they were deeply rooted in the African tradition of storytelling. Their wisdom and artistic flourish contributed very much to Morrison's work. In the African-Yoruba tradition, women are regarded as the custodians of *Oriki* (praise poetry of individuals and lineages that are rendered by women on certain occasions such as marriage, naming, and burial ceremonies). This tradition comes out very clearly in Morrison's writing, and so does the role of women as custodians of the homestead. Morrison, on both sides of her family, both the paternal and maternal lineages, inherited this oral griot tradition. Morrison is one whose *Oríkì* (if we were to invent one for her in Yoruba tradition) would have been Ọmọ Òpítandìran, that is, where a storytelling becomes an inheritance.

In conclusion, we can ask ourselves, How much of Toni Morrison's work can African scholars engage from the African perspective? Second, how much of her work reflects a continuity between the African and African American identities within her writing and literary imagination? Morrison could be perceived as building a bridge between the African heritage lost and the African American identity created, but she could also be acknowledged as a compass pointer gesturing toward a world where the two are once again reconciled. Whereas her storytelling and narrative sharing creates a cultural heritage for African American folks in the United States, it opens up a new world in which the Africanist presence can become a depiction of blackness and a way to uplift the perception that the world has of African people today. This Africanism, however, must become more inclusive of alternate and other forms of blackness if it is to thrive in a fast-changing globalized world. Perhaps Toni Morrison's writing will provide a way for all of us to imagine it, create it, and live in it.

NOTES

1. See my edited volume *African Spirituality: Forms, Meanings and Expressions* (2000) and my single-authored book *City of 201 Gods* (2011) and *A Very Short Introduction to African Religion* (2014).
2. See Joan Daya's article "Erzulie: A Women's History of Haiti," in "Caribbean Literature," special issue, *Research in African Literatures* 25, no. 2 (Summer 1994): 5–31.
3. See Morrison's reference to and use of "Africanism" and "Africanist" in *Playing in the Dark* (1992) and other works.
4. Jacob Olupona, *African Immigrant Religions in America* (New York: New York University Press, 2007), 22–190.
5. Another textual site to consider here is the recurrence of the lost mother/daughter under conditions of slavery. Beloved has flashing memories of slave ships that are powerful movements between time and generations. Look at page 90 and the two chapters told in Beloved's voice (248–56).
6. She's also addressing the white production of Africanist presence in ways that are not about actual African or African American people but rather serve the white imagination. My focus, however, is on her use of "Africanist" as contra to V. Y. Mudimbe's definition of the term.
7. Toni Morrison, *Playing in the Dark* (Cambridge: Harvard University Press, 1992), 5.
8. And one reaching far beyond the particular debates in Morrison's writings.
9. See James H. Meriwether, *Proudly We Can Be Africans: Black Americans and Africa, 1935–1961* (Chapel Hill: University of North Carolina Press, 2002); Henry L. Gates and Gene A. Jarrett, eds., *The New Negro: Readings on Race, Representation, and African American Culture, 1892–1938* (Princeton: Princeton University Press, 2007); Keith B. Richburg, *Out of America: A Black Man Confronts Africa* (New York: Houghton Mifflin Harcourt, 1991); Geneva Smitherman, "'What Is Africa to Me?': Language, Ideology, and 'African American,'" *American Speech* 66, no. 2 (1991): 115–32; E. B. Higginbotham, "African-American Women's History and the Metalanguage of Race," *Signs: Journal of Women in culture and Society* 17, no. 2 (1992): 251–74; and others.
10. Morrison, *Playing in the Dark*, 6–8. The fantastic hegemonic imagination as defined by Emilie M. Townes in her book *Womanist Ethics and the Cultural Production of Evil* (London: Palgrave Macmillan, 2006) refers to "the set of ideas

that dominant groups employ in a society to secure the consent of subordinates to abide by their rule. The notion of consent is key because hegemony is created through coercion that is gained using the church, family, media, political parties, schools, unions and other voluntary associations — the civil society and all its organizations. This breeds a kind of false consciousness (the fantastic in neo-cultural and sociopolitical drag) that creates societal values and moralities such that there is one coherent and accurate viewpoint in the world" (20).

11. Martin Luther King, *I Have a Dream: A Speech* (Kingston, Ontario: Thee Hellbox Press, 1985).

12. Shirley Ann Stave. "Jazz and Paradise: Pivotal Moments in Black History," in *The Cambridge Companion to Toni Morrison,* ed. Justine Tally, 59–74 (Cambridge: Cambridge University Press, 2007).

13. Francis M. Beal, "Double Jeopardy: To Be Black and Female," *Meridians: Feminism, Race, Transnationalism* 8, no. 2 (2008): 166–76.

14. Cheika Anta Diop, *Cultural Unity of Black Africa* (Chicago: Third World, 1959).

15. See Betty Friedan, *The Feminine Mystique* (New York: Norton, 2001); Simone de Beauvoir, *The Second Sex* (New York: Random House, 1961); Mary Daly, *The Church and the Second Sex* (Boston: Beacon, 1985); Judith Butler, *Undoing Gender* (London: Psychology Press, 2004); among other works.

16. Lynn Abrams, *Ideals of Womanhood in Victorian Britain,* http://www.bbc.co.uk/history/trail/victorian_britain/women_home/ideals_womanhood_01.shtml.

17. Toni Morrison, *God Help the Child* (New York: Knopf, 2015). The mother, Sweetness, is embarrassed by the darkness of her daughter's skin and owns her colorism: "Some of you probably think it's a bad thing to group ourselves according to skin color — the lighter, the better — in social clubs, neighborhoods, churches, sororities, even colored schools. But how else can we hold on to a little dignity?" The daughter, Bride, goes on to become a successful executive at a cosmetics company. The reader follows her on a journey from civilization to nature that tracks with changes to the body of Bride. Yet only the character can perceive the metamorphosis.

18. Fela Kuti, "Lady" (1970).

19. Jacob K. Olupona, *African Religions: A Very Short Introduction,* vol. 377 of *Very Short Introductions* (Oxford: Oxford University Press, 2014), 56.

20. As coined by Mark Dery in "Black to the Future" (1994), the term "Afrofuturism" refers to a "flurry of analysis reframing discussions on art and social change through the lens of science and technology in the 80s and 90s." It seeks to unearth the missing history of people of African descent by "unchaining the mind" and spurring critical thinking (Womack) to imagine possible futures through a black cultural lens. It encourages experimentation, reimagines identities and activates liberation (LaFleur). (This is a composite definition drawn from Afrofuturist

author Ytasha Womack, artist-activist Ingrid LaFleur, and other proponents of Afrofuturism.)

21. Toni Morrison, *The Origin of Others* (Cambridge: Harvard University Press, 2017), 58.

22. Morrison, *The Origin of Others,* 36.

23. Morrison, *The Origin of Others,* 37.

24. Morrison, *The Origin of Others,* 38

25. See V. Y. Mudimbe in *The Invention of Africa* (Bloomington: Indiana University Press, 1988), 37, 167–68; V. Y. Mudimbe, *The Idea of Africa* (Bloomington: Indiana University Press, 1994), 38–41.

Structures of Stone and Rings of Light

Spirited Landscapes in Toni Morrison's *Beloved*

TIYA MILES

"124 was spiteful."

In this opening line of her novel *Beloved,* Toni Morrison presents us with a street address and a state of being. We can envision, through Morrison's bleak and balletic prose, the lone house painted in stormy grays that hosts the irrepressible memory of slavery. The house does things, like overturn kettles and fracture mirrors; the house feels things, like rage and a lust for revenge. The moody structure on Bluestone Road plagues beleaguered African American family members — Sethe, the protagonist; her children, Denver, Howard, and Buglar; and her mother-in-law, Baby Suggs. This house draws its ferocious energy from the spirit of a ghost — Sethe's murdered and beloved baby girl. Saved from a life in slavery by her own mother's killing hand but banished to a realm of spiritual unrest, Beloved haunts those left behind. Beloved's spirit possesses the house on the outskirts of Cincinnati, bringing it to life. Animated by this greedy spirit, the house wrests a range of reactions from its residents, who run away (Howard and Buglar), pass away (Baby Suggs), waste away (Sethe), and find a way back to community (Denver). The house at 124 Bluestone Road is spirited, alive with consciousness and verve, as are many other places in the world of this majestic novel. By turning a house into a character with presence, affect, and efficacy, Morrison fixes this haunted spot upon our memories and establishes place as core to her conception of story as well as the African American experience. Here Morrison reimagines what places are (animate rather than inanimate), what places do (act in the world of humans), and with whom they relate most intimately (fugitives seeking asylum). African Americans and Native Americans populate Morrison's living places, disrupting the geomythology that rejects these groups' histories on the land.

This essay follows the rocky course that Morrison lays in *Beloved* to and through pain-ridden places that reveal the presence of helping powers beyond this earthly plane and anchor the possibility of radical secession from the strictures of othering that underlie this nation's twin original sins: the severing of both African and American indigenous people from their respective land bases and the reduction of human beings to beasts of burden. To work through these notions, the essay reprises a black feminist rebuke to traditional Western geographical understandings and then offers readings of three scenes in *Beloved* that, first, reveal natural places in Morrison's story-world to be supernaturally alive; second, show how animated natural places function as conduits for spiritual entities to aid people in need; and third, suggest the fundamental benevolence of nature in Morrison's vision.[1] The essay will argue, by its close, that Toni Morrison draws not only on Afro-diasporic strains of animistic and Christian belief but also on Native American understandings of spiritual allyship to create a good natural world in which fugitives from slavery can acquire help from nonhuman spirits and gods.

Beloved, a work of penetrating historical fiction, is Nobel Laureate Toni Morrison's fifth novel. The book made the *New York Times* bestseller list in its first week in press (1987) and inspired a feature film directed by Jonathan Demme (1998) as well as the opera *Margaret Garner* (2005), composed by Richard Danielpour with a libretto by Morrison. Decorated by multiple honors including a Pulitzer Prize, the novel is roundly classified as a masterpiece of American literature that captures in mesmerizing prose the intangible psychic dynamics of chattel slavery as well as the human condition.[2] Through interwoven and spiraling stories of a black household that knows the terrors of bondage and is forever stained by that experience, Morrison retells a history of the multiracial American family that is violent, deeply corrupt, and traumatized by a past that it wishes to forget but cannot. *Beloved* is a spiritual and psychological drama about the lasting wounds of cruelty and the wrenching difficulty of holding together damaged selves and human relationships in the aftermath of unspeakable tragedy.

Morrison famously conceived this novel while working as an editor at Random House, where she came across the story of Margaret Garner in a digest of African American history.[3] Margaret Garner was a young African American woman enslaved in rural Kentucky and likely sexually abused by her owner, Archibald Gaines, since her teenage years. Permitted to marry, Margaret partnered with Robert Garner, an enslaved man on the nearby Marshall plantation. Margaret had four children and was pregnant again by the time she reached the age of twenty-two. These children were the progeny of her husband, Robert, and also, all indicators suggest, of Archibald Gaines. In the frigid month of January in 1856, Margaret and her husband set in motion a hazardous escape plot. Along with Robert's parents and four young children, the couple approached the frigid banks of the Ohio River via a wagon and two horses that Robert had taken from his owner. The river had frozen over that month, permitting the fugitive family to walk across it. The Garners were not the only people held in bondage who took advantage of the frozen waterway that winter. Nine others also escaped that evening in what the *Chicago Tribune* newspaper disparagingly called a "stampede of slaves."[4]

But the Garner story of border-state slavery sinks into further despair after this remarkable crossing. The Garners made their way to the home of Margaret's free cousins, Joseph, Sarah, and Elijah Kite, who lived by the riverside in Ohio. The plan had been for Elijah to make contact with Underground Railroad activist Levi Coffin and then send the family on to another safe house. But before such steps could be ventured, Archibald Gaines and armed officers surrounded the small wooden structure, threatening violence and recapture under the authority of the Fugitive Slave Act of 1850. Margaret, surely thrown into a morass of fear and sorrow at the specter of a return to a physical, social, and sexual bondage that her offspring would inherit, began to assault her daughter and sons. She was seeking, as revealed in later court testimony, to "kill the children." Margaret sought to rescue those under her care from lives of slavery and did so through the only means at her disposal. "Before my children shall be taken back to slavery, I will kill every one of them," Margaret reportedly shouted. She took the life of her toddler daughter, described in court testimony as being "almost white" in appearance, and injured her other children before being physically restrained. Robert Garner had been firing shots at the slave catchers during Margaret's defensive attack on the children, only later realizing that the youngest girl had been nearly decapitated by his wife. Officers took the Garner family into custody. A sensational two-week trial followed that hinged on whether Margaret could be considered a person and hence held accountable for murder, or whether she should be defined as a thing, the property of her owner, who had merely dispossessed Archibald Gaines of another one of his assets — the two-year-old child, Mary.[5]

The federal commissioner acting as judge, John Pendery, ruled out Margaret's personhood and therefore refused to charge her for murder. Margaret and her family were returned to Gaines, who promptly shipped them down river to Arkansas, New Orleans, and Mississippi in order to protect the value of his property, and, as scholars Steven Weisenburger and Nikki Taylor have argued, to protect the honor of southern men and white society. During a steamboat accident en route to the Deep South, Margaret "lost" her infant to the Mississippi River in what was likely a desperate final attempt at suicide and infanticide. Two years later, Margaret died of typhoid fever. Her husband, Robert, would go on to fight in the Civil War.[6] The Garner story, unique in its particulars but representative of collective traumas that slavery inflicted on black women and families, has been chronicled most feelingly by black women writers, first in the verse of nineteenth-century poet Frances Ellen Watkins Harper and most recently in the fiction of Toni Morrison, who recovered Garner's story for twentieth-century readers and brought to it immense emotional perception.[7]

Morrison's novel *Beloved* offers an imaginary, revelatory, and painful rendering of the life of Sethe, a character inspired by Margaret Garner. While *Beloved* begins north of the Mason-Dixon Line in Reconstruction-era Ohio, it continually returns through memory to a place called Sweet Home, the Kentucky plantation that created the condition for the convergence of the central characters' lives. Sweet Home was a house of horrors, a place, as Morrison's characters unveil, of terrible mental and physical assault and glorious agrarian beauty. Here, a small band of black people struggled to maintain life and personhood under the ownership of Mrs. Garner and the punishment of her sadistic brother-in-law, known as schoolteacher. Sethe, the novel's protagonist, tries but fails to forget Sweet Home, where every "leaf on that farm" made her "want to scream." Sethe never had the chance to know her own mother on the plantation where she was born in the indigo-producing Southeast. At the age of fourteen, she came to Sweet Home as property of the Garners. She was purchased as a "breeder" intended to replace Baby Suggs, the only black woman on the plantation prior to Sethe's arrival and the mother of Halle, who bought Baby Suggs's freedom through years of extra labor. Baby Suggs removed to southern Ohio, where she settled in among painful memories of all the children she had lost and served her small, rural community of formerly enslaved people as a lay preacher. Among Sethe's new companions at Sweet Home were Baby Suggs's two sons and two other black men called Paul D and Sixo. Sethe partnered with Halle for six years. Together they had three children who all belonged to the Garners by law.[8]

The enslaved residents of Sweet Home endured a hell of tortures: perpetual fear, brutal beatings, confinement in iron, sexual and emotional assault, murder, and the helpless witnessing of the abuse of others. They lost their minds and risked their lives in the throes of escape plots, leaving Halle mad, Sixo dead, and Paul D eventually yoked to a nightmarish chain gang while Sethe and Halle's young children, and later, a pregnant Sethe, escaped to Baby Suggs's home on Bluestone Road. There, Sethe began a slow process of physical healing from a brutish sexual assault in which schoolteacher's sons forcibly drained her breastmilk, from a back lacerated by whipping, from fleeing across wide terrain with no shoes, and from giving birth along the way to the infant Denver. But peace was not to be had for Sethe, whose troubled mind was repeatedly seized by horrible memories of Sweet Home and her abuse there. When, one day, Sethe saw a man she took for her former owner approaching the yard to snatch her and her little ones back into slavery, she snapped, grabbed her children, and tried to protect them by taking their lives. She succeeded in killing her toddler, a little girl whom she loved to no end. The black community punishes Sethe for what they view as an inhuman act and shuns the family and the house on Bluestone Road, isolating its inhabitants, including their preacher, Baby Suggs, and the innocent infant born along the harrowing journey of Sethe's escape.

Sethe's experience of Sweet Home and the killing of her daughter occur in the past time of the novel, which begins in the shattered aftermath of violence and abandonment. In the fashion of a poltergeist, the murdered child haunts the house once thought to be a reprieve from slavery but revealed to be a repository of its unrelenting traumas. The book begins in 1873. Baby Suggs has died. Sethe and Halle's sons have fled. Only Sethe and Denver remain in the frightful house. Paul D, whom Sethe calls "the last of the Sweet Home men," escapes and seeks out Baby Suggs's last known address. After Paul D arrives and begins a tender relationship with Sethe, he learns, as do they all, that the ghost of Beloved has been made flesh. The murdered child materially appears as a dark and shining young woman, representative of the past that will always return and pregnant with the promise of still more emotional suffering. Beloved seduces Paul D and possesses Sethe, who takes deathly ill. Through the desperate courage of Denver, who regathers the support of the community's women, Sethe and Denver are returned to a circle of communion and protection once led by Baby Suggs. It is black women who exorcise the ghost by shouting her away, making it possible for Denver to imagine a life and for Sethe and Paul D to imagine a love in the tainted place that is America.[9]

BLACK FEMINIST CRITICS have labored to puncture the geo-mythology of the Americas, the pervasive, transcontinental view of place that separates black and indigenous peoples from the land as well as from national histories of soil and sea. In the canonical literatures and histories of the United States, Canada, and Caribbean islands written during and after colonization, narratives of the land feature heroic, masculinized, racialized white figures who tame or claim it much as they would a woman. There is no room for blackness or redness in these stories, nor for women, nor for preexisting rights or continuing attachments claimed by marginalized peoples. Beyond stereotypical renderings that emphasize defeat, passivity, infantilism, or romanticism (such as the unkempt "pickaninny" chased by alligators or the stoic "Indian brave" riding a horse into the sunset of disappearance), people of color are written out of national landscapes.

In her foundational study *Demonic Grounds,* geographer and black studies scholar Katherine McKittrick established that only one place exists for blacks in the imagined geographies of the diaspora: the place of "racial captivity" or "geographical confinement" constructed by processes of "dispossession" and "social segregation." Separated from their natal continent and forced into personless status and homeless station, black people come from nowhere and can claim nothing beyond the gates of their bondage. Because black people are deemed unworthy and incapable of occupying, and certainly, possessing land in slaveholding regimes and segregated states, black presence and experience are evaporated from the materiality of the land, even as black people are rendered and represented as both "displaced" and "placeless." Into the absence of blackness that structures all of what McKittrick calls "traditional geography," a white presence is assumed, articulated, and elevated. Therefore, in order to accomplish the difficult task of making black experience visible in a whitened landscape, the "topographies of something lost" — stories, meanings, and knowledges — must be recognized. These voided lands must be "remapped."[10]

As her evocative title *Demonic Grounds* suggests, McKittrick insists that reclaiming landscape stripped of histories of blackness is a demonic act. By "demonic," McKittrick does not mean to denote evil in a biblical sense, though the moral stain of land theft and murder clings to the landscapes of North, Central, and South America. Instead, she borrows her language from Jamaican theorist Sylvia Wynter, who carved out space for a "demonic" approach in black feminist cultural studies in her classic essay "Beyond Miranda's Meanings." Here, Wynter argued for an application of physicists' use of the term "demonic models," or readings inexplicable from conditions of the natural world, to studies of race, gender, and hierarchy in the Caribbean. This scientific understanding as interpreted by Wynter defines the "demonic" as utterly beyond the norm, as exterior to existing human space-time positions. To adopt a demonic model, in Wynter's sense, is to seize an entirely new standpoint unclouded by existing consolidations of knowledge, or the "present mode of being/ feeling/knowing."[11] Demonic ground, in McKittrick's usage as inspired by Wynter, is a landscape shaped anew by an outlying and outlier approach that compels us to see blackness in place. The landscape revealed by this approach is necessarily polluted by exploitation but also punctuated by stories of surprising strength and survival.

The places in *Beloved*'s pages can be read as demonic in both Sylvia Wynter's and Katherine McKittrick's senses—unfamiliar, discomfiting, and embedded with unforeseen stories of blackness. McKittrick highlights the spatial quality of Toni Morrison's writing, and of *Beloved* in particular, which she analyzes as a textual example of thoroughly mined demonic ground. McKittrick observes that Morrison maps "painful places," creating in them a "site/sight of memory." Memories recovered in this way, McKittrick asserts, have the authority to thwart "a broader geographic project that thrives on forgetting and displacing blackness" and "returns a "black absented presence" to the land.[12] Environmental historian and divinity scholar Dianne Glave also features *Beloved* in a discussion of African Americans' historically close, and even sacred, relationship to the land, calling attention to the centrality of the "environment" in Morrison's story, as evidenced by "spiritual references to the woods, water, and animals."[13]

Equally important to her location of black people in place, Morrison respects an indigenous claim that remains on this stolen ground. She gestures to this Native claim through the assertion of Native American presence in a landscape that holds a memory of indigenous belief systems as well as through Miami Indians buried beneath the soil and Cherokees who continue to walk their usurped land as a band of resisters.[14] Morri-

FIG. 3. Ronny Salerno, *Looking down the Tributary towards the Ohio River,*
2013. (Courtesy of the artist)

son's remapped places are red as well as black, stained with the blood let
by colonialism as well as slavery. Literary critic Virginia Kennedy drills
down on this point, elucidating "share[d] experiences" and "bloodlines"
that join black and Native people on the landscapes conjured by Morrison. In *Beloved,* African-descended characters and indigenous American
characters dwell in all manner of places, making their presence felt to one
another and the reader. In positioning her characters as people of color
with relationships *to* land and relationships with one another forged
through land, Morrison disrupts an American national geo-mythology
that displaces, disappears, or disqualifies these populations from belonging. As Kennedy asserts, "Morrison demonstrates the coming together
of blacks and Indians on the land, suggesting powerful resistance to the
exploitation of bodies, and of the earth, for material gain."[15]

But Morrison makes her fictional grounds even more demonic, or
strange, than this, pushing beyond radical topographies of black and red
peoples in material places. In *Beloved,* the buildings and grounds them-

selves come alive; the landscape is inspirited, animated by the presence of multiple unseen forces and figures. Ghosts are among the beings that stock her demonic landscape. And alongside the ghosts, discrete elements of the land crowd in. In the world of *Beloved,* rain, wind, woods, and rocks are invested with spirit, giving them power that can be transmitted to humans in need. Morrison creates a multifaceted placefulness that brings African Americans, Native Americans, and women of various racial backgrounds together on a landscape enlivened by supernatural presences. Among Morrison scholars, Kennedy best captures this fusion of place and spirit, writing: "Morrison's characters resist the imposition of the dominant culture's mapped boundaries, both in the physical and in the spiritual sense. They go beyond these imposed boundaries into a wilderness that is not 'wild' in the Western sense of the world but that encompasses an alternate reality. It is a space where, if people pay attention, land and the spirits of the people who have lived and died are not silent."[16]

In *Beloved,* places have life force and agency. The gray and white house where Sethe lives is animated, as we know, by a ghost. Here spirit and structure merge in the haunted house archetype of American southern gothic literature. But as McKittrick, Glave, and Kennedy have observed, Morrison's natural landscapes are alive as well, and differently so, than the haunted house on the edge of town. For it is within nature's coulees and crevices, rather than inside the walls of a building, that places gather their strongest force. The importance that Morrison assigns to spirited landscapes inspires a series of questions: How are these natural places animated, or invested with spirit, in the novel? What makes a given place special, or sacred? What transpires in these spirited landscapes? What does their force give rise to?

MORRISON SIGNALS REPEATEDLY in *Beloved* that particular places are special. These places share the characteristic of being "natural," as in undeveloped by perpetrators of white supremacist slaveholding systems and colonial settlement. These places are also set apart physically, and by indication, morally, from dominant American society. Natural sites thus distinguished appear in the novel as spirits themselves or the dwelling places of spirits. We encounter one of these special places early in *Beloved* and can begin to identify through its description how Morrison represents and understands them.

Denver, Sethe's daughter born on the banks of the Ohio, grows up on Bluestone Road in social isolation. Her sad life is steeped in secrets shrouded by shame, and her greatest solace is a circle of shrubs far beyond the perimeter of the house. Denver's special place is distant from civilization, located past a field that is the last strip of cultivated land before a wood and stream appear. Here, "in these woods, between the field and the stream, hidden by post oaks, five boxwood bushes, planted in a ring, had started stretching toward each other . . . to form a round, empty, room." The shrubs of this room are animated, as indicated by the anthropomorphic characteristic of voice when the leaves "murmur" to Denver as she enters the "bower." Inside, Denver perceives a striking illumination, described as an "emerald light." In addition to being set apart, vocal, and luminous, the boxwood room is aged. It carries a primeval quality captured by the words "quiet, primate and completely secret." Through descriptions of separation, sound, light, and maturity, Morrison signals the sacred. Denver's "refuge" in the woods is animated by a spiritual force that she cannot see. Here, the "live green walls" "veil" and "protect" her from the killing spirit of loneliness, offering in its stead peace and "salvation." In addition to guarding Denver, the boxwood bower offers lessons connecting her to others and the past. One fall while Denver nested inside the arbor, a cold wind touched her perfumed skin and brought with it a sudden snowfall that reminded Denver of the tale of her birth, as told to her by Sethe. In this moment, the emerald enclosure draws on other elements of nature — wind and snow — to arrest Denver's attention, warn her of a coming danger, and point toward a hidden source of strength — her birth story. After experiencing this chill in the wood, Denver returns to the house and sees for the first time an apparition of the ghost kneeling beside her mother. In the boxwood bower, Denver has communed with a spirit that seeks to help her, offering succor and priming her as yet unfound resolve for the coming fight with the family's ghost of the past.[17]

Morrison's construction of the boxwood bower is steeped in an African and African diasporic religious influence that infuses much of her writing. Spirits are multiple in this perspective, diffused as opposed to strictly hierarchical, and often entwined with nature. The Africanity of the boxwood closet is expressed through its circularity. Morrison's highlighting of the "ring" harkens back to an essential shape of ritual motion in west and central Africa, as well as to Caribbean and American enslaved peoples' practicing of the "ring shout," a rhythmic dance believed to open communication with ancestors.[18] In this presentation of the animated arbor, which appears in the first thirty pages of the novel, Morrison establishes her vision of the spirited landscape: a place exterior to the modern built environment and infused with a preternatural power of protection that it bestows on a certain kind of person: the fugitive from suffering. Humans may enter these places with caution and even reverence, like Denver, who "bent low to crawl into" the boxwood sanctuary, in the pose of the prayerful.[19]

Spirited landscapes in *Beloved* share qualities of wildness and seclusion but diverge in the ways that they host supernatural presences. Denver's boxwood bower is a natural place brought alive through an unnamed force represented by the odd "emerald light." Here, the place and its spirit are fused as a single entity. In other moments of the novel, landscapes are animated differently, by spirits in league with nature but mobile in it, and by spirits that exert influence over natural elements and laws such that they might be most accurately described as gods. In the latter two forms of spirited landscape, nature cooperates with individuated spirits, enabling assistance to sufferers. Historian of religion Davíd Carrasco has identified this kind of action—supernatural help, or spiritual allyship—as a feature that Morrison adopts from shamanic narratives. Shamanic characters, Carrasco explains, come to realize "the vital importance of finding a spiritual ally who enables the seeker to transcend the terror of one's historical condition." In Morrison's fiction, these allies take the physical form of animals, as Carrasco has shown, or reside in naturalistic realms, as I am suggesting in this essay. As Carrasco elucidates in an analysis of Morrison's third novel, *Song of Solomon,* spiritual allies often manifest as birds. It is no coincidence that *Song of Solomon* also explores the connective tissue between black and American Indian experience by highlighting an indigenous woman ancestor named Sing in the family lineage of main character Milkman Dead.[20] Indeed, Morrison's formulation of spiritual helpers linked to nature suggests a subtle religious influence on her literary imagination: the faith traditions of Native Americans.

Environmental historian Rosalyn LaPier (Blackfeet/Métis) has formulated a clarifying articulation of the relationship between spirit helpers and nature in a case study on the Blackfeet Nation of the present-day US Northern Plains and Rocky Mountains. While her analysis is specific to Blackfeet history and includes an arresting argument about a long-standing Blackfeet belief in their people's ability to control nature, LaPier's fundamental picture is expandable to a broader American Indian understanding of the intimate overlap between nature and religion. LaPier reasserts and demonstrates the well-established finding that Native people of the pre-European contact period and into the twentieth century did not perceive a separation between spiritual practice and everyday life. Ritual was not contained by "church" or a sense of division between body, mind, and spirit. Rather, religious belief infused the experience of daily consciousness, social relations among people, and interaction between people and the natural world. For the Blackfeet, the omnipresent spiritual world was "invisible" and organized into an intricate, three-dimensional order, including an Above World, a Below World, and a Water World, realms characterized and bounded by natural elements. As LaPier explains, "The Blackfeet understood that within the earth, water, and sky reside a great variety of natural and supernatural beings." In order to thrive, human beings, who were weaker than many other beings, were required to seek out supernatural power. Their only means of acquiring such power was through the establishment of relationship, even "friendship," with supernatural persons. In LaPier's words: "The Blackfeet believed that humans had to create alliances with the supernatural to live life to the fullest." Individuals could forge these relationships through three methods: being sought out by an entity; finding revelation through dreams; or purchasing spirit-infused sacred objects. Access to the supernatural through relationship enriched and strengthened a person's efficacy even amid devastating colonial intrusion.[21]

Toni Morrison's storytelling in *Beloved* and other novels suggests that she writes with a consciousness of these integrated elements of Native religious traditions. Her landscapes are populated by spiritual allies who dwell above, below, and behind the human plane of existence. And where her places are most spiritually potent, indigenous people — living and dead — appear. In *Beloved,* Morrison presents sites touched by Native presence as the places where humans can most readily access powerful spiritual allies. Nature first appears as a conduit for special relations between human beings and supernatural beings in the dramatic episode of Sixo and Patsy, also known as the "Thirty-Mile Woman." Sixo, a man of intellect and daring, was among the enslaved owned by the Garners on Sweet Home Plantation. He felt a feverish love for Patsy, a woman who lived many miles distant on her owner's estate. Starving for a connection both mental and physical that was denied him at Sweet Home, Sixo laid plans with Patsy to meet between the plantations where they were each held. It is not surprising that Sixo chose a spot in the woods, as undeveloped wildlands were spaces of secrecy for the enslaved, who used them to escape surveillance for short bursts of time as well as for communal religious observance. But this was not just any patch of forest. This was "a place he knew" and a place also known by Native people long before his arrival. Sixo's chosen spot had been recognized as sacred ages ago, perhaps millennia ago, by indigenous people. Although this unnamed Native population was long gone, most certainly due to the collapse of moundbuilder societies in the Southeast and riverine Midwest after Europe's first exploratory imperial forays in the late 1400s and 1500s, the people had left their mark on the land. Sneaking through the woods one night, Sixo found "a deserted stone structure," the architectural relic of another era. He came to "know" this place, to appreciate and revere it, through physical and oral communion. The stone site was first revealed to him on an occasion when he was engaged in a mysterious spiritual practice, described as "dancing to keep his bloodlines open." Upon Sixo's initial encounter with the place, he spoke to it, asking "its permission to enter." Once inside, "having felt what it felt like, he asked the Redmen's Presence if he could bring his woman there." Sixo recognized the stone structure, built of the natural element of rock and, importantly, reminiscent of a cave and therefore the below-ground dimension, as something alive. He identified that animating force as an extant and personified "Presence" of Native people. Literary critic Virginia Kennedy writes about this passage: "The dwelling is concrete physical evidence of a people removed by those who now enslave both Sixo's body and the land he is forced to work." In response to Sixo's respectful request for entry, "It"—the spirit of the Redmen—"said yes." But on the evening when Sixo was to meet Patsy, confusion befell them. The couple could not locate one another, and to be alone and wandering at the rise of the dawn would mean certain recapture and punishment. Overcome with concern for Patsy's safety, Sixo wandered the woods for hours in search of her. In a last desperate moment, he "stood in the wind and asked for help." Then, "listening close for some sign, he heard a whimper." Sixo ran to the sound sent to him by the helper wind and discovered that sound to be the voice of his lost lover. Sixo and Patsy found one another on that terrifying night with the aid of two spiritual allies: the Presence in the stone who welcomed them, and the element of wind that guided them. After the rendezvous, Patsy arrived back at her plantation safely, and Sixo "melted into the woods." Over the course of the novel, Sixo meets his death at the hands of slave catchers, but not while under protection of the Redmen's Presence, and its aider and abettor, the wind.[22]

Paul D, who remembered Sixo's encounter with the Presence and witnessed Sixo's eventual death in their joint attempt to escape from Sweet Home, also finds saving grace in a place of nature. After attempting to kill a new owner to whom schoolteacher had sold him, Paul D was imprisoned, yoked to a chain gang, and bound by iron to forty-five other African American men. White wardens treated these black men worse than chattel, locking them up nights in wooden pens dug into a trench, forcing them to perform unwanted sex acts, humiliating them with caustic words of defilement, and working them in an unrelenting grind. Paul D lost his spirit while bound to the chain gang and began to court death. Then something changed. Nature acted. In Morrison's words that occupy a single paragraph on the page: "It rained." Immediately after the rain began, "Snakes came down," signaling an occurrence with biblical echoes. A deluge pummeled the chain gang camp in a wooded area of Georgia where the guards had locked the men into submerged wooden pens. The men might have died there, should have died there, drowned by the weight of the chains that held them below the rising waters. But this rainstorm, this flooding, altered the course of their fate. Instead of sinking, the chained men rose through a terrified but elegantly choreographed movement of their tethered bodies. And, as Morrison writes, "Great God, they all came up." The chained men escaped the camp due to the flood and picked their way through the woods. As they "huddled in a copse of redbud trees," the men prayed for "the rain to go on shielding them." Soon thereafter, they came upon another band of runaways, a group of Cherokee men, women, and children who were fleeing President Andrew Jackson's Indian Removal Act and the armed enforcement of its requirements by federal troops and state militias. This Cherokee band had chosen "a fugitive life" over forced relocation to Indian Territory, and they acted to aid the black escapees. The Cherokees, who were themselves struggling against illness and fatigue, cut the chains of the forty-six men. One by one, the chain gang men departed for known destinations, but Paul D remained, a lost soul. He asked his Cherokee hosts for directions to the "Magical North." They told him to "Follow the tree flowers," a natural pathway made possible because "the flood rains of a month ago had turned everything to steam and blossoms."[23] Paul D tracked the pink and white flowers from Georgia to Ohio, making his way to Sethe's doorstep. His escape was orchestrated by a spiritual helper, perhaps the highest of them all—the "Great God" whose name was evoked as the men rose from their earthbound cells. In Paul D's escape from convict slavery, the landscape shifts from the fields to the woods of Georgia. But even in his coffin in the bowels of earth, nature is a spirited presence. Natural elements come to his aid in the form of intentional rain, directed, it seems, by a divine hand. The southern landscape—its earthen bowels, its rain clouds, reptiles, and forests—provides a stage for God to act on behalf of the suffering fugitive.

In addition to creating the conditions of Paul D's escape, nature forges a bond between Paul D and the Cherokee band, who enter the narrative as though in answer to the prisoners' prayer. Adrift in the woods following their miraculous raising from the dead, the chained black men had been "hoping for a shack, solitary, some distance from its big house, where a slave might be making rope or heating potatoes." They dreamt of aid from fellow captive blacks but found "instead a camp of Cherokee resisters who have fled to the shelter of the woods." Native people, desperate and die-hard Cherokees on the run from forced removal, enter Paul D's story as if by divine intervention. They know, as Paul D must discover through his escape experience, that the woods provide a form of protection more powerful than any shelter attached to a plantation landscape.

If *Beloved* were a different story, centered on expelled American Indians rather than on enslaved blacks, we would surely follow these Cherokees, themselves "sick and decimated" and hovering near a spirit zone between life and death, on their journey.[24] We would then ask whether and how the God that saves Paul D will work in the lives of indigenous fugitives from suffering. And this is no small question, as Native American stories are often sidelined in literature of American landscapes, leaving Native people to serve only as foils for white American dramas and even for black American tragedies. We must therefore press on whether the novel promotes black advancement on the backs of American Indians or represents Indian-inflected places devoid of actual Native presence.

In *Beloved,* Morrison's black characters do not gain entry to the settler colonial economy without indictment. The primary example of her awareness of this trap is her portrayal of Paul D in an urban environment. When Paul D first reaches Cincinnati, also known as Porkopolis, he works in a meat factory to earn necessary wages. Through its very existence and expansion, including over Indian graves, the city has committed a wrong against the original inhabitants. Paul D is implicated in this wrong through his acceptance of work in the city's chief industry. When Paul D leaves the pig factory each day stinking of animal feces, he passes through "a cemetery as old as the sky" where the ghosts of Miami Indians, voicing their protest, "growled on the banks of Licking River, sighed in the trees on Catherine Street and rode the wind above the pig yards." Paul D hears the voices but ignores them in order to keep his job. His lack of attentiveness to these supernatural messengers comes at a cost. Not long after he dismisses the Miami ghosts, Paul D is seduced by another ghost, Beloved, who nearly ruins what is left of his ravaged life. Morrison does not allow her black characters in *Beloved* to claim what Caribbean studies scholar Shona Jackson has termed a "Creole indigeneity," which is an identity politics of replacement in which black people claim authenticity on the land through labor and at the expense of indigenous people.[25] Neither does Morrison conjure vestiges of Indianness on the landscape that only signal indigenous absence. Even as Native spirit animates Morrison's landscapes, Native people still occupy these places and make a claim to histories there. Morrison presents indigenous figures as alive as well as dead, as active in the troubled world of the now. Native people are not only ghosts of the past but also figures with bodies, thoughts, emotions, histories, and powers.

In Toni Morrison's *Beloved,* all kinds of places are enlivened. Structures of slavery (like Sweet Home Plantation) and colonial settlement (like urban Cincinnati and the house on Bluestone Road) are soaked in violent memory and therefore dangerous. But these malevolent spaces are countered by equally potent opposing forces, special places in nature rendered as sacred good. Helping spirits frequent nature's recessed realms and stand ready to interact with desperate fugitives who can enter these natural spaces with respect and find resources for renewal. In her interview with David Carrasco published in this volume, Toni Morrison reveals that nature, in her story-worlds, is a place essentially oriented toward good: "The moral imagination of nature in my writing is about recognition, revelation, and somehow, love." Katherine McKittrick has used the term "demonic ground" to capture what Morrison does with place in *Beloved.* This application is illuminating of the strange alterity that Morrison herself has pointed to in her work. But at the same time, spirited landscape in this novel might be called angelic ground, in reflection of the fiercely good work of spirit guardians. It is upon such benevolent ground, liberating ground, and healing ground that the characters in *Beloved* approach salvation.

NOTES

1. Although humans have long lived in an altered environment where the border between "natural" and "unnatural" is notional, I am choosing to use the terms "nature," "natural world," and "wild," usually without quotation marks, to indicate spaces that Morrison presents as distant and different from modern settlement zones and built structures of the colonial-slavocracy.

2. Nellie Y. McKay, introduction to *Toni Morrison's "Beloved": A Casebook,* ed. William L. Andrews and Nellie Y. McKay (New York: Oxford Unversity Press, 1999), 3, 4; Richard Danielpour and Toni Morrison, "Notes on Margaret Garner," Cincinnati Opera 2005 Summer Festival program (Cincinnati, OH: Cincinnati Opera, 2005), 20–21.

3. McKay, introduction to *Toni Morrison's "Beloved,"* 5.

4. "Stampede of Slaves," *Chicago Tribune,* January 28, 1856; "Negro Stampede," *Covington Journal,* as cited by Steven Weisenburger, *Modern Medea: A Family Story of Slavery and Child-Murder from the Old South* (New York: Hill and Wang, 1998), 307, 56, 297n75.

5. Weisenburger, *Modern Medea,* 157; Nikki M. Taylor, *Driven toward Madness: The Fugitive Slave Margaret Garner and Tragedy on the Ohio* (Athens: Ohio University Press, 2016), 20.

6. Weisenburger, *Modern Medea,* 224–25, 242; Taylor, *Driven toward Madness,* 15–16, 109; "The Slave Case in Cincinnati," *National Anti-Slavery Standard,* February 16, 1856; "Delivery of the Cincinnati Slaves at Covington," *Liberator,* March 7, 1856; "The Case of the Slave Mother, Margaret, at Cincinnati," *Liberator,* May 16, 1856.

7. Frances Ellen Watkins Harper, *A Brighter Coming Day: A Frances Ellen Watkins Harper Reader,* ed. Frances Smith Foster (New York: Feminist Press, 1990), 60, 84–86; Kristine Yohe, "Enslaved Women's Resistance and Survival Strategies in Frances Ellen Watkins Harper's 'The Slave Mother: A Tale of the Ohio,' and Toni Morrison's *Beloved* and *Margaret Garner,*" in *Gendered Resistance: Women, Slavery, and the Legacy of Margaret Garner,* ed. Mary E. Frederickson and Delores M. Walters (Urbana: University of Illinois Press, 2013), 102–3. For a comparison of Harper's poems on Margaret Garner and the character Eliza Harris of *Uncle Tom's Cabin,* see Melba Joyce Boyd, *Discarded Legacy: Politics and Poetics in the Life of Frances E. W. Harper, 1825–1911* (Detroit: Wayne State University Press, 1994), 62–63.

8. Toni Morrison, *Beloved* (New York: Plume, 1987), 6.

9. As with all ghost stories, divergent accounts can coexist. The damaged figure who appears from the blue and wreaks havoc on this family may or may not be spectral in the material world beyond Sethe's mind. Rumors in the community indicate that a young black woman has escaped years of imprisonment and sexual abuse at the hands of two white men in the countryside. This is a second kind of haunting just as powerful and more prevalent than the one to which Sethe succumbs.

10. Katherine McKittrick, *Demonic Grounds: Black Women and the Cartographies of Struggle* (Minneapolis: University of Minnesota Press, 2006), 9, 4, 5.

11. Sylvia Wynter, "Beyond Miranda's Meanings: Un/silencing the 'Demonic Ground' of Caliban's 'Woman,'" in *The Black Feminist Reader,* ed. Joy James and T. Denean Sharpley-Whiting (Malden, MA: Blackwell, 2000), 119.

12. McKittrick, *Demonic Grounds,* 33.

13. Dianne D. Glave, *Rooted in the Earth: Reclaiming the African American Environmental Heritage* (Chicago: Lawrence Hill, 2010), 55–56.

14. Morrison, *Beloved,* 155, 111.

15. Virginia Kennedy, "Native Americans, African Americans, and the Space That Is America: Indian Presence in the Fiction of Toni Morrison," in *Crossing Waters, Crossing Worlds: The African Diaspora in Indian Country,* ed. Tiya Miles and Sharon P. Holland (Durham, NC: Duke University Press, 2006), 198, 199.

16. Kennedy, "Native Americans, African Americans, and the Space That Is America," 200.

17. Morrison, *Beloved,* 28, 29.

18. Michael A. Gomez, *Exchanging Our Country Marks: The Transformation of African Identities in the Colonial and Antebellum South* (Chapel Hill: University of North Carolina Press, 1998), 118.

19. Morrison, *Beloved,* 28.

20. Davíd Carrasco, "Magically Flying with Toni Morrison: Mexico, Gabriel García Márquez, *Song of Solomon,* and *Sula,*" in *Toni Morrison: Memory and Meaning,* ed. Adrienne Lanier Seward and Justine Tally (Jackson: University Press of Mississippi, 2014), 148, 150; Toni Morrison, *Song of Solomon* (New York: Plume, 1977).

21. Rosalyn R. LaPier, *Invisible Reality: Storytellers, Storytakers, and the Supernatural World of the Blackfeet* (Lincoln: University of Nebraska Press, 201), 28–29, 43, 98.

22. Kennedy, "Native Americans, African Americans, and the Space That Is America," 202. For more on the depopulation of Mississippian chiefdoms, see Charles Hudson and Carmen Chaves Tesser, eds., *The Forgotten Centuries: Indians and Europeans in the American South, 1521–1704* (Athens: University of Georgia Press, 1994). Morrison, *Beloved,* 24, 25.

23. Morrison, *Beloved,* 111, 112.

24. Morrison, *Beloved,* 111.

25. Shona N. Jackson, *Creole Indigeneity: Between Myth and Nation in the Caribbean* (Minneapolis: University of Minnesota Press, 2012), 2, 4, 9; Morrison, *Beloved,* 155.

II Putting Goodness Onstage

Evocations of Intimacies

Comments on Toni Morrison's *Home*

CHARLES H. LONG

INTRODUCTION

Let us conjure and meditate on the title of the novel itself—Home. "Home" is a word that communicates its meaning directly and immediately. The adages, sayings, and proverbs of our culture employ it easily: "Be it ever so humble, there's no place like home." "Home sweet home." And since I'm from North Carolina, I don't dare forget to mention Thomas Wolfe's 1940 novel, *You Can't Go Home Again.* Its paperback cover shows a hat hanging on the edge of chair, silently suggesting that "home is where you hang your hat."

"Home" is a familiar word. But it is not an easy word. Home begins pointing almost immediately to the deeper philosophical, political, and religious meanings that are held within it. These meanings are present in the refrains of Negro spirituals: "*O Lord, I have no friend like you. If Heaven's not my Home, what shall I do,*" or, "*I heard of that city called Heaven, and I'm trying to make Heaven my home.*" The profundity of home's eschatological and apocalyptic meanings are matched in philosophical thought about home, extending from Immanuel Kant's Enlightenment treatise[1] on cosmopolitanism that brought us the language of "being at home in the world" to Gaston Bachelard's *Poetics of Space*[2] in which he studies how small and cozy places can become exquisite containers for the intimacies related to being and feeling at home.

Toni Morrison's novel *Home* takes the form of a novel or novella that often moves in the direction of an epic poem. Such a genre is usually discussed under the rubric of literary criticism. I will take a different point of view—that of the historian of religion. I don't identify this position as theological criticism. I see theology as different and distinct from the work I do.[3] As a historian of religion, I understand "religion as orientation—orientation in the ultimate sense, that is, how one comes to terms with the ultimate significance of one's place in the world."[4] Implied

FIG. 4. Jeff Bell Photography, *Wild Horses Battle for Dominance.* (Courtesy of Shutterstock.com)

in the notion of orientation are the empirical and imaginative meanings of the time and space that a person or community occupies. For the purposes of this essay, home *is both a space and a time.* My view of home as a space/time emerges from an awareness of the ways Africans became an "involuntary presence" in the Americas. They were ripped from their homes and their calendars, their lineages and ancestors through the slave trade. Those who survived the Middle Passage found themselves struggling to live in a new world, a new space and time.

Further, I bring a certain personal perspective to bear on this text which in part is about a veteran of the Korean War. I am an African American male, a native of the South. I served in the USAAF in World War II, I volunteered for military service, and I have experienced what it means to be a black person in the United States. Insights from this perspective will also inform my interpretation of the text.

By employing a method derived from the study of religion to Toni Morrison's novel, I don't imply that this is a religious novel or that the author was attempting to write such a novel. I am stating, however, that approaching the novel from the perspective of the history of religions uncovers valid and possible meanings of the work. In what follows I will interpret the novel's epigraph and explicate three powerful orientations of the ritual order within the text as the keys to the religious meaning of the novel.

ORIENTATION ONE: WHO AND WHERE AM I?

Home is a short novel, but its construction is complex. The narrative unfolds in a twofold way: through the language of a narrator (which appears in nine chapters with normal font) and, in seven italicized chapters, the voice of a traumatized black Korean War veteran, Frank Money. Frank is the chief protagonist, and we follow him as he moves across the land motivated by an urgent message to return home to Lotus, Georgia, to aid his sister Ycidra, called Cee. The material and literary structures of the novel are intriguing. The narrative itself is disjunctive — something is mentioned in one place but not carried through, but then the continuity of this narrative is taken up again three or four chapters later in a very different context.

Examples of this can be seen in the epigraph to the novel and then in the lack of any immediate or obvious relationship between this epigraph and the first chapter. In a sense, one does not know where to begin, or more precisely, where Frank Money begins as the protagonist. Where does he take on his potency as a character? Is it in the early scene of chapter 1, or in Korea, or on the journey back to Lotus to be with Cee? These ambiguities and complexities are not cited to reveal the failure of the author; on the contrary, they show how she has crafted the structure of the novel onto the disjunctive content and style of the experiences she is attempting to render. More adept literary critics will be able to make more of these issues than I. My comments arise out of an interest in the religious meanings revealed in the work, and especially from the point of view of religion as an epistemological, hermeneutical, and performative expression of the ultimate significance of one's place in the world.

THE EPIGRAPH: THE LOCK THAT FITS THE KEY

I begin my discussion of the novel with the epigraph:

> *Whose house is this?*
> *Whose night keeps out the light*
> *In here?*
> *Say, who owns this house,*
> *It's not mine*
> *I dreamed another, sweeter, brighter*
> *With a view of lakes crossed in painted boats;*
> *Of fields wide as arms open for me.*
> *This house is strange.*
> *Its shadows lie.*
> *Say, tell me, why does its lock fit my key?*[5]

The epigraph sets the stage for what I am calling "a context of anomic con-tradictions." The narrator has a key to a house that holds only toxic and negative meanings. It is the key to a house that does not have the capacity for intimacy. This is a very ambiguous statement — an ambiguity border-ing on the critically negative. It is a statement of deep concern. There is nothing in or about the house that is pleasing, yet the speaker seems to possess legitimate access to the dwelling since the lock on the door fits the speaker's key. Morrison's reversal of the usual way of access — "my key fits the lock" — suggests that the "lock," perhaps a symbol of a prison, is the active part, a magnetic instrument that is trapping the speaker into the night, the strange, lying place. The speaker is describing a place and time that embodies no intimacy at all; it is a space of alienation. Given that, let us leave this epigraph for other anomic contradictions in our discussion.

For example, there are the names Toni chooses for her characters and spaces — first of all, "Frank Money." At the end of chapter 6, Frank has just abandoned his partner, Lily, when she finds a money purse on the sidewalk outside. She scoops it up and later spreads out the contents of coins, "cold and bright," on the side of the bed where Frank had slept. We read: "In Frank Money's empty space real money glittered. Who could mistake a sign that clear? Not Lillian Florence Jones." "Money," Frank's last name, is also the word for currency, a mode of exchange, and the term "Frank" can be used as a synonym for "Truth" or "Truly." In conjuring his name in relation to the truth of the novel, that he is flat broke and living with lies he tells us and himself, we are able to imagine or suspect other meanings and contradictions will be emerging within the text.

Note also the name of the AME Zion minister who aids Frank Money in his reverse Underground Railway, the Reverend John Locke. You will recognize that this is the same name of the eighteenth-century English philosopher who wrote, among other works, *Essay on Understanding and Two Treatises on Government,* and *The Constitution of Carolina.* He was read by and influenced the American Founding Fathers and could be called the philosopher of modern colonialism and the theory of property that gave philosophical justification for slavery. A black Christian minister bearing the name John Locke is as ridiculous as a poor black man in America with the name Frank Money.

"Orientation" is derived from the Latin term "orior." Romans employed this term or one of its derivatives when they spoke or performed actions that had to do with designating locations in space. One meaning of "orior" referred to the rising of the sun in the east. That is, if one looked toward the rising sun, one could then determine the other directions: West is its opposite, and north and south are at its left and right hands. The earth underneath one's feet, and the sky above give us the basis for the determination of all other directions and spaces. Through the experience of one's own body, the stability of one direction enables one to establish all the other directional divisions. This experience of orientation in the cosmos allowed people to feel a sense of a center in relation to other key directions. People know how to leave in secure directions and return home to their center. In other words, space must become effectively intimate if it is to sustain a viable form of human community.[6] Toni Morrison makes this point in the interview in this volume where she speaks of home this way: "For me it's not things. It's place. You know when you've arrived, a person knows when he's arrived. Home can be anywhere; it can even be outside, on a beach. It's where the comfort is, and the knowledge of belonging. This place is mine, mine, and will always be, that's all." But in the novel we are confronted again and again with dis-orienting displacements, painful losses of homes.

These basic structural elements of human orientation and the knowledge of belonging seem to be missing in the case of Frank Money and his family lineage. The family was expelled under extreme duress from a small town in Texas, moving on to another place in Louisiana, from whence they moved on to Lotus, Georgia, to take up residence with Frank's father and Salem's sister, Lenore, a spiteful, mean woman who resented their encroachment on what she had assumed was her ordered life.

The larger space of the town of Lotus, Georgia, offered no surcease; it was a wretched place for black folks. We must not overlook the novel's allusions to the even larger spatial area of the United States of America as participation in the wretchedness of temporal and spatial orientation as far as black folks were concerned. In chapter 7, Frank Money compares Lotus to the army and the battlefield:

> *Lotus, Georgia, is the worst place in the world, worse than the battlefield. At least in the field there is a goal, excitement, daring, and some chance of winning along with many chances of losing. Death is a sure thing but life is just as certain. Problem is you can't know in advance.*
>
> *In Lotus you did know in advance since there was no future, just long stretches of killing time.*[7]

Given all these contradictory circumstances, how is it possible for Frank Money to be humanly oriented — to experience that locus in time and space that might have been the place that affirmed his preconceptual primordial sensibility as the basis for order in his life? How is it possible for him to experience that place called home? His minimal sense of human community in the United States in general and in Lotus, Georgia, in particular, allowed him to act and perform at a level of survival, but it could not sustain the weight of either a future or a goal. He tells us:

> *I don't miss anything about that place except the stars.*
> *Only my sister in trouble could force me to even think about going in that direction.*
> *Don't paint me as some enthusiastic hero.*
> *I had to go but I dreaded it.*[8]

The source of dread appears in the first chapter, where we read of the very young Frank Money taking Cee, his sister, through the tall grass of Lotus to see horses in combat. It is also there that they observe a group of white men unceremoniously burying a black man who had most probably been murdered. The violent combat of the horses and the secretive burial of the black man are profoundly moving. In the case of the horses, we see "nature in the raw" — the life and death agony for the domination of the herd. The struggle is furious and loud and conveys an authentic and even necessary dimension of nature.

Through the horses, nature reveals that there is something worth fighting for. The unceremonious burial of the black man expresses the evil of human nature. The man's murder and burial are deceitful, surreptitious acts. These two moving acts are what hold Frank and Cee together, however far apart they become in space, until the end of the novel. It is intimated that all the ambiguous, unpleasant, and forced moments of this time and space with his sister Cee constituted a miniature niche that affirmed his humanity, gave him a sense of purpose. Frank speaks about their togetherness in the crawl space: "*The reward was worth the harm grass juice and clouds of gnats did to our eyes, because there right in the front us, about fifty yards off, they stood like men.*"[9] It affirmed the preconceptual feeling of beneficence of being-in-a-world as a viable venture. The empirical and symbolic amalgam of violence — natural and human, balanced by the caring of Frank for Cee — creates a mode of realistic intimacy that allows the vulnerability and the need to care and protect another person to become a part of his character. This original experience of dread and caring will ultimately structure the soteriological meaning of the time, space, and mode of being we call home and Morrison calls *Home.*

ORIENTATION TWO: LABYRINTHINE PEREGRINATIONS

Three explicit journeys are described in the novel. There is first the tragic expulsion of the black families, including the family of Ida and Salem Money, the parents of Frank Money, from a small Texas town to a small town in Louisiana. The next movement is from the town in Louisiana to Lotus, Georgia. They initially take up residence in the house of Lenore, Salem Money's sister. In Lotus, the movements shift to those involving Frank Money. Frank's first move takes place when he volunteers for the United States Army and leaves Lotus to join the army in Kentucky. The final and definitive movement is that of Frank Money, who, after his service in the Korean War, is discharged from the army and finds himself in a veterans hospital in Seattle, Washington, due to recurring episodes of trauma, a residue of the war. Upon receiving the urgent note, "Come fast. She be dead if you tarry," from Sarah, a friend of his sister, Cee, he escapes from the hospital without shoes and, relying on his street smarts and the aid of several black people, undertakes the journey south to Lotus. The literary structure of the novel is built around this movement of Frank Money from the veterans hospital back to Lotus, Georgia. This journey is also the religious structure that allows all the various tales about the lives of the characters to be told.

These movements exemplify various religious motifs. The first movement—the expulsion from the town in Texas—reminds one of the expulsion of the Jews from Israel to Babylon. Frank Money's volunteering for the army may be seen as the first step of an initiatory ritual. Instead of moving from a vague innocence into a knowledge of the wider world and its meaning, Frank Money's flight from the numbness of life in Lotus into the lively adventuresome world of the US Army is full of lessons learned that can be likened to an initiation into a different world with possibilities. He seems to have been forced out by sheer *ennui* of the mediocrity and wretched evil of Lotus, Georgia. It is not a place where his life could have been nurtured. Morrison makes this clear when Frank tells us in chapter 7, "*There was no goal other than breathing, nothing to win and, save for somebody else's quiet death, nothing to survive or worth surviving for.*"[10]

From another perspective, the initiatory ritual structure is the basis for its derivative, the literary form of the *bildungsroman,* a novel concerned with a young person's coming of age. The origin of this literary form is usually attributed to Johann Wolfgang von Goethe's novel *Wilhelm Meister's Apprenticeship.* The literary form and meaning became a favorite topic for Romantic novelists and philosophers. It is clear, nevertheless, that behind this literary form lie the religious notions and practices of pilgrimage on the one hand and initiatory rituals on the other.

Allow me to specify the central motifs of these religious and literary forms. In the initiation rituals, the young person, who up until this point lives a completely neutral and powerless life in the community, is abruptly taken out from the community, confined in some place away from communal existence, undergoes various ordeals under the guidance of specialists, and finally returns to the community. With this return, the young person is endowed with gender-sexual identity, the knowledge and lore of the community, and the obligations and responsibilities he bears as a member of the group.[11]

I see the scene in chapter 1 describing Frank and Cee's observation of the violence of the horses and the burial of the black man as the first part of an initiatory pattern that is later taken over by the initial stage of Frank's pilgrimage away from Lotus. The horse and burial scene never leaves him. Much later, when he returns to Lotus after his long sojourn, he still remembers the beauty of the horses. And in Lotus he solves the mystery of the secret burial. The novel concludes when he and Cee carry out a ritual of reburial for the murdered black man, only now with a cross and writing that repeats the theme of the standing horses. The geographic pilgrimage through space—from Lotus into the world and back to Lotus—has been equally a revealing of identity, knowledge, and wisdom.

The pilgrimage structure in like manner is based upon a departure from "home." In the case of the pilgrimage, those undertaking it are already adults in the community and often led by ritual specialists. The ritual specialists, like Miss Ethel Fordham, possess the knowledge and ritual powers that make the community work. They are, for the most part, responsible for the viability and security of the social group. At particular intervals of time, younger members of this group will depart from the safety and security of their homes to undertake a journey containing ordeals to a sacred or holy site to worship and venerate a mythical being, a god, or a significant event that took place there.[12]

In many rites of passage the departure from home creates different spatial, temporal, and societal situations for those on the pilgrimage. They have left their statuses and prestige, their roles in society, and thus they appear as "new persons" in this new space/time of the pilgrimage. In addition, they meet people, animals, and sometimes spirits from several different towns and villages that are unknown to them. The old rules and habits that defined their life at home are no longer in force. New names and forms of address are taken on in the pilgrimage. The time/space of the pilgrimage is a temporal spatial locus that is, in the words of anthropologist Victor Turner, "betwixt and between." The total situation created in the pilgrim journey is referred to by Turner as *communitas*—a liminal space and time where improvisations are the rule and rubric. One tends to adopt modes of address that express not old statuses but egalitarian meanings that identify others as equals on the pilgrimage and not as members of any particular society or hierarchy. Furthermore, within this new modality of time/space, the events and ordering forms of the places they have left are reinterpreted within the mixture of a polyglot of unfamiliar persons, and thus new and different meanings of their past are spoken within the contingencies of the pilgrimage.

Some analogues to the major elements of the ritual of pilgrimage are present in the journey of Frank Money, except these motifs take place on his return to Lotus, not his departure. We are also reminded of the journey of the enslaved Africans in the United States escaping from enslavement to a "free state" through the Underground Railroad. These journeys, like Frank Money's, were dangerous, subversive passages and required social and even spiritual allies along the way. Let us remember that the geographical goal of this "reverse pilgrimage" is that wretched place, Lotus, Georgia; Lotus is not a place of transcendent value worthy of veneration. Within the liminal space of passage, Frank Money finds himself dependent on hitherto unknown persons who appear at every turn to aid him on his way. Through them another topography and another geography of the country come into view. He's helped by John Locke, who leads him to Reverend Maynard, who gives him a list of safe places to stop and eat. A train waiter named C. Taylor encourages him to go to Booker's Diner, where he meets Billy Watson, who takes him home and offers a room to sleep. It is there that he has a dream in which the zoot suiter appears, as though a ghost with a message. He takes this appearance as a "sign trying to tell him something." It is only then that he begins to realize the ultimate significance of his life through this journey.

Maybe his life had been preserved for Cee, which was only fair since she had been his original caring for, a selflessness without gain or emotional profit. Even before she could walk he'd taken care of her. The first word she spoke was "Fwank."[13]

It is not only a network of persons and places revealed in his trek. Rather, he gains knowledge of the arc of his life through an amalgam of his past expressed in his traumatic episodes of memories and reveries. We travel with him as Morrison and the voice of Frank in the italicized chapters reconstruct his time in Korea, and with Lily, and the little Korean yum-yum girl, all played against a backdrop of the awfulness of that place in Georgia called Lotus and the mysterious magnetism of Cee. When Frank decided to leave Lotus, "He tried to tell her the army was the only solution. Lotus was suffocating, killing him and his two best friends. They all agreed. Frank assured himself Cee would be okay. She wasn't."[14]

PRIMORDIAL PROPENSITIES:
THE GIVEN AND THE POSSIBLE

In the epigraph, Morrison contrasts the "given" and the "possible," what I call the "primordial propensities" of Morrison's writing. Her contrast between the house in which she finds herself and the house she "dreamed" points to the broader interaction of the nonhuman powers of the created world with those of human beings. The notions of "creation" and the deeper structure of the created order come to the fore here.

The created order is *given* but not in the manner of a mute or passive container inside of which humans dwell. In many mythological traditions, the created order of the world makes its appearance precisely when the first humans are in the midst of some creative act that may also involve an ordeal. It is in this environment that access to the potency of the givenness of the created order becomes possible and available in acts of imagination, dreams, and conjurings. In the epigraph, Toni describes both a negative "given" and a positive "possibility": "*This house is strange / Its shadows lie / Say, tell me why does its lock fits my key?*" She contrasts this house-container with another image of a place in which to dwell: "*I dreamed another, sweeter, brighter / With a view of lakes crossed in painted boats; / Of fields wide as arms open for me.*" So the house of night is the world as *given* to the black people in the novel. It's empirical, dangerous, a lie. But the other house, the imagined house, the dreamed-of house, is the center from which a sweet and embracing nature awaits the black people in the novel.

Lotus and Korea are the house of night in most of the novel. Frank's companions from Lotus—Mike and Stuff—who joined the army with him and served with him Korea, are his only stable companions after leaving Lotus; they were both killed in Korea. The only white person with whom he had a sustained relationship was "Neck," a poor white who made himself a part of the Lotus soldiers in Korea. He too was killed. It is significant to note that "Neck," short for "Redneck," is the only white person he has known, and the US Army is the only institution where he has been treated in a manner approximating equality. As a matter of fact, the Reverend John Locke remarked on the fact that the only integrated American institution was one dedicated to killing and death and that after service, they came back to a society that had no regard for them. Locke says: "An integrated army is integrated misery. You all go fight, come back, they treat you like dogs. Change that. They treat dogs better."[15]

What begins to bring the other, imagined house alive for Frank is the journey he takes from the hospital back to the house of night. The persons—beginning with the Reverends John Locke and Maynard in Portland, the porter on the train, the family of Billy, Arlene, and their son, Thomas, in Chicago—all of them singularly and as a network form the *communitas* of his reverse pilgrimage to that wretched site of Lotus. They treat him not so much equally as humanly and with justice. They discern and take care of his needs as he has defined them; they nurture him and provide him with resources for the continuation of his journey. They are his allies.

In the ritual studies of Victor Turner we learn that a radically different form of human community is experienced on certain pilgrimages. Turner calls this form of human togetherness *communitas*. It takes place in a liminal space/time — the in-between time/space of the "no longer" but also "not yet." New and other modes of intuition, perception, and later conceptions emerge from this situation. Reality as "given" and reality as "possible" appear quite differently in this liminal space/time. For Frank, his first experience of reality showing itself in radically different ways takes place when he and Cee are confronted by the horse violence and the human killing. At the end of chapter 1, after the powerful description of the horses fighting, the narrator expresses Frank Money's consciousness in this way: "*I really forgot about the burial. I only remember the horses. They were so beautiful. So brutal. And they stood like men.*" This parallels Morrison's juxtaposition of the dark house and the bright house in the novel's epigraph.

What impresses Frank Money at this early stage is not the evil inflicted on the murdered man but the brutality and beauty of the nonhuman power of horses battling. He intuits here a reality more powerful than the oppressors who have killed another black man. For Cee, the rescue from the house of darkness is even more harrowing. Her dwelling in Lotus was not a place of security and safety. She experienced the place called home in the house of a very mean aunt. She marries Principal (Prince), a ne'er-do-well loser who neglects her and steals from the family. Prince takes her to Atlanta, where he abandons her. Cee is able to find work in various restaurants but eventually ends up as a maid in the home of a prominent white physician, Dr. Beau. The work there goes well for a while, but in time Cee learns that she has been recruited, without her knowledge, to serve as a human subject for certain experiments that Dr. Beau was performing on the bodies of young black females. Based on Dr. J. Marion Sims, the "father of gynecology," who experimented on the bodies of enslaved women, Dr. Beau nearly kills Cee.

Upon his arrival in Atlanta, Frank Money goes to the home of Dr. Beau.

In a dramatic scene he confronts the doctor in his office. Dr. Beau threatens Frank with a gun that misfires. Frank finds the room where Cee is suffering, picks her up, takes her back to Lotus, and places her in the care of Miss Ethel. Miss Ethel and a group of black women comment on the action like a Greek chorus, minister to Cee with herbs, and expose her to the sun for healing. Cee and Frank slowly become aware that, even in Lotus, Georgia, the healing resources of nature and black people are available. The place they had believed to be deathly is now revealed to be life-giving.

ORIENTATION THREE: COMING HOME

After placing Cee in the hands of Miss Ethel and the country women, Frank Money walks through town. For the first time, he can see beauty in Lotus. The sun, the flowers, the butterflies, the sight of a woman fishing in a stream named Wretched, animate one of the few scenes of well-being in the novel. "This feeling of safety and goodwill, he knew, was exaggerated," the narrator tells us, "but savoring it was real."[16] This scene, like Baby Suggs's sermon in *Beloved,* is a kind of aggregation, a recognition and enjoyment of community: "Soon as the blossoms began to fall, Frank headed down the rows of cotton to the shed that the farm manager called his office. He had hated this place once."[17]

The rituals of *Home* do not express a particular doctrine; they express the epistemological structure of the world of the novel. Within this structure, the human body serves as the basis for the determination of the more abstract notions of geographical space. Frank Money's bodily movement through space is a mode of coming to knowledge of himself and his world. With his rescue of Cee from the experiments of Dr. Beau, it begins to dawn on Frank Money that his memory of Cee as a little girl enables him to imagine a community that confirms his early bodily intuitions of both the Given and the Possible in a world that is authentic — his own-life-in-the-world. It is clear that Frank Money's return to Lotus, Georgia, constitutes his first experience of home. The novel makes it clear that home is not identical to the place where one was born and spent one's early life. Home is simultaneously a structure of human consciousness as well as a geographical site. Home establishes our fundamental orientation in time, space, and imagination; home orients us to our world. This realization comes most clearly on one of Frank's walks. Just before the chapter in which he speaks about his abuse and killing of the Korean girl, he finds himself at home in Lotus: "Waving occasionally at passing neighbors or those doing chores on their porches, he could not believe how much he had once hated this place. Now it seemed both fresh and ancient, safe and demanding."[18] Having seen the sights, rituals, and festivals of other places, the pilgrim Frank Money is now able to make use of the knowledge of these other spectacles to deepen his understanding of the nature and meaning of home.

The movement of Frank's body through the world provides the structure for the novel. It is an American novel by an African American woman. It is a story about Frank Money and his family in the early 1950s in the United States. These simple facts are enough to involve us in the issues of long-distance geographical movements by Africans, the African Diaspora. Morrison's novel involves us in the story of Africans who were brought into the Americas as enslaved persons — people who were stolen from a home and taken to a place where they could never be at home. That is one American story of movement.

The other story of long-distance movement in the United States is the movement of a significant group of Europeans across the Atlantic on a religious pilgrimage to America as a "place of freedom." Two voyages to America, one to enslave and the other to establish a home for freedom. These are separate and diametrically opposed meanings, but, in America, they were identical and simultaneous. One query raised by the novel is whether the United States is capable of being a home for all of those who inhabit its spaces. The aboriginal populations have been dispersed, their cultures disrupted and subjected to genocide, and they have been made to feel as aliens in their traditional homes. The European "pilgrims" quickly transformed themselves into Yankee businessmen in league with southern plantation owners who enhanced the slave trade and the South as an empire of human slavery. So the American "house" has been built, but whose home is it?

One of the early theoretical works on the American republic was *Democracy in America,* the observations of the French aristocrat Alexis de Tocqueville, who visited the United States between 1835 and 1840.[19] The chapter entitled "Some Considerations Concerning the Present State and Probable Future of the Three Races That Inhabit the Territory of the United States" is one of the few texts that speaks of the United States as composed of three races and raises the issue of their common habitation in the land. As far as the three races sharing a common culture, Tocqueville surmises that this might be accomplished through the blood mixtures of the three races. Such blood mixtures took place in unprecedented ways, but they were never legitimated in terms that related to the land, labor, or time. Through legal constitutional means and customary practices, the category of "white" as the designation of the European ancestry of the United States became identical with the notion of America.

Sidney E. Mead's essay "The American People: Their Space, Time, and Religion" relates the historical experience of Europeans in America to the way in which the conquest of the land impinged on their notions of time and space.[20] Mead makes no reference to what Tocqueville referred to as "the three races" that inhabit the land. This avoidance or denial is adumbrated in the attention he gives to the failure of Americans to express what he calls "the inner experience," vital and somber. I take it that this unexpressed inner experience is, in fact, the interrelated lives of the three races. In the creation of a new country, Americans eschewed a liminal period — a time of the betwixt and between, a time of the no longer and the not yet, a time when the racial and cultural mixtures could be recognized. At the time of the Founding of the American republic, there was indeed "world enough and time" to attempt the creation of a new form of the human world that took seriously the land and the peoples who inhabited it. The possibility of liminal time went unacknowledged, and thus there was no real *communitas* upon which to found the republic. This is the shadow that continues to haunt the American endeavor. This is "the night that keeps out the light," in Morrison's opening words.

The ambiguous relationship to that intimate space called home has been expressed again and again by African Americans poets, novelists, and musicians. Ray Charles's rendition of the American patriotic hymn "America, the Beautiful" has been reconfigured, reordered, and sung as a stern reminder of the underlying freedom that is too often denied in the American state. Charles renders the music as an incantation against an alienation that seems to be a threat to the possibility of the beauty of the land flowing over into the beauty of the relationships between the peoples of the land. Charles began his rendition with the third verse of the song that carries an admonition. In Charles's version, the relationships of those who people the land must be refined before its natural beauty can be understood and enjoyed.

The intensity of this longing for the intimate space called home can be heard in the plaintive passivity of Otis Redding's "Sitting on the Dock of the Bay." He's just "sitting on the dock of the bay, wasting time, wasting time." Redding's poignant resignation is reversed in Nina Simone's "Mississippi, Goddam!" Simone's aggressive denunciation of the alienated evil that has cursed this land is wild, fierce, and revolutionary. And so the issue is posed once more. Can there ever be an intimate external space in the land that matches the intimate internal spaces of the human? This, in part, is the impetus of this novel and the one constant resource of intimacy that holds it together.

EPILOGUE: KNOWING WHERE ONE STANDS

Cee's rescue and healing is the harbinger for the transformation of the sterile and wretched town of Lotus, Georgia. Through her therapy under the guidance of Miss Ethel, Frank Money experiences the confirmation of the communal nature of human society but also discovers an inner life that had been obscured and distorted. Frank Money is able to see how the repression of his inner life had contributed to the traumatic episodes of memory. Frank Money is now capable of facing his inner life as a soulful self. He confesses his abuse and murder of the little Korean girl and comes to terms with the death of his companions in Korea: "My mourning was so thick it completely covered my shame."[21]

There is also rectification. In his conversation with the old-timers in Lotus, he finally learns the horrible and gruesome truth of how white men had forced a black son to murder his father. These murderers are the ones he and Cee saw piling the black man into a hole at the novel's beginning. In the final scene of the novel, Frank returns with Cee to rebury this man with human dignity under a tree: "Quickly they found the sweet bay tree — split down the middle, beheaded, undead — spreading its arms, one to the right, one to the left." This tree with its arms spread reminds us of those fields with wide-open arms in Morrison's dream. The correct directions of Frank Money's life have been confirmed; his orientation has been confirmed in nature and reconfirmed by humans in his hometown who with him reconfigure the creative orientations of their own lives. Frank pounds a piece of wood he had sanded onto the tree trunk. On it he had carved, "Here Stands a Man":

I stood there a long time staring at that tree.
It looked so strong
So beautiful
Hurt right down the middle
But alive and well.
Cee touched my shoulder
Lightly,
Frank?
Come on, brother, let's go home.

NOTES

1. Immanuel Kant, *Idea for a Universal History from a Cosmopolitan Point of View,* trans. Lewis Beck (New York: Bobbs-Merrill, 1963); see also Chenxi Tang, *The Geographical Imagination of Modernity* (Stanford, CA: Stanford University Press, 2006), esp. part 2. For the relation of race to geography in Kant, see David Harvey, *Cosmopolitanism and the Banality of Geographical Evils,* davidharvey.org/media/cosmopol.pdf.

2. See Gaston Bachelard, *The Poetics of Space*, trans. Miria Jolas (New York: Penguin, 2014).

3. See my "Perspectives for a Study of Afro-American Religions in the United States," 173–84, and "Freedom, Otherness and Religion: Theologies Opaque," 185–99, in *Significations: Signs, Symbols, and Images in the Interpretation of Religion,* 2nd. ed. (Aurora, CO: Davies Group, 1999).

4. Charles H. Long, *Significations* (Aurora, CO: Davies Group, 1995), esp. the foreword and proem, 7.

5. Toni Morrison, *Home* (New York: Knopf, 2012), 1.

6. See Chenxi Tang, *The Geographical Imagination of Modernity,* 8–9.

7. Morrison, *Home,* 84.

8. Morrison, *Home,* 84.

9. Morrison, *Home,* 1.

10. Morrison, *Home,* 83.

11. For a comprehensive description and interpretation of initiation rituals, see Mircea Eliade, *Birth and Rebirth: The Religious Meaning of Initiation in Human Culture* (New York: Harper and Brothers, 1958).

12. Victor Turner has written quite extensively on the topic of pilgrimage. Among his works are "Pilgrimage as Social Process," in *Drama, Fields, and Metaphors: Symbolic Action in Human Society* (Ithaca, NY: Cornell University Press, 1974); and with his wife, Edith Turner, *Image and Pilgrimage in Christian Culture: Anthropo-*

logical Perspectives (New York: Columbia University Press, 1978). The most comprehensive and succinct statement is probably "The Center Out There: Pilgrim's Goal," *History of Religions* 12, no. 13 (February 1973): 191–230.

13. Morrison, *Home,* 34–35.

14. Morrison, *Home,* 35.

15. Morrison, *Home,* 18.

16. Morrison, *Home,* 118.

17. Morrison, *Home,* 120.

18. Morrison, *Home,* 132.

19. Alexis de Tocqueville, *Democracy in America,* trans. George Lawrence (New York: Doubleday, 1969), 316–407.

20. Sidney E. Mead, *The Lively Experiment* (New York: Harper and Row, 1963), 1–15.

21. Morrison, *Home,* 133.

Morrison's Pietàs as Participatory Loss and Love

MARA WILLARD

When the young and gifted Chloë Wofford brought herself to the Roman Catholic church in her Ohio neighborhood, she took herself across a threshold into a world of embodied and imaginative participation. She was twelve, she said in an interview.[1] That marks an entry into what is now termed "pre-Conciliar" Catholicism, which is to say before the profound liturgical changes that followed the meetings of the Second Vatican Council.

Historian of Catholicism Robert Orsi describes the power of devotional Catholicism through "its smells, textures, tastes, and sounds." Sensory media "formed the very way Catholic bodies existed and moved," he says, "the poise and bearing of these bodies, a distinctly Catholic kinetics, inside church and outside, in schools, playgrounds, and workplaces, on city streets and in rural communities."[2] A Catholic learns to receive the Eucharist with bodily knowledge. "Take this, all of you, and eat of it: this is my body which will be given up for you" is a speech act that prompts a flow of bodily movements. The hands fold, the chin tilts up. The mouth moistens to receive the consecrated host, and the lips open so that the tongue may emerge. The forefinger flies up for the sign of the cross.

Homilies will go on, and of a Sunday morning a child is apt to find her eyes drifting from the pulpit. But for Catholics, this too is devotional work. Orsi describes how although some children were restless and bored, "many children loved going to mass, their imaginations captured by its mystery and splendor and pleased to share in their community's distinguishing sign of recognizing God's real presence on the altar."[3] The Stations of the Cross that hang around the walls of the sanctuary compound the power of homilectics in fourteen pictures or sculptures that present the Passion of Christ. These fourteen panels are "narrative pictorial strategies," drawing the devout "into the images by virtue of their very bodies."[4] Painted, or carved to have depth and perspective, the images invite those in the pews to take in the Last Supper, the journey to Golgotha, the stumbles, the crown of thorns, the Crucifixion. When received by the devout, "the senses had cognitive status . . . in which the intellect was materially engaged."[5] The encounter is not well described by any use of distinctions between mind and body, or thinking and feeling. Here again, "it was in their bodies that children were made to know the realness of God."[6]

A well-worn path by which Catholics have moved into the event of the cross is by joining Mary the mother of God by in her sorrow. In the "Lamentation," Mary often holds her grown son upon her lap, brought down after the crucifixion. This is a pietà. Its variation is the mother standing beneath the cross, the *stabat mater dolorosa.* The "Stabat Mater," a thirteenth-century poem and later hymn, calls for participation in the event of the cross: "*Quis non posset contristári / Christi Matrem contemplári / doléntem cum Fílio?*" "Can the human heart refrain / from partaking in her pain / in that Mother's pain untold?" The singing encourages the devotee to produce within her own body the grief felt by Mary in mourning the death of Christ. Her maternal agony of the violent death suffered by her grown son merges with the theological crisis of the *deus absconditus,* the hidden God.

ENTERING A NARRATIVE WORLD

Roman Catholicism's participatory and affective modes of practice, in which the devout are drawn by bodies and images to participate in a world made real, provide one strategy for learning from and about the religious and ethical imagination in the novels of Toni Morrison. The observation that readers are called upon to be active participants in her fiction is neither new nor controversial. Morrison has described her method of writing as providing "places and spaces so that the reader can participate."[7] In this, she receives and remakes a particularly African American method of collective storytelling. Readers, like congregants, must be affective participants in order for a story or preaching to function successfully. They join in generating the emotions that carry the movement of characters. Lips must hum appreciation of a verity; shouts, tears or laughs mark the turning of events. The community draws memory into the present, and projects hope into what comes next. Like the call-and-response structure of storytelling and preaching in the African American tradition, the spaces and silences in Morrison's novels are sites for ethical formation. Young people, guided by elders, participate in making the sense or the nonsense of an event. A Morrison novel often "insists upon the reader's participation in its meaning, through its perspectivist point of view and the construction of its ending," says literary critic Ann E. Imbrie.[8] Without the reader's interpretive agency, the fragmented experiences and events could not become a story.

Of her experience of being drawn by memory to participate in Morrison's works, scholar of African American history Barbara Smith describes how "the music and paintings she makes with words stun the reader's senses."[9] In the same essay, Smith gives a personal account of how memories of participating in a community in mourning flood the past into the present and open up the religious imagination. Listening to the singing of "What a Friend We Have in Jesus" at her grandmother's funeral, Smith says, "made her think of her grandmother herself, singing the same words." This, in turn, "brought back Church and how important it had once been to me simply because it was so vitally important for the women who brought me up." Here, the experience of mourning participates in an "ambiguous corporeality."[10] While listening to the hymn that honored her grandmother, Smith says that she "imagined all the women in my family, now gone, greeting her with joy in a secure realm where Black spirits dwell." Mourning is an occasion to experience the corporeality of a loving and nurturing community of black women.

The unique consideration here is how readers are invited to enter Morrison's novels in events of lamentation and specifically at the work of the tableau of the pietà. There is no one depiction. Each iteration is distinct. We will move to stand before three instances of this Station of the Cross. In *Song of Solomon,* Milkman sings to Pilate as the warmth drains from her body. A pietà closes the great novel *Paradise,* with the song and embrace of Piedade running her fingers through the tea-colored hair of a grown woman. In *Sula,* we stand before Eva holding and rocking in her arms her opiate-hazed and war-traumatized man-boy son.

In her 2012 Ingersoll Lecture, however, Morrison nominates another ethical imperative under which she works, which is to put goodness onstage. The pietà may seem to be a strange place to behold goodness or mercy. Yet we will find as we go how deeply we feel the registers of humanity in these the pictoral narratives. Many demand participation in the embodied emotional work of love that feeds lamentation, even as

FIG. 5. Sandra Hansen, *The Emmett Till Memorial Triptych.* (Licensed under CC BY 2.0)

emotions invoked by intersections of race, death, and the maternal are often fraught.

THE PIETÀ

The pietà commands perception because it has a status in the hegemonic culture. Although the Christian tradition does not define the limits of its powers to signify, a pietà requires some stability of form. Only when thus activated by recognition can its religious-artistic-political power be felt. Once recognized, its deviation and its subversion can also be felt.

In *American Pietà,* Ruby C. Tapia gives broad scope to a "pietà status." She identifies it in any tableau at the "intersection of race, death, and the maternal." Tapia further proposes that an "ascription of pietà status . . . compels viewers to look outside the frame of the image-event."[11] That is to say, anytime that a pietà is recognized, another act must follow. Tapia tells us to look critically at the occasion that prompted the death being mourned and to undertake a political and ethical analysis of the norms that the pietà is tacitly promoting.[12] What interests are being served by a particular invocation of the bereaved embracing the fallen? How are they racialized and gendered?

For instance, American "war memorial pietàs" invite participation in the values of nationalist military adventurers. Male soldiers "replaced Christ and feminized figures stood in for grief-stricken but resilient nations."[13] The pietà proliferated as a European symbol around the First World War, implying the approval of a sacrifice by God and/or the nation-state. It functioned in a secularized form to valorize and even to sanctify ideals of whiteness, masculinized military valor, feminized honor and acceptance, and the worthiness of patriotic sacrifice. Implicitly, the pietà can also be charged with the conviction that death is made meaningful as a sacrifice in an economy of greater redemption.

There are other reasons to be wary of tropes of the pietà and the *stabat mater*. Feminist criticism of this representation expresses particular concern about its participation in displaying norms of race and gender. The most famous is the iconography of Michelangelo's 1499 marble statue in St. Peter's Basilica in the Vatican. Carved in white marble, Mary is slight and stylized as European. Some feminists object that this pietà presumes and satisfies consumption of passive, silent, compliant female beauty. French feminist Julia Kristeva has a related critical concern. She observes how Christianity facilitates imaginative representations of the female subject in ways that exceed, say, biological sciences or philosophical reasoning. Kristeva says that while Christianity "is no doubt the most sophisticated symbolic construct in which femininity, to the extent that it figures therein — and it does so constantly — is confined within the limits of the *Maternal.*"[14] Possible representations of Mary may be rich, but they are not wholly elastic.

Just as the death of Jesus on the cross had historical origins in state violence, the pietà is a pictoral narrative of a young person's death grieved by a living parent. As such, it has significance for political and ethical protest. The mourning parent with dead child is available as a signifier for those who are subject to violence. To read the significance of any instance of the pietà, says Tapia, we must look "outside the frame of the image-event to understand the historical matter of long-standing racial social death."[15] A painting of Emmett Till, entitled *Mother, Behold Thy Son,* both depends upon and exceeds the significance of a Christ figure.[16] The same could be said of *Liberation of the Peon* (1931), by Diego Rivera. A 2015 Associated Press photo of paramilitary police officer who carries the lifeless body of three-year-old Alan Kurdi off the coast of Bodrum, Turkey, had the effect of pulling millions of Western viewers into bodily participation. All become occasions for "visceral seeing" of sorrow and ethical implication.

The pietàs of the Morrison corpus can function to similar effect as pictoral narratives of "the intersection of race, death, and the maternal." Beyond the image-event, the reader knows the contingent history of this family loss. She also perceives the culpability of the structural violence behind the singular incident. Morrison renders her readers witnesses to the extreme conditions and untimely deaths of Africans and African Americans in the Middle Passage, sexual violence, the afterlife of war, and misguided racialized efforts to realize some ultimately security.

SONG OF SOLOMON

> *Eja, Mater, fons amóris / me sentíre vim dolóris / fac, ut tecum lúgeam.* (O thou Mother! Font of love! / Touch my spirit from above, / make my heart with thine accord.)[17]

In *Song of Solomon,* a grown man holds a grown woman. She is not his mother and not even yet his friend. She is dying of a gunshot wound meant for him. Her response to the coming of death is to ask the man to sing: "'Sing,' she said. 'Sing a little somethin for me.'" He doesn't want to. He "knew no songs, and had no singing voice that anybody would want to hear, but he couldn't ignore the urgency in her voice." The grown man, Milkman, cradling the dying woman, must give her this.

So the man goes on, the narrator describes, "Speaking the words without the least bit of a tune, he sang for the lady." The words are new, but recognizable. It is a nursery tune we know from earlier in the novel, whose words of loss he has adjusted: "Sugargirl don't leave me here / Cotton balls to choke me / Sugargirl don't leave me here / Buckra's arms to yoke me." Milkman's sorrow and voice grow together. He "could not stop the worn old words from coming, louder and louder as though sheer volume would wake her."[18] He sings her away to the lyrics that are suited just to her:

> *"Fac, ut árdeat cor meum / in amándo Christum Deum / ut sibi compláceam."*

"Make me feel as thou hast felt; / make my soul to glow and melt / with the love of Christ my Lord."

Inside the frame, love and goodness come onstage. Before dying, the older woman speaks of her daughter and gives a voice to love. "Watch Reba for me," she says. And also: "I wish I'd a knowed more people. I would of loved 'em all. If I'd a knowed more, I would a loved more."[19] Her expression of superabundant love enters the plot, changing the bodily choices of Milkman in the coming pages. One reader of the novel observes, "The responsibility of love presents itself at every death scene in *Song of Solomon*."[20] Morrison is showing us goodness, the African American courage to retain humanity, remain present to death and loss, to mourn and console. Mary need not be a birth mother. Mary need not be a Christian. Mary need not be Mary. Milkman was the one who nursed, but now he is the one who cradles.

"Solomon done fly, Solomon done gone" is an example of "body-words," Latina theologian Mayra Rivera Rivera would say. Colonized or enslaved peoples communicated in ways that exceeded the linguistic tools of slave owners and colonizers. The "Song of Solomon" includes African words. The "tale of a slave who flew home to Africa, a song not entirely intelligible yet fully recognizable," is one that Morrison recounts having heard from her grandfather.[21] Its body-words "are not entirely intelligible to Solomon's descendants, the African-Americans who people the world of the novel."[22] Yet for Milkman, the "worn old words" become utterly meaningful. They teach him his family history. They shape his actions. Milkman keeps the song living, too, renewing its life as he cradles and sings away Sugargirl.

Rivera would have her readers learn new skills of perception of body-words. Doing so would open up these texts. As a scholar, she would have us mine connection with the biblical Song of Songs, which has the power to "both intersect with and unsettle Christian metaphors, inciting the present reinterpretation of spirit and flesh."[23] But this kind of interpretive work would require attention to the intelligence of affect and embodiment and refuse an inheritance that tells us that bodies distract us from wisdom. The wisdom of the racial social-political conditions that inform the pietà in *Song of Solomon* is also experiential, emotional, and embodied. In the USA, huge numbers die each year by gun violence. In 2016, 38,658 people were killed by guns. More than 116,000 others suffered nonfatal injuries.[24]

PARADISE

Quando corpus moriétur, / fac, ut ánimæ donétur / paradísi glória.
(While my body here decays, / may my soul Thy goodness
praise, / Safe in Paradise with Thee.)

The tableau from Morrison's oeuvre that has received by far the highest
degree of critical recognition as a pietà is the closing scene from her novel
Paradise. In this still, quiet scene, the reader encounters female protagonists.

"In ocean hush a woman black as firewood is singing." Again, silence.
"Next to her is a younger woman whose head rests on the singing woman's
lap. Ruined fingers troll the tea brown hair. All the colors of seashells —
wheat, roses, pearl — fuse in the younger woman's face. Her emerald eyes
adore the black face framed in cerulean blue." Color, too. To draw this
scene, my own young child would have to reach for his tremendous sixty-
four pack of Crayola crayons: for wheat, rose, tea brown, emerald, cerulean blue, charcoal.

According to one reader of *Paradise,* the lap that holds Consolata, the
hands that untangle her hair, the voice that sings to her is "the spiritual
mother from her homeland, Piedade, who now sings a song of 'solace.'"[25]
Another says that she is "a real or imagined figure who represents a bliss-
ful childhood memory to Consolata and whose singing is generally held
to render solace to shipwrecked survivors."[26] Other interpreters stress the
ways in which this figure blends imaginations across continents. "*Piedade*
is Portuguese for 'pity' or 'compassion,'" says one reader, "and the image
of her cradling Consolata constitutes a revised version of the pietà, the
conventional depiction of the Christian Madonna and child."[27] Another
says that she is the shape-shifting African goddess Yemanja, who in the
Afro-Brazilian religion Candomblé became conflated with the Virgin
Mary.[28]

Pointing our attention to body-words, Rivera would again not be sur-
prised at this amalgam. She says that it is through discourses about bodies
that "mythology is often creatively reinterpreted."[29] She teaches outsiders
to the colonized worlds of the Caribbean and South America to glean
how human bodies participate with bodies of water. "Questions of bodies, foreign words, and fragrant seas," she tells us, "are not distractions to

be overcome." Salt water and sensual bodies are medium and message. Allies in the work of decolonizing must learn how "the sea as symbol of fluid, rhythmic connection is a recurrent image in Caribbean philosophy." In the tableau of the pietà, the sea is among the consolations. Diasporic communities sing and move in "geographies of a country they have left behind," but which consolations renew again in song and connected bodies.[30]

The younger woman is the object of the solace of the sea, as well as touch and song of the older. The narrator of *Paradise* draws us back and reveals a bit of landscape: "Around them on the beach, sea trash gleams. Discarded bottle caps sparkle near a broken sandal. A small dead radio plays the quiet surf." It plays not static, but the waves. Morrison keeps her reader in a modern time and place, even as she cannot know when or where.[31] The bricolage of "sea trash" refuses sentimentalism. The wreckage of the past is always with us.

The narrator of *Paradise* shoots a quiver full of words, issuing emerald energy to the body of the reader. Go slowly, reader. Hear the teaching out loud. Know that "There is nothing to beat this solace which is what Piedade's song is about, although the words evoke memories neither one has ever had: of reaching age in the company of the other; of speech shared and divided bread smoking from the fire; the unambivalent bliss of going home to be at home — the ease of coming back to love begun."[32] Sing to us, too, console us, play on the surf. The song calls us onward to create another order: "Now they will rest before shouldering the endless work they were created to do down here in Paradise."[33] Work to do. How many excess deaths in Puerto Rico after the storm? 2,975.[34] Lives that matter.

SULA

Juxta Crucem tecum stare / et me tibi sociáre / in planctu desídero. (By the Cross with thee to stay, / there with thee to weep and pray, / is all I ask of thee to give.)

Morrison depicts maternal-filial relationships as singular. She can signal this singularity through prerogatives of bodily accesses. "We are in the presence of mystery, a virtually biblical rite of fleshly acknowledgement," says literary scholar Philip Weinstein of maternal care in *Song of Solo-*

mon.[35] Eva, a mother in *Sula,* cleaned the orifices of her son Plum when he was a child. But their intimacies of infant care persist past prenatal fluidities to a "thick love" and shared fluids of bodily intimacies.

> Eva swung over to the bed and propped her crutches at its foot. She sat down and gathered Plum into her arms. He woke, but only slightly.
> "Hey man. Hey. You holdin' me, Mamma?" His voice was drowsy and amused. He chuckled as though he had heard some private joke. Eva held him closer and began to rock. Back and forth she rocked him, her eyes wandering around his room. . . . Rocking, rocking, listening to Plum's occasional chuckles. . . . Eva lifted her tongue to the edge of her lip to stop the tears from running into her mouth. Rocking, rocking. Later she laid him down and looked at him a long time.[36]

Plum is grown, and his seeking again the unmitigated intimacy of his mother's body is near-unseemly. Just as Milkman gains his nickname from being too long at his mother's breast in *Song of Solomon,* so the scene of *Sula* is uncanny when a diminutive, lame woman rocks an outsized baby, a man who would return to the womb.

The devotional practice of cradling is a bodily, emotional response to "powerlessness and vulnerability," says scholar of religion Jennifer Scheper Hughes. In her study "Cradling the Sacred," she identifies the demand for presence and care by that which is "small, powerless, and in need of care." The devotees respond in a kind of rocking. This "cradling gesture underscores the nature of these object-entities as vital matter: they are 'beings,'" says Hughes.[37] Although living presence may defy observation by modern Western scientific methods, the claim of need upon the emotions and bodies of the devotees yields a cradling of mercy and goodness.

The reader does not yet know, from inside the frame of *Sula,* why the mother weeps. Only in retrospect does the reader appreciate how Eva is anticipating and beginning to mourn her son's untimely death. Similarly, the peculiar birth gifts, funeral spices of frankincense and myrrh, have significance only with foreknowledge of the Passion of Christ. In what way does Mary understand this?

Katy Ryan, a keen reader of Morrison, convincingly argues the ethical demand that universality of bodily arrangements cannot be read in ways that efface the particularity of black experience in America.[38] In the instance of Plum Peace, Ryan would have us know that when he went off to fight in World War I in 1917, he would have been one of four hundred thousand black Americans who served in a segregated army. He returned from his tour in 1919. This was also the peak year for lynching in the United States. Between 1917 and 1923, white Americans murdered 363 people of color.[39] Ryan also points out that Morrison wrote *Sula* in the context of the US war in Vietnam. African Americans served, were killed, and returned home veterans in numbers highly disproportionate to their white counterparts. In 1965, the US war intensified, Malcolm X was assassinated, and the Watts riots began.

Eva may be pondering these things in her heart as "her eyes wander[ed] around his room." She puts together the taste of a red drink beside his bed, sipping, perhaps, Plum's blood. The writer may think of the bent spoon. Together, mother and reader are putting together that opioid use is taking her son, and move through the spaces that Morrison's sentences hold open. Like Mexican and Mesoamerican devotees, she is responding in ways that cannot parse embodiment from affect.

In the "Stabat Mater," we address Mary directly, petitioning her to let us join her in the companionship of grief by the cross, "there to weep and pray."

Fac, ut portem Christi mortem, / passiónis fac consórtem, / et plagas recólere.

(Let me, to my latest breath, / in my body bear the death / of that dying Son of thine.)

Many mothers and lovers and sisters and others participate in this pain, this mourning, of slow suicide through opioid use. The disorder affected 2.1 million people in the United States in 2016,[40] and overdoses involving opioids killed more than 42,000 people. How to bear the death / of that dying Son of thine? So many share in the grief of Eva.

Plum on the rim of a warm light sleep was still chuckling. Mamma. She sure was somethin'. He felt twilight. Now there seemed to be some kind of wet light travelling over his legs and stomach with a deeply attractive smell. It wound itself — this wet light — all about him, splashing and running into his skin. He opened his eyes and saw what he imagined was the great wing of an eagle pouring a wet lightness over him. Some kind of baptism, some kind of blessing, he thought. Everything is going to be all right, it said. Knowing that it was so he closed his eyes and sank back into the bright hole of sleep.

Eva stepped back from the bed and let the crutches rest under her arms. She rolled a bit of newspaper into a tight stick about six inches long, lit it, and threw it onto the bed where the kerosene-soaked Plum lay in snug delight. Quickly, as the whoosh of flames engulfed him, she shut the door and made her slow and painful journey back to the top of the house.[41]

The narrator of *Sula* renders Plum's experience in birth metaphors, associated with reconciliation and security. But this liquification is also an ambiguous murder. It is an auto-da-fé enacted by the mother. The cradled child becomes a death pyre. Was it a mercy, that Plum's death follows this pietà of the grown son on the lap of his weeping mother. Was it a woefully misguided extension of maternal prerogative to give and take life? What is goodness in the state of emergency?

The pietà, says Tapia, can "invite readers to construct meaning from what they read."[42] But other readers insist that the inclusion of the reader in responding must incorporate study of how generations of African Americans who were subject to a system so violent that mothers' emotions and actions around life and death became extreme.[43] Her method of storytelling requires the reader to participate, yes. However, the openings in the text also function to defy mastery by the participating reader. One critic nicely observes the effectiveness of Morrison's strategy "to produce or represent a series of marked absences — the absence of a narratable meaning, of a history that can be fully experienced or adequately known — around which is then allowed to circulate a deep sense of loss." The reader's affective confrontation with loss is paired with a powerlessness for full assimilation. Participation becomes a lesson in humility at the points of Morrison's novels that "move beyond merely problematizing meaning to the more radical position of questioning the very possibility of narrating, of relating a history, of making events speak."[44] Attention to how bodies come together in a mixing of love and death in the novels of Morrison can function to privilege an ethics of empathy and compassion over an ethics of judgement.

CONCLUSION

Reading Morrison under the guidance of scholars of religion who move also in critical race and gender theory, we learn how to read in the survival of the humanity of the colonized and the enslaved. We learn that these spaces are open to our participation. The body-words of Sugarman, "done fly," sing on. On the beach is real presence of loving oceanic being out of "ancestral memories," and the consolations of color, touch, and song.[45] Their texts resist totalizing powers of the colonizer, or the slaveholder, to maintain the hegemonic powers of representational language. Like other postcolonial and diasporic writers, Morrison mixes the Christian tradition with pre- and postcolonial traditions of Brazil, African religions. Her "variations of the pietà are fused with precolonial religious sites and practices." With the pietà, Morrison poses "considerably different possibilities for gendered, nationalist signification."[46]

Participation in a Morrison pietà acts upon the reader. Perhaps we give fresh emotional attention to the once-unwed mother of ancient Palestine, holding her Jewish son executed by an order-demented Empire.[47] What does Mary ponder in her heart? With what complex affective blend of grief and rage does she feel the weight of her complex relationship to the man-child in her lap? He who denied her in the marketplace. From whose body may drift a potent aroma of myrrh, that embalming scent that brings her back to childbirth?

Then again, in Morrison's novels, the particularities of manifestations of love and grief over an untimely death refuse the shell of the pietà as a stable universal. In *Sula* and elsewhere, maternality is no assurance of security. Kristeva's demand for a maternal that signifies more than "envelope" is met. The birth mother is not the privileged figure of mourning in *Song of Solomon* or in *Paradise,* where other abundant presences hold and rock.[48] This is in part a comment on the severing violence of colonialization, genocide, when "the dislocating effects of the Middle Passage that make any attempt to identify one's ancestors difficult, if not impossible."[49] It can also be ethical instruction that we offer our own presence to the dead. That we become the abundant presence for those who are broken. "There she is, Miss America," said Toni Morrison at the Museo Nacional de Antropología in Mexico City. In her brokenness. Let us hold her, we who outlive her, in love and song, elevating of the ethic of embrace in love and lamentation.[50] Death does not mark the end of presence. New beginnings can be produced "within the contract of a pietà."[51] Plum continues to speak to Eva about the living and the dead.

At a funeral in *Sula,* the mourning congregation slips through its memories from the drowned child to "the slim, young Jew." In ambiguous corporeality, he "for them was both son and lover and in whose downy face they could see the sugar-and-butter sandwiches and feel the oldest and most devastating pain there is: not the pain of childhood, but the remembrance of it."[52] Deep pain is present here. The mind cannot name the demands that grief makes upon the heart. The "downy face," the body of the past, the lean revolutionary extends an erotic tug, assures knowing companionship, calls out to be taken up, held, rocked, and loved.

NOTES

1. Morrison converted to Roman Catholicism when she was twelve. Listen to her tell the story in "'I Regret Everything': Toni Morrison Looks Back on Her Personal Life," *Fresh Air with Terry Gross,* April 20, 2015, http://www.npr.org/2015/04/20 /400394947/i-regret-everything-toni-morrison-looks-back-on-her-personal-life.

2. Robert A. Orsi, "The Many Names of the Mother of God," in *Between Heaven and Earth: The Religious Worlds People Make and the Scholars Who Study Them* (Princeton: Princeton University Press, 2005), 55.

3. Orsi, "Material Children: Making God's Presence Real for Catholic Boys and Girls and for the Adults in Relation to Them," in *Between Heaven and Earth,* 96.

4. This term was coined by Patricia Cox Miller, who writes on medieval Catholic devotion. She also speaks of the "sensory realism" invoked when the devout presented themselves to the lives of the saints. The faithful are drawn "into the images by virtue of their very bodies" (Miller, "Visceral Seeing: The Holy Body in Late Ancient Christianity," *Journal of Early Christian Studies* 12, no. 4 [2004]: 392, cited in Mayra Rivera Rivera, "Thinking Bodies: The Spirit of a Latina Incarnational Imagination," in *Decolonizing Epistemologies: Latina/o Theology and Philosophy,* ed. Ada María Isasi Díaz and Eduardo Mendieta, 207–25 [New York: Fordham University Press, 2011]).

5. Miller, "Visceral Seeing." A powerful example of Morrison's work upon the reader as integrated mind and body is the injunction of the final lines of *Jazz:* "Look where your hands are. Now."

6. Orsi, "Material Children," 96.

7. Toni Morrison, "Rootedness: The Ancestor as Foundation," in *Black Women Writers: A Critical Evaluation,* ed. Mari Evans (New York: Anchor-Doubleday, 1984), cited in Ann E. Imbrie, "'What Shalimar Knew': Toni Morrison's *Song of Solomon* as a Pastoral Novel," *College English* 55, no. 5 (September 1993): 473–90.

8. Imbrie, "What Shalimar Knew."

9. Barbara Smith, "Beautiful, Needed, Mysterious: Review of *Sula* by Toni Morrison" (1974), in *Ain't Gonna Let Nobody Turn Me Around: Forty Years of Movement Building with Barbara Smith,* ed. Alethia Jones and Virginia Eubanks (Albany: State University of New York Press, 107), citing Stephen Henderson, *Understanding New Black Poetry* (New York: Morrow, 1973), 44.

10. Miller, "Visceral Seeing."

11. Tapia, *American Pietà: Visions of Race, Death, and the Maternal* (Minneapolis: University of Minnesota Press, 2011), 6.

12. In early medieval representations, Mary is generally represented as Mother Church, the Queen of Heaven. She is distant and divine, with foreknowledge of the sacrifice required for human salvation. Later medieval depictions of the pietà present Mary's sorrow became an entryway for devotional participation in the sorrow of the cross (see the *Röttgen Pietà,* ca. 1300–1325, painted wood, 34½", Rheinisches Landesmuseum, Bonn, an altarpiece in a German convent). The emotional response of Mary posed an opportunity for affective connection with the Passion. Christian mystics such as Hildegard and Francis meditated upon devotional media in order to foster presence to suffering.

13. Tapia, *American Pietà,* 5. Tapia points us to Jay Winter, "War Memorials and the Mourning Process," in *Sites of Memory, Sites of Mourning: The Great War in European Cultural History* (Cambridge University Press, 1995), 78–118.

14. Julia Kristeva, "Stabat Mater," in *Tales of Love* (New York: Columbia University Press, 1983), 234–64.

15. Tapia, *American Pietà,* 6.

16. The mother of Emmett Till insisted on his coffin being open. In *Song of Solomon,* men listen to the radio announcement of the murder of Emmett Till in Tommy's barbershop. "When Jesus therefore saw his mother, and the disciple standing by, whom he loved, he saith unto his mother, Woman, behold thy son!" (KJV, John 19:26).

17. This translation by Edward Caswall, Lyra Catholica (1849).

18. Toni Morrison. *Song of Solomon* (New York: First Vintage International, 2004), 336.

19. Morrison, *Song of Solomon,* 337.

20. Katy Ryan, "Revolutionary Suicide in Toni Morrison's Fiction," *African American Review* 34, no. 3 (Autumn 2000): 395.

21. Imbrie, "What Shalimar Knew," 488.

22. Imbrie, "What Shalimar Knew," 488.

23. In "Thinking Bodies," Rivera credits Moraga's account of a "theory-in-the-flesh."

24. Amnesty International USA.

25. Morrison, *Paradise* (New York: Knopf, 1998), 318.

26. Morrison, *Paradise,* 318.

27. Tessa Roynon, *The Cambridge Introduction to Toni Morrison* (Cambridge: Cambridge University Press, 2012), 73.

28. Naomi Katz, "For Love of a Sea Goddess," *Américas* 38, no. 4 (1986): 40–45.

29. Rivera, "Thinking Bodies."

30. Referencing specifically poems of Gabriela Mistral and Marjorie Agosín. Rivera

points us to Antonio Benitez Rojo's *La isla que se repite: El Caribe y la perspectiva posmoderna* and Édouard Glissant's *Poetics of Relation*.

31. For a nice analysis of the role of music and the oral traditions that Morrison invigorates in her novels, see Nada Elia, *Trances, Dances and Vociferations: Agency and Resistance in Africana Women's Narratives* (New York: Garland, 2001).

32. Morrison, *Paradise*, 318.

33. Morrison, *Paradise*, 318.

34. "Ascertainment of the Estimated Excess Mortality from Hurricane Maria in Puerto Rico," George Washington University Milken Institute School of Public Health, https://publichealth.gwu.edu/sites/default/files/downloads/projects/PRstudy/Acertainment%20of%20the%20Estimated%20Excess%20Mortality%20from%20Hurricane%20Maria%20in%20Puerto%20Rico.pdf.

35. Philip M. Weinstein identifies pre-Oedipal somatic care between black mothers and their sons in *Song of Solomon* (137) and *Beloved* (23) (Weinstein, *What Else but Love? The Ordeal of Race in Faulkner and Morrison* [New York: Columbia University Press, 1996], 29–30).

36. Morrison, *Sula* (New York: Knopf Doubleday, 1973), 46–47.

37. Jennifer Scheper Hughes, "Cradling the Sacred: Image, Ritual, and Affect in Mexican and Mesoamerican Material Religion," *History of Religions* 56, no. 1 (August 2016): 55–107. Here "the term 'cradling,' embodies, evokes, and performs the emotions of tenderness and affection for the material world and the numina within them." Hughes's attention is upon affective and embodied ritual encounters with "small, three-dimensional religious images in Mexico, throughout Central America, and in Latino immigrant communities in the United States." She identifies it with "devotional manifestations of the infant Jesus" but also "with devotions to a range of adult saints, from Saint Jude to the skeletal saint of death, Santa Muerte."

38. Katy Ryan, "Revolutionary Suicide in Toni Morrison's Fiction," *African American Review* 34, no. 3 (Autumn 2000): 395.

39. Ryan, "Revolutionary Suicide in Toni Morrison's Fiction." For these statistics, Ryan cites Eileen Barrett, "Septimus and Shadrack: Woolf and Morrison Envision the Madness of War," in *Virginia Woolf: Emerging Perspectives, Selected Papers from the Third Annual Conference on Virginia Woolf*, ed. Mark Hussey and Vara Neverow (New York: Pace University Press, 1994), 29.

40. *The National Survey on Drug Use and Health Mortality in the United States: 2017*, https://www.samhsa.gov/data/sites/default/files/nsduh-ppt-09-2018.pdf.

41. Morrison, *Sula*, 47–48.

42. Tapia, *American Pietà*, 176.

43. Ryan's insistence that ethical evaluation be held at bay is most pointed in her reading of *Beloved*: "Just as Sethe's actions (and her mother's flight) cannot be evaluated outside the context of U.S. American slavery, the black woman's decision

to jump overboard cannot be approached outside the context of captivity, murder, and rape by white men" ("Revolutionary Suicide in Toni Morrison's Fiction," 395).

44. Phillip Novak, "Signifying Silences: Morrison's Soundings in the Faulknerian Void," in *Unflinching Gaze: Morrison and Faulkner Re-Envisioned* (Jackson: University Press of Mississippi, 1997). "The aim in the case of both novels is not, thus, a proliferation of significations, but a kind of articulated, deeply meaningful silence," he continues (200).

45. Marcella Althaus-Reid, "Feetishism: The Scent of a Latin American Body Theology," in *Toward a Theology of Eros: Transfiguring Passion at the Limit of Discipline,* ed. Virginia Burrus and Catherine Keller, 134–52 (New York: Fordham University Press, 2006), 137, cited in Rivera, "Thinking Bodies." She also points to resources for reading of spirit as a figure of memory in her "Ghostly Encounters: Spirits, Memory, and the Holy Ghost," in *Planetary Loves: Gayatri Spivak, Postcoloniality, and Theology,* ed. Stephen D. Moore and Mayra Rivera (New York: Fordham University Press, 2010).

46. Tapia, *American Pietà,* 5

47. See Beverley Foulkes, "Trial by Fire: The Theodicy of Toni Morrison in *Sula,*" in *Toni Morrison and the Bible: Contested Intertextualities* (New York: Peter Lang, 2006), 8–25.

48. Brenna Moore argues for opening the affective and embodied religious imagination, saying that it "must include not only face-to-face bonds, but bonds that existed across a wide range of human experiences, including memory, dreams, fantasy, and imagination" (Moore, "Friendship and the Cultivation of Religious Sensibilities," *Journal of the American Academy of Religion* 83, no. 2 [June 2015]: 437–63).

49. Ryan, "Suicide," 396.

50. In *Love,* the intimacy of a pietà informs a particular bodily encounter of two women: "She races down the ladder, along the hall, and into the room. On her knees again, she turns, then gathers Heed in her arms. In light sifting from above each searches the face of the other. The holy feeling is still alive, as is its purity, but it is altered now, overwhelmed by desire." Toni Morrison, *Love* (New York: Knopf, 2003), 177. Thanks to Davíd Carrasco for this reference.

51. Michael Ondaatje, *Anil's Ghost,* cited in "Burgher Writing: Aesthetics as Resistance to Secular in Carl Muller's and Michael Ondaatje's Fiction," in *Secularism and the Crisis of Minority Identity in Postcolonial Literature,* ed. Roger McNamara (Lanham, MD: Rowman and Littlefield, 2018), 22. This embrace "could be the beginning of a permanent conversation with [the dead] Sarath."

52. Morrison, *Sula,* 65.

The Ghost of *Love* and Goodness

DAVÍD CARRASCO

> But I want you to know that the religion of the people I write
> about is so very important to me.
> —TONI MORRISON in Mexico City
>
> The holy feeling is still alive, as is its purity.
> —TONI MORRISON, *Love*

The Mexicans said it best about Toni Morrison. When she arrived at the Universidad Nacional Autónoma de México in 1995 to give a public lecture, she and her companions could barely make their way to the lecture hall, surrounded by a pulsating throng of students and teachers along the outdoor walkways. There were green signs, like huge leaves, pasted to every wall and column to mark and guide Toni's pathway. Each green sign had a photograph of Morrison's smiling face and name joined to two powerful words in Spanish. Each announced:

Toni Morrison Entre Nosotros

(Toni Morrison Among Us)

When Toni was introduced to the overflowing crowd in the Sala Magna, with students having to use even the stairways as seats, one of the hosts asked the audience if they wished her to translate Toni's comments and reading into Spanish. Members of the audience bellowed out, "NO, Por Favor No! We came to hear Toni Morrison's voice. We can understand her in her language because we are in her novels. Toni Morrison Entre Nosotros."

This cry that Morrison is "among us" speaks to the questions about human belonging with which Morrison is engaged in her work, *in* her writings. Throughout Morrison's writings, she is engaged with the question of who is on the inside, and who is on the outside of the black community. Who is among us? Who belongs to us? Who among us will be our friend,

FIG. 6. Fabrizio Leon, *Writer, Jungle, Stone.* (Courtesy of the artist)

enslaver, protector, ally, enemy? This focus on community has been brought home to us with great force in her recent Norton Lectures, *The Origin of Others*. As Nell Irvin Painter notes in her review of these essays, Morrison is deeply concerned with tracing "through American literature, patterns of thought and behavior that subtly code who belongs and who doesn't, who is accepted in and who is cast out as 'Other.'"[1] According to Painter, Morrison's "humanist imagination" places black people, and especially African American women, on the center stage in her novels. She gives these racialized and gendered "others" a home where their full, complex humanity appears among us.

My eyes are drawn to the phrase "origin of others" because I see *another species of others and otherness* in her writings as well: the spirits, the ancestors, the dead, the invisible who sometimes play pivotal roles in her novels and to whom she refers in essays and interviews.[2] In Morrison's worldview, vital companionships and potent alliances extend beyond the interactions of living humans to include elements of the natural world, spirit helpers, and spirited places. In her novels, we encounter dead people who come back to life and take material form and reminiscences of other times and places that possess a tactile and visible presence in the here and now (*Beloved*). There are water spirits who can save (*Tar Baby*) and kill people (*Love*), plus sacred birds who communicate in dreams and death scenes (*Song of Solomon*). Birds can serve as metaphors for language (Nobel Prize speech), and, in one novel, a ghost narrates the climax of a novel (*Love*), telling the reader secrets that even the characters in the book don't know. Drawing on the work of Giles Gunn, whose scholarship on the "imagination of otherness" has yielded invaluable insights into "new world metaphysics" in American literature,[3] I call this aspect of Morrison's writing the spiritual imaginary of matter. In Gunn's view, a spiritual imaginary "releases the energies of the imagination from the confines of its own inherited boundaries and inhibitions so that they might become freer to discover whatever spiritual possibilities and liabilities might lie beyond them."[4]

Working as a historian of religion, I build on Gunn's "spiritual imaginary" by adding the phrase *of matter* because Morrison never fails to anchor her discovery of spiritual possibilities and liabilities in the material, tactile, dynamic existence of African American people, culture, suffering, thriving. Bodies, tears, scars, sounds, sky, water, stones, plants, houses, animals, and relationships *among these matters* are animated with spirit and the living presences that inhabit matter.[5] We see a splendid example of this dynamic between matter and spirit, as well as a "release" in Morrison's imagination to discover a new spiritual possibility in her novel *Love*.[6] In *Love,* Morrison uses the voice of a female ghost narrator to write scenes of a "holy feeling" between two other female characters, Heed the Night and Christine. She tells us of her discovery in the interview found at the end of this book: "I wanted to discover and write about the best lovers. I thought, 'Who are the people who really love,' and it occurred to me, it was children. When one child falls in love with another, it doesn't care if the other has any money, what the other looks like. It's pure. It's goodness before socialization."[7]

The love in this novel goes beyond the sexual and the love of parents, neighbors, friends. Morrison writes about a higher love that resonates with what Christians call *agape,* a selfless love of one person for another, a love that exercises a thorough bias for the well-being of another.[8] With this love between the two girls, Morrison provides us with a "spiritual possibility" beyond what we've seen elsewhere in her work. She mixes historical narrative with a second ghost narrator's spirited interventions, and turns this narrator, known only as "L," into the spiritual ally *of the reader*, helping us acquire special knowledge and moral clarity about both the novel and Morrison's views on love.

In what follows, I will first summarize the complex plot of *Love* and then explore Morrison's spiritual imaginary of matter in passages about nature, the supernatural in nature, and the destiny of the holy feelings of the children in *Love*. We'll see how this novel is a special example of her statement to me in our interview: "I do strive to give goodness its own speech in my novels." This goodness takes the form of love among three females, and in reading *Love* we come to understand yet another literary and spiritual way that Toni Morrison is among us.

THE PLOT

Love is narrated by two storytellers who cover a sixty-year period (1930s–1990s) in the life of an African American family that revolves around the paradoxical Bill Cosey — *"you could call him a good bad man or a bad good man"* — and his Hotel and Resort in Up Beach somewhere on the east coast.[9] Menace also lurks just offshore in mysterious water-cloud monsters called "Police-heads" who kill wayward children and philandering adults. The central drama is a childhood love, "a holy feeling" between two little girls, Heed the Night and Christine, that is twisted into adolescent hatred and destroyed by Bill Cosey and his daughter-in-law, May, the mother of Christine. An alluring "sporting woman" named Celestial catches the attention of everyone who sees or hears her on the beach, near the hotel, or out on Cosey's boat, where whites and blacks sample her charms. Meanwhile, Heed and Christine, turned into mortal enemies by May's twisted prohibitions to their friendship and sexual molestations by Cosey, inhabit different floors of the deceased Cosey's house on Monarch Street in the present-day of the novel. This hate-filled living arrangement results from Bill Cosey's vague will, scribbled on a menu, leaving his estate to that "sweet Cosey child." Both elderly women (Christine is his granddaughter; Heed was his child bride whom he married when she was eleven years old) claim that title and scheme to get the other removed from the house. Into this place of painful memories and present hatreds comes a twenty-year-old woman named Junior, who uses her smarts and sexuality to maneuver her way into the house as Heed's caretaker, even while she romps with the young handyman Romen. Meanwhile, Junior smells, sees, and communicates with Bill Cosey's ghost, who emerges from his large portrait in the house, the ghostly presence she calls "my Good Man." Heed plans, with the aid of Junior, to find and forge another Cosey will, giving her control of the property and evicting Christine.

The physical and psychological violence suffered by African Americans during these years is symbolized by several references to the murder of Emmett Till in Mississippi in 1955. Cosey's daughter-in-law, May, the mother of Christine, sinks into madness, believing that every black activist from Martin Luther King to the Black Panthers is out to destroy her life and the success of her father-in-law's hotel and resort. Within this pervasive atmosphere of racial danger, Cosey's Hotel and Resort caters exclusively to well-off African Americans, who come to hear and dance to the best black blues and jazz musicians of the time.

The ghost narrator, a female cook for Cosey's resort and protector of the two girls, known only as the letter "L," acts as a spiritual messenger to the reader.[10] She "hums" her version of the story, providing extra details and, finally, secret knowledge about Heed and Christine. She communicates only to the reader how her paradoxical acts of love led to a luminous scene toward the end of the novel in which Heed and Christine are brought together and express their love. L is the key instrument of Morrison's spiritual imaginary and is closest to Morrison's voice and view of goodness in the novel.

NATURE AND SUPERNATURAL IN MORRISON'S *LOVE*

In April 1994, the National Orchid Society had a celebration in honor of Toni Morrison at the Cathedral of St. John the Divine in New York City. The church was packed that night with several thousand people, including the celebrities Harry Belafonte, Ozzie Davis, Ruby Dee, Bill Cosby, Peter Yarrow (who all spoke or performed) and nearly a thousand blooming orchids whose yellow, pink, blue, purple, and dappled petals softened the stone walls of the cathedral, adding comfort to the worshiping crowd. When it was announced that a new strain of orchid had been named after Morrison, a thunderous applause filled the cathedral and bounced back upon the crowd. At one point, Toni ascended the pulpit and read from her works. To the surprise of many, Toni's selections focused on passages and scenes of nature — the forests, flowers, birds, waters, trails, trees, fields, and the skies and storms amid which her characters lived, suffered, and survived. We heard her read memorable passages about Pecola, Sula, Milkman, Stamp Paid, and Beloved and were thrilled that her careful change of focus revealed that she was an exquisite writer of nature and the natural world. The orchids seemed to be flirting with the crowd as we heard that Morrison's views of nature encompassed hope and danger, biology and the supernatural, nurture and neglect. In what follows and as a pathway to her spiritual imaginary of matter, we encounter examples of Morrison as a nature writer who infuses nature with the supernatural, and as a writer of a ghost narrator who reflects her own view of goodness and mercy. Along the way, I'll introduce a surprise source from Latin America who influenced Morrison's magical writings.

The natural world is central to the story Morrison tells in *Love*. Consider this passage where Morrison links earthly poverty and celestial riches, the desires of fishermen and imaginary umbrellas whetting our appetite for reading more about the ecology around the African Americans who partied and suffered in the world of the novel: "*No matter what your place in life or your state of mind, having a star-packed sky be part of your night made you feel rich. And then there was the sea. Fishermen say there is life down there that looks like wedding veils and ropes of gold with ruby eyes. They say some sea life makes you think of the collars of schoolteachers or parasols made of flowers.*"[11] Animals can be symbols and metaphors for the human characters in her novels as in this scene about turtles crossing a dangerous road in *Love*. One of the hate-filled women, Christine, is driving to her lawyer's office to launch a legal maneuver against her rival, Heed, when she fears she has run over one of two turtles. Instead of driving on, Christine stops the car in a near panic to run back and survey the damage to these "others." Rattled at the thought of having crushed one of the pair to death:

She stopped and looked in the rearview mirrors — left one, right one, and overhead — for a sign of life or death; legs pleading skyward for help or a cracked immobile shell. Her hands were shaking. Seeing nothing, she left the driver's seat and ran back down the road. The pavement was blank, the orange trees still. No turtle anywhere. Had she imagined it, the second turtle? The one left behind, Miss Second Best, crushed by a tire gone off track, swerving to save its preferred sister? Scanning the road, she did not wonder what the matter was; did not ask herself why her heart was sitting up for a turtle creeping along Route 12. She saw a movement on the south side of the road where the first turtle had been heading. Slowly she approached and was relieved to see two shiny green shells edging toward the trees. The wheels had missed Miss Second Best, and while the driver was shuddering in the car, she had caught up the to the faster one. Transfixed, Christine watched the pair disappear, returning to her car only when another slowed behind it.[12]

In these two turtles crossing a dangerous road, Morrison shows us Christine and Heed creeping through the last years of their lives. We are left to ask who, in Christine's mind, was the nearly crushed to death "Miss Second Best."

Morrison intensifies her description of the nature world in this passage imbued with celestial images that carry a tinge of science fiction: *"Jade and sapphire waves fight each other, kicking up enough foam to wash sheets in. An evening sky behaves as though it's from some other planet — one without rules, where the sun can be plum purple if it wants to and clouds can be read as poplar pies. Our shore is like sugar, which is what the Spaniards thought of when they first saw it. Sucra, they called it, a name local whites tore up for all time into Sooker."*[13] Morrison's description of the world as at once material and celestial is the fruit of the African American traditions in which she was raised. This other planet, the one without rules, is both a material place and celestial place. Morrison gives the sky an earthbound character at first — it "behaves." Quickly we read that it behaves "as though it's from some other planet," and the skies above Cosey's Hotel and Resort are from out there in the solar system revolving around a sun that turns plum purple when "it wants to."

It has often and rightly been noted that one source for Morrison's nature and magical writing is the African American community in which she was raised. However, as the interview with Morrison in this volume reveals, Latin American writing has also played a generative role in her writing about spirits, ghosts, nature "without rules," and the "strange stuff" that animates nature and human nature. When I asked her about the ways she writes the "supernatural" into the natural and historical world in her novels, she recalled the impact of first reading Gabriel García Márquez:

> When I read his book *One Hundred Years of Solitude,* I literally said, "Oh, my God, you can do this" — meaning magic, strange stuff — and be deadly serious. So, that freed me up in my writing. I realized that I could have somebody flying, or a version of it, or have people burn each other up, and

more. I felt for the first time that I could follow the emotional train and close it with something that's not in nature, something outside of that. I became aware of a freedom in writing. Reading him unlocked something important for me.

Alongside the African American ghost story traditions that shaped her as a writer, a Latin American writer also helped her become "aware of a freedom in writing" as she progressed in her compositions that included *Song of Solomon, Beloved, A Mercy,* and *Love.* The phrases "something not in nature," "outside of that," and "unlocked" take us back to the central point that Giles Gunn makes about the spiritual imaginary as a practice of "release beyond the confines," "discovery" in writing. It appears that Morrison reading García Márquez released an energy in her imagination so that her writing became freer to further narrate spiritual possibilities and liabilities that lay alongside and in league with the imagination she grew up with.

This new link in her lineage leads to one more surprise that takes us back to where this essay began, Mexico. When Garcia Márquez was asked about which authors freed him up to write *One Hundred Years of Solitude,* he pointed to the Mexican writer Juan Rulfo, and specifically his novel *Pedro Páramo.*[14] Reading this novel, which he claimed he could recite forward and backward, opened the pathway for him to write his great masterpiece. It cannot go unnoticed that, as with both *Love* and Morrison's later novel *Home,* there are two narrators in *Pedro Páramo,* and everyone in the town of Rulfo's novel is deceased and present as ghosts. Whether Toni Morrison was aware of this novel's influence on García Márquez's liberated imaginary or not, the lineage is fascinating to contemplate. Perhaps Morrison's *Love* is haunted by the unseen *Pedro Páramo.*

THE GHOST OF GOODNESS IN *LOVE*

Morrison's religious and moral vision — that is, her spiritual imaginary of matter — is expressed by the narrator, L. L is the creator of what is at the heart of the story and closest to Morrison's voice. L makes a judgment about Cosey's family and world, namely that even with the hatred he felt for the women closest to him, "*his hatred for the women in his house had no level,*" redemption for the girls is possible.[15] Even with a murder, a forgery, and years of envy and hatred between Heed and Christine, reconciliation and love, a higher love, is sought after and achieved. Morrison uses a series of doubles to oppose each other (Heed and Christine, Dark and Bill Cosey, May and Christine, Celestial and L) that do not, in the end, destroy the girls but rather lead to a luminous scene of reconciliation through the aid of what I am calling "*agape's* ghost," that is, the love and actions of L. In Morrison's spiritual imaginary of matters of the heart, a primordial love overcomes the broken, formalized, and oppressed humanity of the African Americans of Up Beach. As we shall now see, L hums, that is, acts as a spiritual messenger to the reader in five storytelling interventions, appearing in the novel in italicized pages, about her secret struggle to give the girls' "holy feeling" a final chapter.

Toni Morrison's quest to discover and write about the "best lovers" led her to invent a narrator who used more than words to tell the story. L acts in two ways — she watches and hums. That her humming is more than just sound making in reaction to what she sees is signaled by the fact that the word "hum" is the last word in the first and last sentences of the novel. In a sense, L hums the key messages of the novel rather than merely speaking them. This use of a low-frequency sound to tell, or accompany the telling, of the story suggests Morrison's insertion of a spiritual worldview. Each of L's five interventions, always signaled by several pages of italicized print, has a single theme that I label in sequence, "women and monsters," "infatuation and love," "belonging and Celestial," "death by sacrifice," and "L the revelator." The thread that runs through each of them is the arduous search for the goodness of love for the two main female characters in the midst of racial and gender violence and destruction.

WOMEN AND MONSTERS

The first matter that L hums to us is the "Cosey women." She uses "*the music in my mouth*" to introduce us to the sad stories of women, each with "*a monster in it who made them tough instead of brave, so they open their legs rather than their hearts where the folded child is tucked.*" The phrases "*my humming encourages people,*" "*my hum is mostly below range . . . what's the deep to you?*" hint at her spectral identity and seduces the reader into her story of the seaside community of Up Beach, where other monsters lurk in the water to make "*women hate each other.*" L tells us of "*an outside evil*" in the forms of "*creatures called Police-heads — dirty things with big*" *hats who shoot up out of the ocean to harm loose women and eat disobedient children,*" killings punctuated by what L alone hears as "*whoops of joy.*" These violent acts illuminate the violence of our own world, in which African Americans continually suffer at the hands of the police.[16]

L's opening story moves back to the land to introduce us to the rise and fall, in the past, of Bill Cosey's Hotel and Resort ("*they came partly for the music but mostly to dance with pretty women*") and his Big House on Monarch Street where, in the present-day, Heed and Christine live in mutual hatred. L tells of the two forces that finally wreck Cosey's world of wealth, family, and resort. First, a hurricane named after another female — Agnes. Then, the even more destructive force was "the Cosey women" — May, Heed, Christine, and Celestial. At the end of her first appearance in the novel, L the ghost leaves us hanging about whether Heed and Christine had "*finally killed each other,*" since she hadn't floated over to their house in a while, and who the monsters were that made them so hateful. The real hook from her hum comes when she tells that this novel is "*a story that shows how brazen women can take a good man down.*" Which brazen women? Which good man?[17]

INFATUATION VERSUS LOVE

The second matter L hums (she now calls it "*singsong*") to us, fifty-nine pages later, is the most potent one for Morrison, infatuation — the "*magic axe that chops away the world in one blow*" —versus love.[18] Morrison has remarked elsewhere that the word "love" appears just once in the novel, toward the end. But L uses the word "love" twice during this earlier critique of youthful infatuation. And in doing so, she begins to build the case for the higher love that is revealed only at the end of the novel. L tells us:

> *People with no imagination feed it* [infatuation] *with sex — the clown of love. They don't know the real kinds, the better kinds, where losses are cut and everybody benefits. It takes a certain intelligence to love like that — softly, without props. But the world is such a showpiece, maybe that's why folks try to outdo it, put everything they feel onstage just to prove they can think up things too: handsome scary things like fights to the death, adultery, setting sheets afire.*[19]

Then L, emphasizing love "without props," shows us part of the way back to the "goodness before socialization," the wonder of nature and of children:

The world outdoes them every time. While they are busy showing off, digging other people's graves, hanging themselves on the cross . . . cherries are quietly turning from green to red, oysters are suffering pearls, and children are catching rain in their mouths expecting the drops to be cold but they're not; they are warm and smell like pineapple.[20]

In this second italicized intervention, L tells us crucial historical details of African American lives at Up Beach including bits of her autobiography, stories of the brazen Junior and inspirational Celestial, and Bill Cosey's criminal father known as Dark. These details appear to us as examples of parental, marital, and sexual love. We learn how sex and love led to L's birth, delivered by both her parents during a coastal storm:

My mother, limp as a rag waiting for this overdue baby, said she suddenly perked up and decided to hang laundry. Only later did she realize she was drunk with the pure oxygen that swept in before the storm. Halfway through her basket she saw the day turn black, and I began to thrash. She called my father and the two of them delivered me in a downpour. You could say going from womb water straight to rain marked me.[21]

Marked her so much she lived a fluid life cooking between Cosey's Resort and then at Maceo's Café . . . ria (the lights went out in the "te" of the Cafeteria neon sign), winning the deep confidence of both men and countless customers even as she worked behind the scenes to watch, to protect, to defy, and eventually to kill and save.

Human love first appears to her when, as a child, she witnesses Bill Cosey, the "good bad man" in the surf holding his beloved wife Julia with great tenderness, a sight that "brought tears to my eyes," watery love. Love's clown swings back into the picture as L tells us her view, from her ghostly perch in the café, of the "*girl with no underwear — she calls herself Junior . . . all her private parts going public.*" Junior rivets the eyes of all the men even as she intimidates the waiter, Theo: "*I see why you need a posse. Your dick don't work one on one?*"[22]

Then L tells us about the beautiful, scared sporting woman, Celestial, whose role as human and ghost returns at crucial points in the novel.

The other revelation in this second narration is the blood money upon which all this love, smart and clownish, was floating in Cosey's world. Floating, that is, until hurricane Agnes swept through and the Cosey women carried out their own blood feud that drove Cosey's wicked self-ishness further over the edge. Cosey's father, known first as DRC, whom the blacks called "Dark" behind his back, was a stooge for the cops, who looked the other way from his gambling, liquored-up world as long as he fed them names of outspoken colored folks, those seeking access to property, and other heads to beat down.

In this section as in the first, the spiritual identity of L comes to us in hints that a ghost is talking to us and telling secrets maybe no one in-side the novel knows. Her ghostly identity gets clearer when she tells that no one remembers her real name beyond the letter L. All guesses at her name are wrong, she tells us, including Louise, Lucile, Eleanor, Elvira. Even children *"treat me like I'm dead and don't ask about me anymore."* *"Standing by,"* she is *"unable to do anything but watch . . . and hum."*[23]

BELONGING TO CELESTIAL

L's spirited voice displays Morrison's taste for supernatural waters and numinous sounds in her third appearance thirty pages later. She has com-mented elsewhere on how music is one of her guides as she writes and imagines: "I know that my effort is to be like something that has probably only been fully expressed perhaps in music. . . . Writing novels is a way to encompass this — this something."[24] We see examples of this "something," this "music," throughout the novel and especially when L tells us that the ocean, with its tenor voice, *"is my man now."* No longer alive, L hints at a sexual relationship with her ocean man as they gaze at each other at sunrise and sunset: *"He knows when to rear and hump his back, when to be quiet and simply watch a woman. . . . His soul is deep down there and suf-fering."*[25] We learn intimate details of African American life and the Cosey family prior to Heed and Christine's young love and later battles. In this section, L builds on the "women and monsters" and "love versus infatua-tion" soliloquies by mapping Cosey's other steps to ruination — marrying the eleven-year-old Heed and later returning, as always, to have sex with the sporting woman Celestial on the beach at night and on his boat.

There are two profound belongings recorded here. First, L says that it *"was marrying Heed that laid the brickwork for ruination. See, he chose a girl already spoken for. Not promised to anyone by her parents. That trash gave her up like they would a puppy. No. The way I see it, she belonged to Christine and Christine belonged to her."*[26] Second, a charismatic, numinous cry on the beach by Celestial brings Morrison's spiritual imaginary to the surface. Morrison has told us repeatedly how the effective and spiritual use of language is central to her view of human identity and goodness: "We die. That may be the meaning of life. But we do language. That may be the measure of our lives," she claimed in her Nobel Prize speech. Elsewhere, she has written of love's challenge in the measure of our lives this way: "Love is divine only and difficult always. If you think it is easy you are a fool. If you think it is natural you are blind. It is a learned application without reason or motive except that it is God."[27] In *Love*, Morrison uses her skill with words to open our eyes and ears to unnatural love through sounds and low-frequency words.[28]

One night, L sees Celestial, after she has had sex with Cosey on the beach, sitting naked on the edge of the surf. The description has the quality of a creation myth when a human first entered the waters to discover life and rose up again to utter primal sounds:

> *Down a piece I saw somebody else. A woman sitting on a blanket massaging her head with both hands. I stood there while she got up, naked as truth, and went into the waves. The tide was out, so she had to walk a long time for the water to reach her waist. Tall, raggedy clouds drifted across the moon and I remember how my heart kicked. Police-heads were on the move then. They had already drowned the Johnson boys, almost killed the cannery girl and who knew what else they had in mind. But this woman kept on wading out into black water and I could tell she wasn't afraid of them — or of anything — because she stretched, raised her arms, and dove. I remember that arc better than I remember yesterday. She was out of sight for a time and I held my breath as long as she did. Finally, she surfaced and I breathed again watching her swim back to shallow water. She stood up and massaged her head once more. Her hair, flat when she went in, rose up slowly and took on the shape of the clouds dragging the moon. Then she — well, made a sound. I don't know to this day whether it was a word, a tune, or a scream. All I know us that it was a sound I wanted to answer. Even though, normally, I'm stone quiet, Celestial.*[29]

These sacred sounds call to mind the radical theological position of the twentieth-century German theologian Rudolph Otto.[30] It was Otto, partly thinking of religious sounds, who said that religious experience, not moral commitments, was the true source of religion and culture. So uncanny and full of energy were the religious experiences recorded in the world's scriptures, songs, and rites of passage that he invented new words to bring us closer to what he called "Das Heilige" (The Holy) — which for him was "wholly other." Instead of "ominous," he wrote "numinous." In place of "mighty," he invented "tremendum." In place of mystery, he insisted on "mysterium." In the face of joyous rapture, he gave us "mysterium fascinosum." Morrison uses this kind of language, that is, numinous sounds to bring out the otherness in the experiences, emotions, and thoughts of her characters. Celestial's sound is not an ordinary cry or noise. It comes from a deeper place within her life and body. Morrison periodically embraces such scope and depth of language and meaning to illuminate the kinds of belongings she cares about — mother and child, child and child, slave and slave, ghost and human. In this case L, while alive, felt she belonged to that sound, for L, like Mr. Cosey, was under the spell of Celestial's awesome utterances. Belonging to Celestial.

DEATH BY SACRIFICE

L's fourth message to the reader is about the death of the belonging shared by Heed and Christine as girls. In her penultimate intervention thirty pages later, L begins, humming to the reader who has caught wind of the damage done to the girls, "*You are always thinking of death.*"[31] While she is addressing Christine's mother, May, it's we who are the other hearers. We read of the death of African Americans by poverty, by posse, by tuberculosis, but she gives the emphasis in this section to the steps taken to kill the love between two children. This killing of the girls' love is the result, in part, of the history of other social and psychological aggressions against black people. We learn that Cosey descended from "*prosperous slaves and thrifty freedmen*" who used their strength and intelligence to survive white supremacy in its most lethal and clever forms. Christine's mother and Cosey's daughter-in-law, May, goes mad when facing the history of risks black people faced when standing up to oppression — so she did her best to kill the girls' friendship: "*If Heed and Christine had ideas about being friends and behaving like sisters . . . May put a stop to them. . . . Raid-spray the air so it couldn't breathe.*"[32] The greatest sacrificial blow to the girls came from the most powerful man on the shore, Bill Cosey, who decided to take the eleven-year-old Heed as his wife, even when she was the very best friend of his granddaughter, Christine. This creates a psychic atmosphere of envy, hatred, and a thirst for revenge that L compares to the spread of tuberculosis: "*All over the world, traitors help progress. It's like being exposed to tuberculosis. After it fills the cemetery, it strengthens whoever survives; helps them know the difference between a strong mind and a healthy one: between the righteous and the right — which is, after all, progress. The problem for those left alive is what to do about revenge — how to escape the sweetness of its rot. So, you can see why families make the best enemies. They have time and convenience to honey-butter the wickedness they prefer.*"[33] With these references to revenge, escape, rot, enemies, and wickedness, we sense L's growing commitment toward some drastic, secret action to protect the little girls even as she witnesses their teenage and young adult years filled with venom, crushing heartbreaks, and total alienation.

L sets the stage for the final revelation of a mystery in the final passage of this fourth section. Ripped apart by mother and husband, the two girls, growing into women "*battled on as though they were champions instead of sacrifices. A crying shame.*"[34] There is that sound beyond words again, "crying" — another reference to how deep and holy is the suffering of these many women in the novel.

L THE REVELATOR OF *AGAPE*

We've known that L is an active ghost at least since chapter 4, "Benefactor," when the main narrator uses the phrase "L haunting Up Beach."[35] But it is only in the final pages that we realize that her purpose has been to haunt the reader and become our spirit-helper through revealing to us how she killed Bill Cosey and forged the will to save Heed and Christine. She becomes a revelator of radical, paradoxical acts of love.

In the final italicized pages of the book, L confesses that she had a *solution* to the crying shame of the destruction of the best lovers. Decades ago, while she was alive and Heed and Christine were in their forties, L made two risky moves designed to give the childhood love of Heed and Christine some potential for a future reprieve. We learn she was provoked into action by the absurd will that Cosey wrote on a menu, leaving everything except his boat to Celestial, thereby cutting off his daughter-in-law, granddaughter, and his younger wife from any financial, domestic security. "*I had to stop him. Had to,*" she tells us. What she had to do, her radical solution, was to follow the conviction of her name, which we now learn comes from the Bible.[36] *"If your name is the subject of First Corinthians, chapter 13, it's natural to make it your business."*[37] Let us go to the Bible for a moment since Morrison has directed us there.

The thirteenth chapter of the Apostle Paul's First Epistle to the Corinthians in the New Testament of the Christian Bible takes as its central subject love of the most profound and pure kind as signaled by the author's use of the Greek word *ἀγάπη* or *agape,* translated into Latin as *caritas. Agape* love is radical love: selfless love, sacrificial love expressing a powerful bias for the well-being of the "other." *Agape* is the kind of love that is to be extended to all people, whether family or strangers — all others, regardless of their origin. In the spirit of the opening section of this essay, *agape* love is the love we strive to have among us all no matter the identity or nature of the others. Morrison has embedded the figure of L as *agape*'s ghost, whose secret actions are revealed to us only at the end.

In I Corinthians 13, we first read that *agape* love is patient and kind, and then we are shown what it is not in a list that describes much of the action in this novel, where pride, boasting, rudeness, anger, and evil abound. Real love, the letter says, "always protects, always trusts, always hopes, always perseveres. Love never fails. . . . And now these three remain: Faith, Hope, and Love. But the greatest of these is Love."[38]

My eyes are drawn to the repetition of the adverb "always"—"always protects, always trusts, always hopes . . . always preserves." The strength this repetition adds to the word "love" is the thrust of L's solution and the key to grasping Morrison's moral vision born of her spiritual imaginary in this novel. With no thought of the danger she was in, or how she might profit from her actions, L protected the girls, acted to give their childhood love a chance to resurface and preserve what they knew as children.

The paradox of her acts of love is that she used her knowledge of the kitchen, of plants and menus to murder Bill Cosey by poison and destroy his menu and forge a new one. But how can poisoning another human being and forging a will be an act of love? L tells us how in one of Morrison's most elegant passages about human belonging.

It's like that when children fall for one another. On the spot, without introduction. Grown-ups don't pay it much attention because they can't imagine anything more majestic to a child than their own selves, and so confuse dependence with reverence. Parents . . . their place is secondary to a child's first chosen love. If such children find each other before they know their own sex, or which one of them is starving, which well fed; before they know color from no color, kin from stranger, then they have found a mix of surrender and mutiny they can never live without. Heed and Christine found such a one.[39]

And that is why L had to stop him, because she shared in the "mix of surrender and mutiny they can never live without." L helps us know what no one in the novel knows — that she practiced a form of Corinthians love, *agape,* in the form of a mutiny against Bill Cosey. It was L who rewrote the menu, destroying the one that left all to "Celestial" to say instead that the recipient of Bill Cosey's wealth will be that "sweet Cosey child." She confesses to the reader: *"My menu worked just fine. Gave them a reason to stay connected and maybe figure out how precious the tongue is."*[40]

With "the tongue" we are back to hums and Celestial sounds and the secret language that Heed and Christine invented as girls, a language they called "idigay." The language consisted of adding a series of letters, some in reverse order to the phrase "idigay" to speak their private and shared thoughts to one another. If one wished to call the other a slave she would say "Ave-slidigay," for instance. And when they wanted to say the equivalent of "Amen" in agreement to the other, they would say "Hey Celestial," a phrase they overheard on the beach one day when the sporting woman was passing by. The final time we hear that language, in a scene before L makes her confession to the reader, it is used to calm and sooth the dying Heed. Christine has gone to the attic of Cosey's ruined hotel with Junior, hoping to find another old menu she can forge showing that the house she shares with Heed really belongs to her. That lethal thinking, "a hatred so pure . . . it feels beautiful, almost holy," is reversed when Heed arrives, interrupts the attic search, slips on the ladder and falls, crushing some bones.[41] She lay in Christine's arms, and death is near in the form of a constant eternity of the present: "The future is disintegrating along with the past."[42] Amid candlelight set up by Christine, the two of them avoid the quarrel they expected and circle back to their childhood love, its destruction, their beach games and Baby Ruths, ham sandwiches, lemonade, fireflies and turtles, a game of jacks and their childhood underwear, family madness and the sacrifice adults made of them. They speak softly to each their secret-code phrase "Hey Celestial," affirming what the other had said. Their final words while both are alive take us back to Morrison's nature writing and its linkage to *agape* love, the deep caring for the other who is with us. Heed is dying, and we read:

> You're crying.
> So are you.
> Am I?
> Uh-huh.
> I can barely hear you.
> Hold my . . . my hand.
> He took all my childhood away from me, girl.
> He took all of you away from me.
> The sky, remember? When the sun went down?
> Sand. It turned pale blue.
> And the stars. Just a few at first.
> Then so many they lit the whole fucking world.
> Pretty. So so pretty.
> Love. I really do.
> Ush-hidagay. Ush-hidagay.[43]

Ush-hidagay. Ush-hidagay meaning Hush, Hush.

This is an example of Morrison's moral purpose in the novel. She states in the interview elsewhere in this book, "I strive to give goodness its own speech in my novels." What she has achieved in this combination of tenderness, L's revelation, and the goodness in this dialogue between the two women is to transport us to a new spiritual location. She does more than just evoke the spiritual imaginary of Heed and Christine so that we can witness it. We experience it in this passage, we feel ourselves inside of Morrison's spiritualized world with its secret code. Somehow, through Morrison's writing, we also undergo the struggle for love's return and sense that goodness has fought through evil and in the end has moved downstage, closer to us.

CONCLUSION

The Mexicans who shouted, "Toni Morrison entre nosotros" in Mexico City that distant afternoon carried out an act of social goodness. They were proclaiming their identity with her and her writings, aware that Morrison brought with her generations of African American people, strivings, betrayals, sufferings, and most certainly spirits. Morrison made it clear to the Mexicans that religion was crucial to her writing when a reporter in the crowd asked her what it was like to be rostered in the Department of Religion at Princeton University. Morrison gently corrected him, "I'm in the department of Humanities but I want you to know that the religion of the people I write about is very important to me." As this book shows, religion and the religious dimensions of African American life permeate her novels, sometimes in Christian tones, sometimes in African tones, always through the strange stuff of existence. In my previous essay on *Song of Solomon,* I pointed out how Morrison had partially hidden in her "narrative thread of magical flight one of the key meanings of shamanic transport and elevation, namely, the vital importance of finding a spiritual ally who enables the seeker to transcend the terror of one's historical condition."[44] She took the theme of a "spiritual ally" to a new place in *Love* by placing one of her narrators, the ghostly L, both inside and outside of history, so L could serve as a human ally to the characters in the novel and as a spiritual ally to the readers, revealing to us and us alone a new version of Morrison's moral vision of love and goodness.[45] In this way and in many others, Toni Morrison has become our historical and spiritual ally.

The depth of the Mexican appreciation of this alliance came clearest on another afternoon, ten years later, when Morrison returned to Mexico for the Guadalajara Book Fair. She was gathered in the "green room" with Mexican colleagues after her appearance before several thousand Mexican writers and readers. A Mexican photojournalist lingered near us and said, "No lo puedo creer" (I can't believe it). When asked "Que es lo que no puede creer?" (What is it that you can't believe?), his response was: "Estar tan cerca de Toni Morrison. Ella es como una divinidad" (To be so close to Toni Morrison. She is like a divinity).

NOTES

1. Nell Irvin Painter, "Toni Morrison's Radical Vision of Otherness," *New Republic,* October 11, 2017, https://newrepublic.com/article/144972/toni-morrisons-radical-vision-otherness-history-racism-exclusion-whiteness.
2. For an excellent collection of many revealing interviews with Toni Morrison, see *Conversations with Toni Morrison,* ed. Danielle Taylor-Guthrie (Jackson: University Press of Mississippi, 1994).

3. Giles Gunn, "Forms of Religious Meaning in Literature," in *The Imagination of Otherness*, by Gunn (London: Oxford University Press, 1979).

4. Giles Gunn, *The Pragmatist Turn: Religion, the Enlightenment, and the Formation of American Literature* (Charlottesville: University of Virginia Press, 2017), 7. Gunn's "spiritual imaginary" is not focused, as I am, on an individual's energies and discoveries but rather on two traditions of expression and reflection (the Enlightenment and Protestantism) in the seventeenth and eighteenth centuries and how those practices nurtured American literature. Yet the phrase and definitional power of "spiritual imaginary" can be used, as I hope to show, to illuminate Morrison's literary energies, resources, and her discovery of a new spiritual possibility in *Love*.

5. When I say a "spiritual imagination of matter," I am speaking of matter in a similar way to how Mircea Eliade wrote about "hierophanies" and of the ways that the material world manifests power, meaning, danger, beauty to the human. The capacity of the natural world to show its power opens the human mind to the primordial and creative natural world in all its forms. See especially the long introduction, "Approximations: The Structure and Morphology of the Sacred," to his *Patterns in Comparative Religions* (Lincoln: University of Nebraska Press, 1996), 4. There we learn that religious texts, myths, rites of passage show the human realization, all over the world, that there was a "religious value of organic life, the elementary forces of blood, sexuality and fecundity." Morrison writes with a similar view in mind and the natural, material world in her novels is periodically spectral and filled with magic. I thank Mara Willard for assisting me with this point.

6. Charles H. Long, *Significations: Signs, Symbols and Images in the Interpretation of Religion* (Aurora, CO: Davies Group, 1986), 187–98, carries the notion of the imagination of matter beyond Eliade's vision into the history of colonialism and African American religions in numerous articles including "Perspectives for the Study of Afro-American Religion in the United States." For one example of how Long's conception of the imagination of matter has influenced other scholars, see James Noel, *Black Religion and the Imagination of Matter in the Atlantic World* (London: Palgrave Macmillan, 2009).

7. Toni Morrison in the interview in this volume, page 231.

8. Two books in particular assist us in understanding the Christian conception of *agape* as a moral and theological practice. First, Gene Outka's *Agape: An Ethical Analysis* (New Haven: Yale University Press, 1977). A more recent exploration is Timothy Jackson, *The Priority of Love: Christian Charity and Social Justice* (Princeton: Princeton University Press, 2009).

9. Toni Morrison, *Love* (New York: Knopf, 2003), 200. Other insightful readings of *Love* include Lucille P. Fultz, "*Love:* An Elegy for the African American Com-

munity, or the Unintended Consequence of Desegregation/Integration," in *Toni Morrison: Memory and Meaning,* ed. Adrienne Lanier Seward and Justine Tally (Jackson: University Press of Mississippi, 2014), 93–106; and Melanie R. Anderson, "The Specter as Possibility," in *Spectrality in the Novels of Toni Morrison* (Nashville: University of Tennessee Press, 2013), 101–30. Anderson's entire book enlarges our understanding of Morrison's writings on hauntings and ghosts.

10. This concept of "ghost narrator" is explored in rich detail by Melanie R. Anderson, *Spectrality in the Novels of Toni Morrison.* In a series of chapters, she shows the various ways that "supernatural events and ghosts are present throughout her novels" (1). An insightful reading of ghosts and hauntings in *Beloved* is found in Kathleen Brogan, *Cultural Haunting: Ghosts and Ethnicity in Recent American Literature* (Charlottesville: University of Virginia Press, 1998), 61–92.

11. Morrison, *Love,* 105

12. Morrison, *Love,* 87.

13. Morrison, *Love,* 7–8

14. Juan Rulfo, *Pedro Páramo* (New York: Grove, 1994).

15. Morrison, *Love,* 201

16. Morrison, *Love,* 3–5.

17. Morrison, *Love,* 6, 9, 10.

18. Morrison, *Love,* 63.

19. Morrison, *Love,* 63.

20. Morrison, *Love,* 63.

21. Morrison, *Love,* 64.

22. Morrison, *Love,* 66–67.

23. Morrison, *Love,* 65, 3.

24. Nellie McKay, "An Interview with Toni Morrison," *Contemporary Literature* 24, no. 4 (1983): 413–29. This interview also appears in *Conversations with Toni Morrison,* ed. Danielle Taylor-Guthrie (Jackson: University Press of Mississippi, 1994), 138–55. The quote above appears on page 152.

25. Morrison, *Love,* 100.

26. Morrison, *Love,* 104–5.

27. Morrison, *Paradise* (New York: Knopf, 1998), 141.

28. For a brilliant exploration of Morrison's use of music and sounds, see Jody Morgan, "The Aural in *Beloved,*" *Osprey Journal of Ideas and Inquiry* 7 (2008): 12, https://digitalcommons.unf.edu/ojii_volumes/12.

29. Morrison, *Love,* 105–6.

30. Rudolph Otto, *The Idea of the Holy* (London: Oxford University Press, 1958). See esp. chaps. 1–3.

31. Morrison, *Love,* 135.

32. Morrison, *Love,* 136.

33. Morrison, *Love,* 139.
34. Morrison, *Love,* 141.
35. Morrison, *Love,* 73.
36. For an excellent survey of how the Bible and a "spiritual-theological nexus" plays a major role in Morrison's novels, see Shirley A. Stave, ed., *Toni Morrison and the Bible: Contested Intertextualities* (New York: Peter Lang, 2006). Especially relevant to this section of my essay is Sharon Jesse's excellent "The 'Female Revealer' in *Beloved, Jazz* and *Paradise:* Syncretic Spirituality in Toni Morrison's Trilogy." A number of articles in Stave's groundbreaking collection assist in understanding Morrison use of biblical and theological themes.
37. Morrison, *Love,* 199.
38. There are many important differences in the translations of the Bible and therefore these passages. I am using the *New International Version* (Grand Rapids, MI: Zondervan, 2015). One alternative translation is the New King James Bible, which translates this passage as Love "bears all things, believes all things, hopes all things, endures all things. Love never fails."
39. Morrison, *Love,* 199.
40. Morrison, *Love,* 201.
41. Morrison, *Love,* 177.
42. Morrison, *Love,* 184.
43. Morrison, *Love,* 194.
44. Davíd Carrasco, "Magically Flying with Toni Morrison: Mexico, García Márquez, *Song of Solomon* and *Sula,*" in *Toni Morrison: Memory and Meaning,* ed. Adrienne Lanier Seward and Justine Tally (Jackson: University Press of Mississippi, 2014), 144–58.
45. I read Morrison's words on this innovation only after writing this article. In her foreword to the 2005 paperback version of *Love* she writes of "L" and her paradoxical love—a love inside and outside of history, a love on the margin between goodness and evil—the following: "The interior narrative of the characters, so full of secrets and partial insights would be interrupted and observed by an 'I' not restricted by chronology or space—or the frontier between life and not-life. Thus the character called 'L' is meant to exhibit and represent the imaginative and transformative nature of her name along with its constructive and destructive talents" (xi).

Demons and Dominion

Possession and Dispossession in Toni Morrison's *A Mercy*

MATTHEW POTTS

In her 2012 Ingersoll Lecture, included in this volume, Toni Morrison expresses worry over the fragility of goodness in modern American fiction while wondering at the attractiveness of evil for contemporary readers and writers. Why, she asks, is evil "so worshiped, especially in literature? Is it its theatricality, its costume, its blood spray, the emotional satisfaction that comes with its investigation more than with its collapse?"[1] And while Morrison is right to ask us why the surreally gruesome, nearly worshipful cinematics of modern novels might hold such appeal, it also must be noted that the fiction of Toni Morrison does not itself shy from violence. An almost gothic, sometimes supernatural threat of suffering haunts much of her fiction, and upon occasion these metaphorical ghosts take on real bodies and inflict real abuse and damage. Perhaps most troubling among these violent acts is the harm done to children by their mothers. Eva sets fire to her son Plum in *Sula;* Sethe draws a handsaw across her toddler's throat in *Beloved;* Sweetness punishes Bride for her dark skin in *God Help the Child.* From Morrison's early novels to her most recent works, children suffer mistreatment, abandonment, and murder at the hands of their mothers. The trope recurs over and over again and loses no power for its recurrence. But these violent events and parental acts are most affecting when the mothers in question believe themselves to be acting out of love for their children. Indeed, what most deeply troubles the reader of these difficult fictions is that these acts of maternal violence, rejection, and abandonment are often construed and justified — by Morrison's characters, at least — as protective acts of desperate but deep love. In Morrison's fictional world, abandonment and abuse are sometimes expressions of dearest affection.

As a student of Christian theology, I cannot but read in these fictions a troubling echo of the Christian West's theological legacy and discern a recognizably Christian ambivalence about violence. Western Christianity takes as its historical centerpiece the abandonment and torture of Jesus of Nazareth and paradoxically interprets this act as peculiarly revelatory of

God's love. What's more, the familial language used in describing God as Trinity, of a Son abandoned and given over to suffering by a Father, finds especially disturbing expression in many traditional theological articulations of Jesus's death. Of course, the prevailing interpretation of this event is by no means universal; these claims are variously argued, justified, and critiqued in and by figures within the tradition.[2] But the idea that Jesus's death somehow compensates as punishment for human sin and is also commanded by Jesus's Father dominates both doctrine and devotion throughout the Christian West. And it's perhaps not difficult to understand why. However distasteful this doctrine of substitutionary atonement may be in its popular articulation — that the loving Father demands a death to offset human sin and to which his loving Son submits — it is tidy enough at least. By way of its own cruel calculus, this doctrine leaves no logical loose ends lying, even if the knotty tangle of love that results is one that remains troubled and troubling at best.

If it is easy to see the nifty algebra of this atonement, it is also not difficult to generate some objections to it. That God in Christ so suffered might be a sign of edifying solidarity but also one of worrisome self-sacrifice. One of the most powerful theological works in recent memory about the death of Jesus is James Cone's *The Cross and the Lynching Tree,* which reads Jesus's suffering as an act in intimate solidarity with black suffering, and which interprets an identity between the trees of America's lynchings and the tree of Jesus's crucifixion.[3] And although Cone insists that Jesus resists and opposes such suffering by and through his own suffering, we can also see how the willingness of Christ to submit to his enemies — or to his Father — might be moralized into worrisome habits of an obligatory self-sacrifice, or weaponized by power as holy subjugation. We might worry, perhaps much like Toni Morrison does with modern fiction, that this sacrifice is too weak, that this goodness is too fragile, that this selflessness too selfless. At Golgotha, evil is theatrical and cinematic with its blood spray (consider Mel Gibson's *The Passion of the Christ,* for example) while goodness — perhaps as in the modern fiction Morrison cites — perhaps remains too weak and frail, maybe even complacent or compliant, and in any case obscured by the spectacle of a gruesome public torture. Indeed, many of the most strident theological critiques of what I have called the traditional model of the atonement in black or feminist or womanist theology have made exactly this argument: Christ's death must not valorize suffering or moralize self-abasement.[4] In much Christian reflection on the cross, such valor and morality remain entirely too available for abuse by power.

But surely a goodness entirely unwilling to put anything at all at risk would become the very definition of frailty and weakness. So which risks are worth taking, and on behalf of whom? Could there be forms of self-sacrifice we might morally endorse without valorizing subjugation and suffering? And what, if anything, might they teach us about the cross of Christ? As Cone confesses, one must "have a powerful religious imagination to see redemption in the cross, to discover life in death and hope in tragedy," as well as "the imagination to relate the message of the cross to one's own social reality."[5] I would add that one needs a powerful moral imagination to recognize the possibility of goodness as hiding in the risks and hazards that surround us.

Toni Morrison's novels are formidable fictions that exert exactly these forces of imagination. Of course, fiction is not doctrine. Whatever my own religious traditions and instincts, I have also to acknowledge that what I hear echoing in Morrison's novels should be distinguished by the narrative particularities of its reverberation. In other words, part of what must challenge any too simply or clumsily dogmatic reading of these difficult fictions is their absolutely and exquisitely rendered historical specificity. As noted, many theologians have read particular political, racial, and gender liberation into and alongside the governing doctrine of Christ's cross. But Morrison's fictions need not be so governed by doctrine, and in their relative dogmatic freedom they can set more pressing questions to theology. Put more simply: although power, race, and gender constantly frame Morrison's depictions of loving abuses and abandonments, hers are always particular powers, races, and genders. The Holy Trinity will not map so easily upon this fiction. These are not fathers and sons, not deities and messiahs. More often than not, they are mothers and daughters. They are fugitives. They are slaves. Love may manifest as abuse and abandonment in Morrison's novels, but it does so in a manner that resists any too-nifty Christian depictions of love even as it sometimes also echoes them.

Still, even if Morrison's novels do not constitute a dogmatic or systematic theology, this does not mean they aren't theological. I'd like to suggest that Morrison's novel *A Mercy* attempts to articulate just what she says she finds missing in contemporary fiction: the unsettling power of goodness, and in particular, the challenging moral value of self-sacrifice and risk. *A Mercy*, of course, is no pie-eyed apology; Morrison allows and admits the pervasive force of evil in the novel and rejects any notion of servile submission to wickedness. But she also shows how a certain willingness to risk one's self might align both with goodness and with freedom, and in so doing, she may suggest a way for Christians like me to wrestle in new ways with the troubling details of my own theological tradition. The logic of Christian atonement is tidy enough at times, but I want here to argue that, in refracting this logic through the fictional experiences of African and Native American slave women, Toni Morrison disturbs any of that theology's simple algebras of suffering. Because so many of the human bodies in this novel, by virtue of their races and genders, are literally possessed, this fiction's considerations of love are also always bound up with the realities of dominion and possession. Where Christian scripture and theology proclaim triumphantly, perhaps too easily, that God is love, *A Mercy* gives us tragic pause and causes us to reassess our loving risks and abandonments. What we discover in reading Morrison's novel is that any concrete, human conception of love must also reckon with the hard realities of human possession, realities articulated in some of the novel's final lines: "to be given dominion over another is a hard thing; to wrest dominion over another is a wrong thing; to give dominion of yourself to another is a wicked thing."[6] In offering this reading, I will not argue that Morrison's novel resolves any of theology's disturbing dilemmas. I will, however, suggest that Morrison's fiction can deepen theology's mysteries, which is perhaps the better purpose for it in the first place. At the very least, when I, as a student of Christian theology, might rather look away, *A Mercy* demands I look again toward the gruesome cross of Christ.

Toni Morrison's novel *A Mercy* is a book both of slavery and of consecutive maternal abandonment. The novel is set in the colonial period in New England and is structured carefully around a narrative of journey. In alternating chapters, a young, black enslaved woman named Florens recounts her mission to find a cure for her dead master Jacob Vaark's widow, Rebekka. Rebekka is bedridden with plague, and her only hope is the medical knowledge of a free black ironsmith several miles away. As the narrative builds, we learn that this smith wrought the iron that gates Vaark's palatial home; that Florens is in love with this blacksmith and has no plans to return to bondage; that her relationship with the smith violently soured at their reunion; that she has returned to her master's mansion rejected; that she haunts the empty building at night and that the story we read is one written on the walls of the house. This mansion, a garish

FIG. 7. *Nieu Amsterdam.* (New York Public Library Digital Collections)

trophy of financial triumph that is unnecessary to shelter Vaark's childless family, is an especially complex metaphor for colonial (and contemporary) America's economic and racial ambivalences. Vaark, for example, finds the practice of slavery personally unsavory and even condemns others for engaging with it. But Vaark is also reflectively content to accept young, female slaves as remittance for unpaid debts, to reason that he has saved them from rougher bondage, as well as to benefit distantly from brutal Caribbean slave labor through his flourishing sugar business.

And while Morrison's astute political critique of colonialist capitalism, structured around the image of Vaark's house with Florens's story written upon the walls of its unoccupied rooms, provides one narrative arc to the tale, the story is actually told in a series of narrative fragments that gather scenes of rejection and suffering and that offer a deeply unsettling corollary examination of love and power. Again, while Florens's first-person recollection structures the novel in alternating chapters, other characters'

experiences interrupt her missive in highly limited and narratively intimate third-person perspectives. The novel begins with Florens's recollection of being given to Vaark by her mother while her young brother
nursed greedily and clutched tightly at that mother's breast. Vaark then
also recalls the same scene as preface to his fond recollection of discovering the lucrative sugar trade through a conversation with a drunk in
a tavern. In later chapters Florens's fellow slave Lina remembers the anni-
hilation of her Indian tribe through disease and her early days of slavery
among Presbyterians. In the midst of a fever, Rebekka recalls her sale as a
wife from an unloving mother and father in England to an unknown husband in America, as well as the surprisingly happy ocean passage she made
in the hold of a ship with a group of similarly dispossessed women. In yet
another fragment, the slave Sorrow mourns the loss of her firstborn child,
whom Lina either delivers stillborn or murders. Toward the novel's end,
even Vaark's indentured servants Will and Scully offer their own short
and unrealistic reflections upon their hopes for eventual freedom from
substantial debts. In every episode of *A Mercy,* financial debts are realized
as bound bodies. Aside from Vaark, who remains indentured only to his
ambition, each major character in the novel is possessed by another and
dispossessed of her- or himself, and love — if and when it arises — does
so only under the troubling circumstances of power and direct dominion
over human bodies. In this way, Morrison's economic and political critique is brilliantly dramatized on an emotional and human scale.

The mapping of this political critique upon the powers and possessions
of love has theological implications as well. At times the novel seems to
suggest that interpersonal love can temper or restrain the devastatingly
acquisitive impulses of American political economy. Early in the novel
Lina tells a fable to the little girl Florens that is rich with aspirational
American imagery while deeply resonant with Morrison's larger critique:

One day, ran the story, an eagle laid her eggs in a nest far above and far
beyond the snakes and paws that hunted them. . . . Her talons are sharp-
ened on rock; her beak is like the scythe of a war god. She is fierce, protecting her borning young. But one thing she cannot protect against: the
evil thoughts of man. One day a traveler climbs a mountain nearby. He
stands at its summit admiring all he sees below him. The turquoise lake,
the eternal hemlocks, the starlings sailing into clouds cut by rainbow. The
traveler laughs at the beauty saying, "This is perfect. This is mine." And

the word swells, booming like thunder into valleys, over acres of primrose and mallow. Creatures come out of caves wondering what it means. Mine. Mine. Mine. The shells of the eagle's eggs quiver and one even cracks. The eagle swivels her head to find the source of the strange, meaningless thunder, the incomprehensible sound. Spotting the traveler, she swoops down to claw away his laugh and his unnatural sound. But the traveler, under attack, raises his stick and strikes her wing with all his strength. Screaming she falls and falls. . . . Screaming, screaming she is carried away by wind instead of wing.

Then Florens would whisper, "Where is she now?"

"Still falling," Lina would answer, "she is falling forever."

Florens barely breathes. "And the eggs?" she asks.

"They hatch alone," says Lina.

"Do they live?" Florens' whispering is urgent.

"We have," says Lina.[7]

Florens is only a girl at the time of this fable's telling, and this is Lina's bedtime tale for her. The moral of this tale is a simple one: that cry of European possession, "Mine, mine, mine," is what incites the eagle and cracks her eggs, what ruins the landscape and leaves her offspring orphaned. But familial solidarity tempers the possessive tragedy of the tale and offers a potentially redeeming counterpoint. Lina and Florens are at once sisters orphaned each by the European man as well as mother and daughter to one another. "Mother hunger," Lina reflects, "to be one or have one — both of them were reeling from that longing which, Lina knew, remained alive, traveling the bone."[8] But, as Lina worries, mother love can also ramify as power and possession when expressed within a system of bound human bodies. This is what Lina's tale glosses by its eager solidarity, and what Morrison's larger tale I think exposes.

Consider two particular scenes of maternal rejection and abandonment complexly portrayed by the novel. Once again, the novel begins as a letter by Florens addressed to the blacksmith she loves, as a missive of longing and recollection written on the walls of Vaark's empty house. But the first part of that letter closes with a memory that will return to haunt the book's conclusion. Florens recounts the circumstances of her sale to Vaark from her previous Portuguese master, Senhor D'Ortega:

Senhor is not paying the whole amount he owes to Sir. Sir saying he will take instead the woman and the girl, not the baby boy and the debt is gone. A minha mãe begs no. Her baby boy is still at her breast. Take the girl, she says, my daughter, she says. Me. Me. Sir agrees and changes the balance due. . . . [M]others nursing greedy babies scare me. I know how their eyes go when they choose. How they raise them to look at me hard, saying something I cannot hear. Saying something important to me, but holding the little boy's hand.[9]

In her innocence and abandonment, Florens believes her mother here to have chosen a son over a daughter. Forced in an instant to decide whether to be separated from her still nursing son or her young daughter, Florens's mother holds the boy close and offers up the girl to permanent separation and slavery. Florens is understandably haunted by the memory of this choice. But when Florens's mother gives an account of the same event, we learn that D'Ortega routinely rapes the mother and that Florens has also lately caught D'Ortega's violent eye. What Florens's mother seeks is not estrangement from her daughter but escape for her: she hopes through abandonment to protect Florens from violence. Florens's mother sacrifices their intimacy for safety. "There is no protection," she explains, no salvation from this commodified plight, "but there is difference."[10] Florens's mother intuits that all unfreedoms are not equal. In that crucial moment, Florens's mother believes that Vaark can see Florens "as a human child" so she kneels "before him. Hoping for a miracle."[11] When he agrees, Florens mother insists "it [is] not a miracle. Bestowed by God. It [is] a mercy. Offered by a human."[12]

I will return to this antimiraculous insistence shortly, but what's crucial here is how Florens and her mother's common enslavement so constrains their choices that even an act of maternal protection and merciful salvation must here take the form of a dominion, a bartering of bodies: Florens's mother must engage in the trade of her own daughter's flesh in order to spare that child rape. And thus we readers are brought to recognize the dramatic irony when Florens's abandonment resurfaces in her relationship with the blacksmith, who is himself raising a young child. Florens's mother hunger makes her long to be possessed entirely and exclusively by the blacksmith, but because Florens knows "how their eyes go when they choose," she becomes inevitably and violently jealous of the smith's boy Malik. When she carelessly dislocates Malik's shoulder, the smith rebukes and rejects her, telling Florens: "Own yourself, woman, and leave us be. . . . You are nothing but wilderness, no constraint."[13]

The smith's accusation is unfair, as Florens intuits: she has been entirely constrained since birth, and constraint is precisely what the wilderness of her passion struggles against. But in either case, her mother's act of abandoning mercy cannot but haunt Florens as dominion and desire. Perhaps this is why the mercy should not, cannot be counted a miracle (though I will suggest other reasons too): because it — and Florens also — remains entirely bound by the brute human violence of slavery.

Florens's trauma is a mercy, not a miracle, we are told: a human rather than a divine thing. Another scene of maternal abuse might shed more light on the (ir)religious valence of this mother's mercy, and the possibilities for goodness and self-possession within systems of structured violence. On her journey to the blacksmith, Florens is sheltered for one night by a woman called the Widow Ealing. Ealing and her daughter Jane live together in a witch-crazed religious community. Jane has a lazy eye, and the witchhunters believe her for this reason to be a demon of the tellingly named "Black Man." Never having seen skin as dark as Florens's, the witchhunters believe Florens to be the Black Man's minion too. The Ealings' home is thus quarantined as a demonic portal to hell. Distressingly, Ealing conceives only one possible proof of her daughter's innocence. She lashes Jane's thighs and calves until a "dark blood" comes "beetling down her legs" so that "the light pouring over her pale skin" causes the wounds to "look like live jewels."[14] When the authorities come to investigate, Florens eavesdrops upon Ealing's explanation from a hiding place in the closet: "The Widow offers the visitors seating. They refuse. A man's voice says this is preliminary yet witnesses are several. Widow interrupts him saying her daughter's eye is askew as God made it and it has no special powers. And look, she says, look at her wounds. God's son bleeds. We bleed. Demons never."[15] The widow lashes her daughter because the running blood should prove she is human and thus save her from judgment. This abuse is meant to save her life; it is a blood sacrifice of sorts. Like Florens's mother, Ealing is caught and constrained by a larger violence and can guard her daughter's body only by mutilating it. The widow and her daughter each are so wholly dominated by their religion and its authorities that their love cannot but trade in the patterns of its domination.

But at dusk, after the investigators have left with a dire warning that no woman leave the house and after the Widow Ealing has gone out in defiance to seek the sheriff's aid, Jane boils some duck eggs, places them in a cloth, gives them to Florens, and then leads Florens out of the village into the darkening woods. At a stream, Jane sends Florens off to safety. Florens recounts the departure: "She explains how I am to go, where the trail will be that takes me to the post road that takes me to the hamlet where I hope you are. I say thank you and lift her hand to kiss it. She says no, I thank you. They look at you and forget about me. She kisses my forehead then watches as I step down into the stream's dry bed. I turn and look up at her. Are you a demon I ask her. Her wayward eye is steady. She smiles. Yes, she says. Oh, yes. Go now."[16] Whatever the significance of the unsettling straightening of Jane's lazy eye, her irreligion here demands a closer reading. What should we make of Jane's demonic possession? How is it linked to the merciful risk she here takes to save Florens?

In his slim but important book *The Gift of Death*, Jacques Derrida meditates upon the nature of religion and responsibility. In a critical appropriation of the work of Czech thinker Jan Patočka, Derrida cites the demonic as a condition of "irresponsibility or, if one wishes, as non-responsibility. It belongs to a space that does not yet resound with the injunction to *respond*, a space in which one does not yet hear the call to explain oneself, one's actions, or one's thoughts, to respond to the other and answer for oneself before the other."[17] What's important here is the relation between response and responsibility. To be responsible is to be answerable to another, to allow the other to be other, to let her speak for herself instead of being spoken for by me. This is why the demonic is prior to responsibility, prior to alterity and subjectivity. The demonic admits no otherness; it is totalitarian. But as the subject realizes it is not alone in an inanimate world, a new selfhood and subjectivity arises. The subject recognizes that there are others who do not speak for it, and for whom it cannot speak, and to whom it is therefore answerable. In this way, self and other arise together. That there is another to whom I must respond becomes the ground of my sense of myself as one who can make a response and then be responded to also. In the somewhat tangled prose of Derrida we might then say that the self becomes simultaneously a subject "who says 'myself'" and can "relate to itself as an instance of liberty, singularity, and responsibility."[18] Freedom, uniqueness, and subjectivity — all three — escape from the totalitarian demonic in this passage toward response and responsibility.

This mix of responsibility toward, and difference from, the irreducible other is what Derrida links to the religious. Since "religion exists once the secret of the . . . demonic mystery has been, if not destroyed, at least integrated, and finally subjected to the sphere of responsibility," religion therefore "is responsibility or it is nothing at all."[19] Responsibility, Patočka asserts and Derrida allows, is thus the root of religion and characterizes religion as the response of the free and unique subject to the irreducible other. To be properly religious is to admit the other's absolute alterity and thus to construe myself as one capable of responding. For Derrida this is all due to the other's unknowability. Because "my neighbor or my loved ones . . . are as inaccessible to me, as secret, and as transcendent as Jahweh," each act of ethical responsibility on behalf of the other is a leap into the unknowable and the unknown, each moral response to the other an act of faith.[20] Responsibility and religious faith "go together, however paradoxical that might seem to some," because both "should, in the same movement, exceed mastery and knowledge."[21] If everyone else is "every bit other," then one can no longer distinguish between" a general ethical obligation to other humans "and the faith that turns to God alone."[22]

Mystery haunts every relation, divine or human. But Derrida notes that a dilemma hides in this free passage through alterity from the demonic to responsibility: since subjectivity arises only through the encounter with, and obligation to, the unknowable other, it remains also always secretly fettered to that other, too. Or, as Terry Eagleton might paraphrase, we "are able to become self-determining, but only on the basis of a deeper dependency. This dependency is the condition of our freedom, not the infringement of it."[23] The self arises out of the demonic into moral freedom only to find itself ethically bound to the other once it arrives there. If human subjectivity is so wholly given over to alterity, Derrida thus asks, does anything then remain uniquely one's own to offer in response? One thing, Derrida argues, remains always and entirely one's own. Everyone "must assume their own death, that is to say, the one thing in the world that no one else can *either give or take:* therein resides freedom and responsibility."[24] No one can die our death for us, and we can die no other's death. Since it is the one thing entirely our own, it remains the only thing we are entirely free to risk on behalf of the unknowable other. Of course, with the harrowing details of this novel as a reminder, one must note that one's life can surely be taken, even if one's death cannot be. Still, the truth that one's death remains entirely one's own to undergo will mean that the choice to risk it — if it is a choice, not a coercion — remains free, unconditioned by the encounter with the other.

A Mercy concretizes Derrida's abstract claims. In this novel where dominion and possession pervade and corrupt most all human relations, it is telling that the particular crime Jane is accused of by her religious elders is demonic possession. She is accused of being bodily possessed by a spiritual force. But what she and even the hapless Widow Ealing fully recognize is that the accusations are, in an important sense, true. Jane is possessed, but it isn't some "black man" who holds her; it is religious authority itself that owns Jane's body. This sort of religious possession is in fact — on Derrida's definition at least — irreligious. This religion is actually demonic because, in their judgment of her, the religious authorities refuse to recognize Jane as a human other. They do not recognize their own answerability and accountability to her, they do not feel obligated to respond to her as a fellow subject, they do not pass into responsibility for her. They do not see her as unknowable, secret, or transcendent. On the contrary, they assume the right to know her and judge her absolutely. They regard Jane as an object of their own fears and desire, not as one to whom they are unknowably accountable and for whom they are ineffably responsible. These elders read and interpret her flesh and determine its unequivocal meaning. They absolutely administer and adjudicate the value and significance of Jane's body, its ailments, its oddities, its wounds, and of Florens's too. For all the elders' wrongheaded fear and foment, it turns out that they are right, that she is, in fact, possessed by demons: she is possessed by them.

But in saving and sending forth Florens, Jane momentarily escapes the gaze of their judgment. She resists their demonic possession and possesses herself — that is, she owns the risk of her chosen actions. As Florens recalls, Jane's "bloody legs do not stop her. She risks. Risks all to save the slave."[25] Taking control of all her body's wounds and of its risks, Jane saves Florens from a demonic religion. In this saving act of response to Florens's humanity, Jane is not possessed, or not only possessed, by others. In risking her own death for Florens, she is self-possessed too, and it is this self-possession that straightens her sight and sets her against her elders' religion as their empowered adversary. If she is demonic, as she claims, then it is only because she knows her human act of risk and responsibility will bedevil her elders' irresponsible religion.

When *A Mercy* ends, Florens's mother imagines an address to her daughter and attempts to justify her abandonment of Florens. She tells Florens, by way of explanation, that "to be given dominion over another is a hard thing; to wrest dominion over another is a wrong thing; to give dominion of yourself to another is a wicked thing."²⁶ Having now followed this complex story's windings to its end, we might gloss that moral's meaning. Love is a hard thing; it operates in a hard world and under conditions of bondage it cannot ever fully escape, and so it might — as with Florens's mother — take the form of abuse and abandonment at times. But this is a different thing than the wresting of dominion from another, which is immoral and brutal rather than merely tragic. But both tragedy and immorality differ from the singularly demonic wickedness of failing to possess oneself through the risking of oneself for the sake of another. Jane here provides a dramatic model for this final moral, an example of owning one's risk even while owned, of responsible religion acting in defiance of knowing demons. For Florens's mother as for Daughter Jane, there is no escaping the twin plights of possession and dispossession, not for women and persons of color in colonial (and contemporary) America, perhaps not for anyone. And yet even under the constraint of these binding terms, to hazard oneself for the sake of another's safety, to risk one's own bound body in order to free the body of another, remains an act of self-possession that even bad religion, bald patriarchy, and brutal racism cannot defy. Love may at times be a risk and an affliction; it may be a separation, an abandonment, a self-sacrifice, a loss. But whatever else it is, it is free. Even when offered under all the undeniable constraints of material and political dominion, because of the death it is willing to risk, it is also fundamentally an act of human self-possession.

The primary and well-founded critique of much Christian atonement theology is set around its valorization of self-sacrifice. This selflessness is too weak, it argues, this vulnerability too feeble. A cross too readily embraced will prove self-abnegating and masochistic. But what Morrison suggests in this haunting novel is that not all sacrifice is the same, that not all risk is reckless. Freely to risk one's life for another affirms life rather than annuls it. It recognizes the terrible stakes of the wager, then hazards the highest for the sake of a likewise reward. But the challenge and promise of this for Christian theology is that a love such as this demands death. Only the mortal can risk dying. The impervious or impassible cannot offer as much. So how will an infinite God love us? At the end of *A Mercy*, Florens's mother insists that the sacrifice that saved her daughter was not a miracle bestowed by God but a mercy offered by a human. And in the beginning of this essay I suggested that *A Mercy* might deepen the mystery of the incarnation for those inclined to look for religion in the cross of Christ. Once again, I don't pretend that this novel resolves any of Christianity's deep dilemmas or that it should. But what haunts the torture and execution of Jesus Christ — for this Christian theologian anyway — is the assertion that a brutal death should be a sign of deepest love. Toni Morrison I think suggests that this deep love might better be reckoned a mercy than a miracle, an act of human freedom than of divine dominion. For Morrison, love is not decreed by an impassible God above; it is risked by a fragile human below. God's Son bleeds. We bleed. Demons never. Love is owned and self-possessed by whomever will embrace its mortal risks against all the demons and powers and dominions arrayed against it. Indeed, Morrison suggests, this is perhaps precisely love's inimitable power. The human miracle of mercy is that alone among all possible acts it cannot be constrained. Because it is so intimately bound to one's own death, human mercy always retains the capacity to resist domination. Love alone can act in freedom while enslaved.

NOTES

1. Toni Morrison, "Goodness: Altruism and the Literary Imagination," in this volume. See also the video of Morrison's Ingersoll Lecture, filmed December 6, 2012, at Harvard University, Cambridge, https://hds.harvard.edu/news/2012/12/11/goodness-altruism-and-literary-imagination.

2. Understandings of Jesus's death in the modern Christian West have been dominated by Reformation understandings of atonement as articulated by John Calvin and (to a lesser and perhaps debatable extent) Martin Luther, themselves indebted to Anselm. These tend to focus on a theory of substitution, that Jesus stands in our place before God's judgment, and (in familiar versions) bears our punishment. Alternative interpretations of Jesus's death in political, feminist, liberationist, and womanist theology are indeed notable, not least for their common dissatisfaction with the dominant, substitutionary model. See especially Delores Williams, *Sisters in the Wilderness: The Challenge of Womanist God-Talk* (Maryknoll, NY: Orbis, 1993); and Rita Nakashima Brock and Rebecca Ann Parker, *Proverbs of Ashes: Violence Redemptive Suffering, and the Search for What Saves Us* (Boston: Beacon, 2001).

3. James Cone, *The Cross and the Lynching Tree* (Maryknoll, NY: Orbis, 2013).

4. See note 2 above.

5. Cone, *The Cross and the Lynching Tree*, 157–58.

6. Toni Morrison, *A Mercy* (New York: Vintage, 2008), 196.

7. Morrison, *A Mercy*, 73.

8. Morrison, *A Mercy*, 73.

9. Morrison, *A Mercy*, 9.

10. Morrison, *A Mercy*, 195.

11. Morrison, *A Mercy*, 195.

12. Morrison, *A Mercy*, 195.

13. Morrison, *A Mercy*, 166.

14. Morrison, *A Mercy*, 127.

15. Morrison, *A Mercy*, 130.

16. Morrison, *A Mercy*, 135.

17. Jacques Derrida, *The Gift of Death and Literature in Secret* (Chicago: University of Chicago Press, 2008), 5.

18. Derrida, *The Gift of Death and Literature in Secret*, 5.

19. Derrida, *The Gift of Death and Literature in Secret*, 4.

20. Derrida, *The Gift of Death and Literature in Secret*, 78.

21. Derrida, *The Gift of Death and Literature in Secret*, 8.

22. Derrida, *The Gift of Death and Literature in Secret*, 84.

23. Terry Eagleton, *After Theory* (New York: Basic, 2003), 189.

24. Derrida, *The Gift of Death and Literature in Secret*, 45, original emphasis.

25. Morrison, *A Mercy*, 188.

26. Morrison, *A Mercy*, 196.

III Giving Goodness a Voice

Ministry in *Paradise*

STEPHANIE PAULSELL

*P*aradise is the third novel in Toni Morrison's richly imagined trilogy of African American life from the years of slavery through the Bicentennial of 1976. Like *Beloved* and *Jazz,* the two novels that precede it, *Paradise* is saturated with open secrets and unspoken histories. Morrison reveals layer after layer of the histories that haunt this novel, reaching back through *Jazz* and *Beloved* all the way to the biblical books of Genesis and Exodus, with their stories of the loss of paradise, the journey of the people of Israel out of slavery, and the longing for a promised land.

In the opening scene of *Paradise,* nine churchgoing men armed with rifles drive from their town to an isolated former convent seventeen miles away and proceed to murder the women who live there. "They shoot the white girl first," Morrison writes in the opening sentence of the novel. "With the rest they can take their time."[1]

The men are from Ruby, an all-black town in Oklahoma founded by the remnant of another all-black town called Haven, which had itself been founded in great hope by formerly enslaved people. But Haven had gone from "dreamtown" to "ghosttown" (5) during the Great Depression. When the men went off to fight in World War II, they cherished the idea of their town and dreamed of founding a new one.[2] Met on their return from the battlefield by a society in which "your children were sport, your women quarry, and where your very person could be annulled" (16), the patriarchs of several Haven families — the "New Fathers" who prided themselves on the purity visible in the deep blackness of their skin — packed up their families and the communal oven that had served as a sacred gathering place in Haven and moved deeper into Oklahoma. There they founded a town called Ruby, ninety miles from any other town. Ruby became self-sufficient and prosperous, a place where women and children could live in safety.

Among the histories that live a "quietly throbbing life" (195) in Morrison's novel is the history of black towns in Oklahoma. From 1865 to 1920, African Americans created dozens of self-governed communities in what

FIG. 8. *Part of District Burned in Race Riots, Tulsa, Oklahoma, 1921.* (Library of Congress)

became, in 1907, the state of Oklahoma, often on the "unassigned land" of Native Americans.[3] As Oklahoma became a boom state, enriched by oil and the railroads, it came to be seen as a kind of Promised Land[4] in which African Americans could thrive in self-sufficient communities.

The history of racist violence inflicted on these communities is an open secret that haunts Morrison's novel. In 1921, a white mob attacked the prosperous Greenwood District in Tulsa, Oklahoma. Known as the "Black Wall Street," its inhabitants built "a self-sufficient community, with a school, a hospital, hotels, grocery, drug, and clothing stores, two newspapers, and two movie theaters."[5] The Greenwood community was served by African American professionals — doctors, dentists, lawyers, ministers. When a young man from Greenwood was accused of assaulting a white woman, and a lynch mob gathered outside the jail where he was being held, men from the Greenwood District came over, rifles in hand. *Paradise* contains an echo of that scene. When carloads of white men threaten a group of young girls, the men of Ruby emerge quietly, but visibly armed, from their homes and businesses to confront them.

In Morrison's novel, the men of Ruby prevail. In Tulsa, however, a white mob responded to the community's attempt to prevent a lynching by attacking the Greenwood District for sixteen hours, sending eight hundred people to the hospital and killing as many as three hundred. Armed Greenwood residents tried to hold the mob back at the boundary of the neighborhood but were eventually overcome. Many residents of Greenwood were rounded up and detained and their homes then looted and burned to the ground. More than a thousand families were left homeless, and thirty-five city blocks in Greenwood were destroyed by fire. Photos of the aftermath, like the one on the facing page, show the district razed and smouldering.

In spite of the scale and violence of this atrocity, the Greenwood massacre became "a public secret" (145), quickly whitewashed by the city. White ministers like Reverend Ed Mouzon took to their pulpits to blame "outside agitators" for the violence leveled against the Greenwood community, and a grand jury issued indictments mostly for Greenwood residents.[6] It was not until 1997 that a full-scale investigation into the massacre began, culminating in a report in 2001. In 2010, a memorial park was built in Tulsa to commemorate the massacre. And in November 2018, the last-known survivor of the Greenwood District massacre died.[7] Dr. Olivia Hooker had been six years old when white mobs attached her neighborhood. She lived to be 103.

Such violent, hidden histories haunt Morrison's novel and shape the actions of the characters. The unspoken fear that the boundaries of their paradise might be violently breached leads the men of the town to transgress the boundaries of the Convent to rid themselves of women they consider "throwaway people" (4). The women's presence, they believe, has destabilized their paradise and made it vulnerable. "God at their side," Morrison writes, "the men take aim. For Ruby" (18).

Morrison portrays the founding of the town of Ruby as grounded in experiences of the vulnerability of women and the anguish of men unable to protect them. When the first families traveled from Fairly, Oklahoma, to what would become the town of Haven, they were rejected multiple times, "turned away by rich Choctaw and poor whites, chased by yard dogs, jeered at by camp prostitutes and their children" (13). Most painful, though, was being denied help by the inhabitants of other black towns, often by light-skinned black people who rejected them because of their darker skin. "It was the shame of seeing one's pregnant wife or sister or daughter refused shelter that had rocked them," Morrison writes, "and changed them for all time. The humiliation did more than rankle; it threated to crack open their bones" (95).

These stories, passed down from parents to children, get hardwired into the new town of Ruby by being ritually reenacted by the town's children each Christmas in the town's Nativity Play. Every year, the cruel innkeeper turns away seven holy families from the inn. The children cry out: "But our wives are pregnant!" "Our children are going to die of thirst!" (210). And so the story is passed on, from generation to generation.

Stories about the vulnerability of women and girls punctuate the novel and define a vision of paradise as a place where no one within ninety miles would see a sleepless woman walking down the road at night as prey.[8] There is the story of the girls who are threatened by a group of white men passing through Ruby in their cars, and the story of Elder Morgan, who sees a black prostitute beaten by two white men in New York City. Elder tries and fails to protect her, but he sees her face and prays for her every day for the rest of his life. Steward Morgan imagines what it would be like if his own wife were denied shelter: "The thought of that level of helplessness made him want to shoot somebody," Morrison writes (96). The women of the Convent, the women who ultimately are shot by Steward and the other eight men from Ruby, carry their own stories of humiliation and violation.

All of these stories gesture further back than the founding of Haven and Ruby. They look toward the first novel of Morrison's trilogy, *Beloved,* and that novel's attention to the sexual violence to which enslaved women were subjected. The men of Ruby cannot tolerate light-skinned people; they insist that one man in the community send the light-skinned woman he loves back where she came from, a loss from which he never recovers. Not only do light-skinned people remind them of those who refused to help their mothers and fathers during their journey from Fairly to Haven, but they recall an even older, even more unbearable memory of enslaved women unprotected from the sexual violence endemic to the system of slavery, a system Sethe kills her daughter to protect her from in *Beloved.*

We meet the inhabitants of the town of Ruby in 1976, the year the United States celebrated its bicentennial. But the history of places like Haven and Ruby and the Greenwood District was not the history being remembered and celebrated. As Leon F. Litwack has written, the bicentennial did not attend to "the history of individual and collective efforts by black men and women to build a community and a culture that could sustain them in a society that refused to acknowledge their humanity."[9] Morrison's novel turns its attention precisely to such an effort and to the ways in which the nation's willful ignorance of that history continues to perpetuate violence.

In 1976, there is no one left in Ruby with a direct experience of slavery. The patriarchs and matriarchs of the town still remember the formerly enslaved founders of Haven who passed on to them the dream of an all-black town where women and children would be safe from harm. But the next generation is further removed from that history and has its own ideas about it. The history the new generation cares about is the more recent history of Martin Luther King Jr. and Malcolm X, of the young people who endured abuse at lunch counters and in the streets in order to move history forward.

Their elders are more interested in preserving the self-sufficient home they have created in Ruby than they are in the civil rights movement. Ruby's elders want a paradise free of white people, free even of light-skinned black people, where they can take care of their own. Steward Morgan, one of the New Fathers, is so disturbed by the idea of young people trying to integrate the lunch counters that he writes an angry letter to the woman who organized the drugstore protests in Oklahoma City. Ten years earlier, he had criticized Thurgood Marshall for his antisegregation work in Norman, Oklahoma.

The young people of Ruby, however, have a much different perspective. For them, Ruby is a "prison calling itself a town" (308) where they are under constant pressure to subsume their individuality into the larger community. They begin to reinterpret the founding stories of Ruby, beginning with the inscription on the Oven that the founders of Ruby brought from Haven. Like a fragment of an ancient manuscript, the inscription over the Oven is incomplete. It reads ". . . the Furrow of His Brow."

The patriarchs of Ruby appeal to the eyewitness account of Miss Esther, who had seen the original Oven when she was five years old and run her finger over the words to argue that the original inscription read, "Beware the Furrow of His Brow." This is a command to live in the fear of the Lord, the elders insist, to understand that God's power is sovereign. The young people respond that the original inscription could not possibly have demanded such subservience from the once enslaved people who gathered around it every day to cook and share meals, to celebrate baptisms, and build up the community. The young people argue that the inscription must have read "Be the Furrow of His Brow." The message delivered from their ancestors, they insist, is not to cower before God but to be God's instrument of justice in the world.

Destry Beauchamp argues for the new reading of the inscription, telling the town elders that "no ex-slave who had the guts to make his own way, build a town out of nothing could think like that." The young man's interpretation enrages Deacon Morgan: "That's my grandfather you're talking about. Quit calling him an ex-slave like that's all he was. He was also an ex–lieutenant governor, an ex-banker, an ex-deacon and a whole lot of other exes, and he wasn't making his own way; he was part of a whole group making their own way" (84).

The argument about the Oven quickly becomes an argument about their shared history. Who gets to say what that history means? The elders whose grandparents had been enslaved? Or the young people searching their ancestors' history for clues to their own identity and purpose? Who are the true heirs of Ruby's founders? The bankers and ministers who sacrificed to preserve their grandparents' vision unchanged? Or the young people inspired by the civil rights movement to change their world?

The young people have grown up acting out the story of their ancestors in the annual Nativity Play. They have been shaped by that story, just as the elders of Ruby hoped. But knowing the story in their bones turns out to be no guarantee that it will mean the same thing to them as it did to their parents. "It's our history too, sir," one of the young people says. "Not just yours" (86). The argument about the Oven's inscription is at once historical, hermeneutical, theological, and ethical. It is an argument that makes a claim on every person in Ruby but perhaps especially the ministers. In their pastoral care and their prayers, in their ritual gestures and their preaching, the town's ministers respond to the town's history and shape how the story is told, understood, and passed on. The story of Ruby's founding is the sacred text they interpret over and over again. The town is full of ministers, and we hear bits and pieces of several sermons in the novel. But there are two ministers in particular whose sermons Morrison allows us to experience in their entirety: one by the older Reverend Senior Pulliam, who stands against the young people, and two by the younger Reverend Richard Misner, who stands with them.

The first full sermon we encounter in *Paradise* belongs to Reverend Pulliam. Although he is in Reverend Misner's church, he has been asked to say a few words to mark the wedding of K.D. and Arnette. This wedding already bears the burden of the community's hope that this union will mend the conflict between two feuding families, the Morgans and the Fleetwoods. Then Reverend Pulliam rises to his feet and puts a little more pressure on everyone.

In her William Vaughn Moody Lecture at the University of Chicago in 1996, "The Trouble with Paradise," Toni Morrison stood in the pulpit of the Rockefeller Memorial Chapel and talked about how difficult it is to write a good sermon. She was in the middle of writing the novel that would become *Paradise,* and she said she was finding it hard not to slip into clichés or familiar phrases while writing the sermons of the town's ministers.[10] In her essay of the same name, recently published in her volume of selected essays, *The Source of Self-Regard,* Morrison writes of the difficulty of making religious language credible and effective in fiction "without having to submit to a vague egalitarianism, or to a kind of late-twentieth-century environmental spiritualism, or to the modernist/feminist school of the goddess-body adored, or to the biblical/political scholasticism of the more entrenched and dictatorial wings of contemporary religious institutions."[11] She discusses her struggle to find language that does justice to the religious lives of her characters and "render their profoundly held moral system affective in these alienated, uninspiring, and uninspired times."[12] Morrison is after a religious language that is fresh and arresting, a language that startles us awake rather than lulling us with its familiar phrases.

She finds that language in Reverend Pulliam's sermon. His long sentences are punctuated by short sentences that land like blows. "Love is divine only and difficult always. If you think it is easy you are a fool," Pulliam proclaims. "You have to earn God. You have to practice God. You have to think God — carefully." The climax of this fierce wedding homily is uncompromising: "You are human and therefore educable, and therefore capable of learning how to learn, and therefore interesting to God, who is interested only in Himself, which is to say He is interested only in love. Do you understand me? God is not interested in you" (141–42).

In his "Divinity School Address," Ralph Waldo Emerson defined preaching as "life passed through the fire of thought."[13] Reverend Pulliam preaches a sermon that sounds more like thought passed through the fire of life. We don't learn much about Reverend Pulliam's history, except that it is knit tightly into the history of Ruby. He uses his wedding sermon to argue with Ruby's young people and with Reverend Misner. But the severity of his language bears the mark not only of his interpretation of the words on the Oven but of the traumatic origins of the town itself.

Morrison resists making Pulliam a caricature of a conversative, cranky old preacher. The transcendent, all-powerful, and wholly mysterious God Reverend Pulliam invokes is a God who judges the arrogance of young people who think they can reinterpret the Oven, to be sure. But Reverend Pulliam's God is also a God out of the reach of lynch mobs, out of the reach of those who would prey on women and children, out of the reach of the police, out of the reach of death. There are no open secrets, no hidden histories with Reverend Pulliam's God. This God sees all and judges all. Pulliam's clipped, ferocious words communicate more than his frustration with Misner and his new ideas. They communicate his desire for a power greater than any earthly power, a God who would, in the end, insist upon justice—not because of the prayers or actions of any frail human but because justice is what God cares about. Reverend Pulliam's refusal to sugarcoat his words looks back to the demanding and unsentimental ministry of Baby Suggs in *Beloved* and ahead to the ministry of Ethel Fordham in *Home*.

This is not how Pulliam appears to Reverend Misner in this moment, however, and Misner responds with his own sermon, a sermon preached in a silence as fierce as Reverend Pulliam's words. "Misner knew," Morrison writes, "that Pulliam's words were a widening of the war he had declared on Misner's activities: tempting the young to step outside the wall, outside the town limits, shepherding them, forcing them to transgress, to think of themselves as civil warriors" (145). So angry that he does not trust himself to speak, Misner grabs the crucifix from the wall behind him and holds it out to the congregation, trying to make them see it. As he holds the cross before him, he preaches a sermon in his head that he hopes his gesture will communicate. He wants the congregation to see the cross as both ordinary and sublime, the mark of a human figure poised to embrace. He wants them to see Jesus as a death-row felon who "moved the relationship between God and man from CEO and supplicant to one on one." He wants them to see that the death of this "one solitary black man" brought human beings into the spotlight, into "the principal role in the story of their lives." Holding up the cross, Misner shouts inside his head to the congregation before him "that not only is God interested in you; He *is* you" (146–47).

Reverend Misner and Reverend Pulliam are at odds with each other, theologically and politically, throughout the novel. But Morrison subverts their antagonistic relationship by linking them together in a lyrical history of ministry that she places at the center of the book. In a long, cascading paragraph that sounds like a sermon itself, Morrison lifts up the history of black ministers: those called to their vocation in the midst of slavery who whispered words of liberation in cabins and clearings; ministers who held onto the Spirit with their teeth and their fists; ministers who "wiped white folks' spit from the faces of children, hid strangers from posses and police, relayed lifepreserving information, faster than the newspaper and better than the radio"; ministers who buried the dead children of brokenhearted mothers, all the while preaching "That death was *life*, don't you know, and *every* life, don't you know, was holy, don't you know, in His eyesight" (159–60). This history of ministers who both fought for, and marveled at, the survival of their people is the sermon around which the whole novel turns.

When we next hear Reverend Misner preaching, he is standing at the grave of little Save-Marie, one of the four of Sweetie Fleetwood's damaged children. These children are ghostly presences in the novel; we don't often see them, but we sense the slow-burning anxiety they create in Ruby, and we see their mother breaking under the burden of their care and the hopelessness of their condition. As he preaches, Reverend Misner's mind drifts. He imagines the future of Ruby—a future in which the young people dream of leaving and the old people are full of regret, a future in which ministers fail to find a language powerful enough to transform their listeners and instead preach eloquent sermons which fewer and fewer people hear and apply to their everyday lives. And when Morrison brings us back into the words of his sermon, we see that they are indeed eloquent and yet somehow detached from what is really happening. The thoughts of the mourners at the grave begin to turn to other matters: what they will cook for Thanksgiving dinner, what they think of their neighbors.

But just as he begins to draw his sermon to an end, Reverend Misner snaps out of his reverie and shouts, "Wait. Wait." And he begins to preach a sermon that blends Reverend Pulliam's fierce questioning of the human tendency to make everything about ourselves and Misner's own love of all the ways human beings manifest their existence on this earth.

"Do you think," he asks, "that this was a short, pitiful life bereft of worth because it did not parallel your own? Let me tell you something. The love she received was wide and deep, and the care given her was gentle and unrelenting, and that love and care enveloped her so completely that the dreams, the visions she had, the journeys she took made her life as compelling, as rich, as valuable as any of ours and probably more blessed" (307). Preaching in the midst of a community that pours its energy into amassing strength and protecting itself from change, Reverend Misner lifts up its most vulnerable, most weak, more unknowable member as the one whose life reveals what goodness is.

For Billie Delia, one of the mourners, Save-Marie's funeral expands to include the women of the Convent, murdered by the men of Ruby who believed their paradise threatened by women whose lives did not fulfill their visions of what a woman ought to be. For Billie Delia, Ruby is not a paradise, but a "backward noplace ruled by men whose power to control was out of control" (308), men who despised the Convent women's self-sufficiency. "They don't need men and they don't need God" (276), the threatened men of Ruby tell each other as they load their guns into their trucks.

There can be no graveside service for the murdered women because their bodies have mysteriously disappeared. Indeed, the dead women seem to have taken off together in Mavis's Cadillac. But Misner's sermon opens a space to remember and honor those lives — lives, like Save-Marie's, that were so different from the lives of the citizens of Ruby. Lives that offered hidden, but unrelenting, love and care. Lives as valuable as anyone's in Ruby, and probably more blessed. Reverend Misner's funeral sermon is a critique of the very idea of paradise upon which Ruby was founded. "How exquisitely human was the wish for permanent happiness," he thinks, "and how thin human imagination became trying to achieve it."

It's that thinning out of the imagination that he resists and critiques in his sermon for Save-Marie. If we can't imagine what the lives of others are like, if we can't feel reverence for the worlds they contain within them, if all we can do is to project our own fears and desires onto them, we become dangerous to them. To lack imagination is to lack the capacity for goodness.

Through the unrelenting policing of its boundaries, what Misner describes to himself as "this hard-won heaven defined only by the absence of the unsaved, the unworthy, and the strange" (306) has thinned out its imagination. The boundaries themselves have become dangerous because what the patriarchs of Ruby try so hard to keep out ends up getting trapped inside.

The Convent, on the other hand, seems boundaryless and marked not by the stability sought by Ruby's town fathers but by constant change. The house itself has an ambiguous history: it began its life as the pleasure palace of a rich embezzler and was then transformed into a school for Native American girls who had been removed from their own culture and set down in a new one. When we encounter the Convent in *Paradise,* it has become a sanctuary for women with no place to go, presided over by Consolata, brought to Oklahoma by Sister Mary Magna when she was a child. Connie is another of the ministers in this story, and the Convent another paradise, but one with boundaries fluid enough to make room for strangers — including citizens of Ruby — when they turn up. The patriarchs of Ruby want to make a paradise that cannot be breached, and who can blame them? They know what lies on the other side of the town limits. Connie knows, however, that unbreachable boundaries erode the most essential qualities of paradise. She knows that the solace we seek in paradise requires goodness and mercy. And goodness and mercy require us to open ourselves to what is not ourselves.

Misner ends his sermon by addressing little Save-Marie directly. "Oh, Save-Marie," he says, "your name always sounded like 'Save me. Save me.' Any other messages hiding in your name? I know one that shines out for all to see: there never was a time when you were not saved, Marie." This child, greatly loved but largely unknown, used by the town as a blank slate onto which they projected their anxieties about the future, turns out not to be a blank slate at all but a text full of hidden messages that the town needs to hear and a mirror of the otherness the town has tried to destroy.

For Billie Delia, Save-Marie's funeral recalls for her the kindness the Convent women showed her when she turned up on their doorstep with her face bruised and swollen. Not only does she remember and miss them, she looks for their Second Coming. "When will they return?" she wonders. "When will they reappear, with blazing eyes, war paint and huge hands to rip up and stomp down this prison calling itself a town? She hoped with all her heart that the women were out there, darkly burnished, biding their time, brass-metaling their nails, filing their incisors — but out there" (308).

The Convent women are, indeed, out there, and we meet them one more time at the very end of the novel. One by one, they appear to those they had left behind at home: fathers, mothers, children. They do not appear ghostly — they eat, they swim, they bleed — but they are not wholly substantial, either. They seem to need to keep moving, and they slip from the presence of those to whom they appear almost imperceptibly. The "throwaway people" imagined by the men of Ruby turn out not to be disposable at all.

The Convent women slip out of our grasp, too, especially if we are still looking for the white girl among them. "They shoot the white girl first," the novel begins. Who is the white girl the men of Ruby see when they enter the Convent? As we search through the Convent women, Morrison exposes the racialized quality of our thinking, the ways in which we invest eyes, hair, speech, clothes, and bodies with racialized meanings. In *Playing in the Dark,* Morrison writes, "I am a black writer struggling with and through a language that can powerfully evoke and enforce hidden signs of racial superiority, cultural hegemony, and dismissive 'othering' of people and language."[14] In *Paradise,* she forces us to confront those same hidden signs at work not only in our language but in our imaginations.

As we read Morrison's novel, it reads us as well. This is part of its religious work. Reading this novel is a spiritual discipline, a practice that keeps revealing the hidden histories within the book and within ourselves. *Paradise* is Toni Morrison's own sermon — as fierce and uncompromising as Reverend Pulliam's and as committed as Reverend Misner's to seeking goodness in the vulnerable, the hidden, the broken, and the unknown. Morrison finds religious language that draws us not toward a life in paradise but toward "sane, intelligent life itself,"[15] the kind of life within which it would be possible to encounter together the open secrets of our shared history.

NOTES

1. Toni Morrison, *Paradise* (New York: Knopf, 1998), 3. Further references to the novel will be placed in parentheses within the essay.

2. For a discussion of the idea of home in *Paradise,* see Cynthia Dobbs, "Diasporic Designs of House, Home, and Haven in Toni Morrison's *Paradise*," *MELUS* 36, no. 2 (Summer 2011): 101–26.

3. For a discussion of Indian Territory as Promised Land for African Americans, see the introduction to Tiya Miles and Sharon P. Holland, eds., *Crossing Rivers, Crossing Worlds: The African Diaspora in Indian Country* (Durham, NC: Duke University Press, 2006), 1–23.

4. Scott Ellsworth, *Death in a Promised Land: The Tulsa Race Riot of 1921* (Baton Rouge: Louisiana State University Press, 1982), 1–11.

5. Alfred L. Brophy, *Reconstructing the Dreamland: The Tulsa Riots of 1921: Race, Reparations, and Reconciliation* (Oxford: Oxford University Press, 2002), 1.

6. Brophy, *Reconstructing the Dreamland,* 69–87.

7. Dr. Hooker's obituary in the *New York Times:* https://www.nytimes.com/2018/11 /23/obituaries/olivia-hooker-dead.html.

8. See Toni Morrison's discussion of this vision in her essay "Home," in *The House That Race Built: Black Americans, U.S. Terrain,* ed. Wahneema Lubiano (New York: Pantheon, 1997), 9–10.

9. Leon F. Litwack, "Trouble in Mind: The Bicentennial and the Afro-American Experience," *Journal of American History* 74, no. 2 (September 1987): 317.

10. Toni Morrison delivered the William Vaughn Moody Lecture at the University of Chicago on May 10, 1996. This description is based on my recollections of the lecture.

11. Toni Morrison, *The Source of Self-Regard: Selected Essays, Speeches, and Meditations* (New York: Knopf, 2019), 275.

12. Morrison, *The Source of Self-Regard,* 278.

13. http://transcendentalism-legacy.tamu.edu/authors/emerson/essays/dsa.html.

14. Toni Morrison, *Playing in the Dark: Whiteness and the Literary Imagination* (New York: Vintage, 1992), x. For a discussion of Morrison's engagement with issues of representation in *Paradise,* see Linda Krumholz, "Reading and Insight in Toni Morrison's *Paradise*," *African American Review* 36, no. 1 (Spring 2002): 21–34.

15. Morrison, *The Source of Self-Regard,* 276.

Luminous Darkness

Africanist Presence and the American Soul

JONATHAN L. WALTON

In 1990 Toni Morrison delivered the William E. Massey Sr. Lectures at Harvard University. These lectures now constitute her pithy yet powerful book *Playing in the Dark: Whiteness and the Literary Imagination*. Morrison's literary analysis in *Playing in the Dark* reminds me of my favorite childhood athlete, boxer Sugar Ray Leonard. Like Leonard, the book's power and strength are not derived from its size but rather from its skill and precision. As evidenced in her award-winning novels and essays of literary criticism, Morrison is an intellectual prizefighter — a people's champion who fights on behalf of those otherwise ignored in the American literary canon.

Playing in the Dark uncovers the many ways the paradoxical invisible visibility of black folk provides an indubitable backdrop of this nation's racial imaginary in early American literature. Even when unnamed, the four-hundred-year presence of Africans in the Americas shaped American self-conception. So even if the prevailing assumptions and pervasive ideology among literary critics of the twentieth century affirmed that the American literary canon was race-free, Morrison argues that the presence of a racialized other, namely an African presence, is essential to understanding American literature.[1]

Morrison questions the marginalizing and curious category of "race literature" to frame the writings of prominent African American writers such as Zora Neale Hurston, Richard Wright, Lorraine Hansberry, and James Baldwin. Similar questions might be asked of how we frame Latin American, Asian American, and all other qualified-American literary production. Such categories work only if one accepts the view that "American" literature is devoid of the presence of the racialized other. Hence, traditionalists can deflect charges of racism against the accepted American literary canon. In their reading, most American classics are innocent of white supremacy since few of the books engage the issue of race at all. Morrison, however, asks us to consider the distinctive themes of the genre — autonomy, authority, absolute power, and a priori innocence. From where do these characteristic markers of American literature extend if not from a comparative conception of a racialized other? This is the question that animates Toni Morrison's efforts. Thus, *Playing in the Dark* takes up the task of uncovering what Morrison refers to as the Africanist presence in American literature.

By Africanist presence, Morrison is referring to the ways "a nonwhite, African-like presence or persona was constructed in the United States, and the imaginative uses this fabricated presence served."[2] The two key terms in this definition are constructed and imaginative. Blackness was a concept informed by the ideology, assumptions, and particular logic of white supremacy. It is a concept defined by those who had both the power to create and the need to define themselves in opposition to such an imaginary black identity. The very concept of whiteness is predicated and dependent on the self-satisfying construction of what Morrison calls "literary blackness." Literary blackness creates the conditions for literary whiteness, as defined by autonomy, authority, power, and innocence. The latter is parasitic upon the former. Not only ideologically useful, the Africanist presence is a metaphysical necessity,[3] a ground of all being, a foundational presupposition from which American attributes of freedom, power, and purity extend.

In her reading of American literary works such as Willa Cather's *Sapphira and the Slave Girl,* Edgar Allen Poe's *The Narrative of Arthur Gordon Pym,* Mark Twain's *Huckleberry Finn,* and Ernest Hemingway's *To Have and Have Not,* Morrison demonstrates that the serviceability of black people to the narrative is sometimes explicit, but more often implicit. For example, Morrison illuminates the "theatrical presence of black surrogacy," in which a particular passing character of African descent is present only as a theoretical foil.[4] An African character, replete with imagined and embellished attributes of dependency, provides a conceptual life of freedom, power, and autonomy for white protagonists. In identifying this dynamic, Morrison flips the familiar script. She pulls our attention away from the intended primary white actors to the racialized bodies who, as human props, define the scene. Morrison's goal is to "to avert the critical gaze from the racial object to the racial subject; from the described and imagined to the describers and imaginers; from the serving to the served."[5]

This shift from object to subject is no easy task. To turn the reader's gaze back on those whose imaginations justify and reify racial hierarchies, Morrison must transform objects to subjects, rendering them real, beautiful, complicated, and tragic people. Here Morrison is at her best. She uncovers the identities of those rendered invisible, offers appellations to the otherwise nameless, and provides a voice to those silenced in prevailing American narratives. These are indeed the central themes of Morrison's corpus: black invisibility, namelessness, and social and civic death. To quote philosopher Cornel West, the Africanist presence conjured by white writers "reduces black folk to abstractions and objects born of white fantasies and insecurities." Through her art, which sheds the spotlight on her beautifully complex characters, Morrison has been perfecting the remedy for this damaging reduction.[6]

To be clear, I am neither equipped nor confident enough to provide a nuanced reading of the texts Morrison engages in *Playing in the Dark*. There is nothing I could contribute to her insightful analysis. Yet I would like to illumine the theoretical framework that Morrison uses to consider the American literary canon in such a courageous and incisive manner. Morrison's method of investigating the dynamics of the black-white binary in American literature is consistent with her examination of goodness and evil. There is a framework of interdependence that makes it impossible to point to the constitutive themes of a prevailing idea without the spectral presence of its opposite hovering in the background. Just as there is no conception of American freedom apart from its imagined opposite, there can be no discussion of goodness apart from the evil we fear.

Morrison's approach is consistent with the work of Harvard sociologist Orlando Patterson, specifically his 1991 text *Freedom in the Making of Western Culture*. Patterson argues that concepts of freedom never emerge in a sociohistorical vacuum. There is a symbiotic relationship between Enlightenment and modern slavery in the Americas. Each thesis of the Enlightenment era was predicated on an appropriate antithesis. The dramatic polarity of free and enslaved, mainly predicated on the binary of black and white, is what cultivated this "fabricated brew of darkness, otherness, alarm, and desire that is uniquely American."[7] In other words, for someone to be free, there needs to be another who is enslaved. Similarly, there is no such thing as the civilized, enlightened, and rational apart from a conception of that which is primitive, dark, and superstitious. Autonomy and self-sufficiency are based upon notions of dependency and subjection. Progress is measured against those deemed traditional. Freedom and slavery are two sides of the same coin.

What is particularly notable for my purpose here is the manner in which Patterson traces this understanding of freedom back to the theology of the Apostle Paul, which informs so many of our social views in the modern West. Patterson notes that slavery was most pronounced in the regions in which the vast majority of Paul's ministry took place, particularly Ephesus and Corinth. It is impossible to live in a large-scale slaveholding society and not have slavery color how one perceives the world. Whether one is in bondage or free, a landowner or a peasant, slavery informs every aspect of society. As Patterson puts it, "it's [slavery] like a cancer in the blood, pervades all, pollutes all, degrades all, and magnifies in all the overwhelming goodness and desirability of freedom."[8] This helps to explain why Paul hoists freedom as the moral ideal while equating sin with subjection. The social significance of such a theological worldview shapes how we categorize the dynamic of power. Those who are wealthy and free are clean and pure. Those who are needy and dependent are deviant and deficient, in need of salvation.

Whereas Patterson employs the terms "pollute" and "degrade," Morrison refers to the "dirtying" process of slavery in her novel *Beloved*. Black folk are dirtied, first, by the racial imagination of white supremacy. Racial visions are then transformed into laws, statutes, and cultural practices that dehumanize and dirty their targets. These are the conditions from which those on the underside of freedom, autonomy, and power seek to break free. These are the conditions from which Morrison seeks to reconsider goodness by reframing who and what we deem as inherently evil.

Consider Morrison's character Sethe. When cornered by slave catchers attempting to return her to the euphemistically named "Sweet Home" plantation, Sethe takes the life of her daughter Beloved. Sethe loved Beloved too much to let her endure the evils of enslavement and sexual abuse. Morrison contrasts the decision of a loving yet desperate Sethe over against those with a perverse freedom to have their way with black life. As Morrison writes:

And though she and others lived through and got over it, she could never let it happen to her own. The best thing she was, was her children. Whites might dirty her all right, but not her best thing, her beautiful, magical best thing — the part of her that was clean. No undreamable dreams about

... whether a gang of whites invaded her daughter's private parts, soiled her daughter's thighs and threw her daughter out of the wagon. She might have to work the slaughterhouse yard, but not her daughter.

And no one, nobody on this earth, would list her daughter's characteristics on the animal side of the paper. No. Oh no.[9]

Sethe's response inverts the moral order and illumines the heinous behaviors of those with the cultural power to define and determine good and evil. Sethe made an ethical choice under conditions not of her choosing. The normative conceptions of freedom and virtue were not available to this grief-stricken mother. Facing the reality of turning her daughter back over to those who would degrade her humanity and defile her body for their sexual pleasure, she resorts to an ultimate act to protect her child. Filicide, then, becomes an expression of mercy. Taking her child's life is not evil, but good, when one considers the alternative. Hence, Morrison concludes the passage mentioned above with, "What she had done was right because it came from true love."[10] Sethe opted for an expression of love set apart from the anemic polarity of Western, or even Pauline, ideals that Orlando Patterson deftly adumbrates.

Sethe is not the only character in *Beloved* whose ethical thinking is done outside of culturally defined binaries of good and evil, free and enslaved. The lay preacher Baby Suggs provides a vision of holiness and goodness that belies the antebellum South's structures of social power and hierarchical authority. Morrison constructs Baby Suggs and her folk theology in stark contrast to the ways a slaveholding society embraced the writings of the Apostle Paul. Whether the oft-quoted Ephesians 6:5 — "Servants, be obedient to them that are your masters according to the flesh" — or Paul's letter to Philemon — where Paul encourages an enslaved Onesimus to return to his slaveholder Philemon — it was through Paul that the South found, in the words of abolitionist Frederick Douglass, "a justifier of the most appalling barbarity, — a sanctifier of the most hateful frauds."[11] Slaveholding Christianity encouraged the enslaved to find spiritual freedom "in Christ" rather than physical freedom in this world (Galatians 5:1) and to accept without question their position in society, as their condition was "instituted by God" (Romans 13:1).

Pauline theology also conveyed strong views concerning corporeality. According to prevailing southern evangelical interpretations, "the flesh" was something to be overcome. Our sinful flesh runs counter to the Spirit, under whose subjection its carnal cravings must be brought (Galatians 5:17). Couple this negative conception of corporeality with the widespread belief that blackness was a curse, passed down through the condemned offspring of Noah's son Ham, and we see how slaveholding Christianity used Paul's sacred imprimatur to cast descendants of Africa as ontologically evil. Enslavement and pigment become mutually reinforcing markers of evil that need to be contained or, failing that, destroyed. Slavery and freedom, darkness and light, flesh and Spirit enter a symbiotic relationship insofar as the former make the latter possible. Life in the Spirit demands constant denunciation of the flesh.

In contrast, consider how Morrison presents Baby Suggs. Neither her spiritual power nor religious authority comes from any official sanctioning body. She was, in Morrison's words, "Uncalled, unrobed, unanointed."[12] Rather than offering an unattainable vision of goodness juxtaposed against an explicit or implicit black evil and inferiority that too many clergy still preach, Baby Suggs inverts and affirms. She finds goodness in the very bodies that the power structure depicts as aberrant. Baby Suggs encourages her congregation — a congregation gathered together outside of the walls of a church in a wooded clearing — to love that which society hates: black flesh. Baby Suggs exhorts her listeners:

> In this here place, we flesh; flesh that weeps, laughs; flesh that dances on bare feet in grass. Love it. Love it hard. Yonder they do not love your flesh. They despise it. They don't love your eyes; they'd just as soon pick em out. No more do they love the skin on your back.... Love your hands! Love them. Raise them up and kiss them. Touch others with them, pat them together, stroke them on your face 'cause they don't love that either. You got to love it, you![13]

Through Baby Suggs, Morrison invites readers to reimagine Christian faith as predicated on self-love, not self-abdication. Morrison encourages us to reject Pauline proscription in favor of a gospel ethic that uncovers goodness in the most unlikely of places and among the most vulnerable. Here the life of one sheep is equal in value to ninety-nine (Matthew 18:12). Those furthest away from sources of healing command God's attention (John 5:1–6). Our care of the hungry, poor, and imprisoned determines our relation to the sacred (Matthew 25:31–46). Moreover, loving one's self is a precondition for loving God and others — an ethical principle that is usually deficient among the most vulnerable and in excess among the powerful (Mark 12:31). These are the teachings that emerge from the one thing that Baby Suggs had to offer the community: her heart.[14]

Essential insights regarding goodness, then, spring forth from Morrison's literary analysis in *Playing in the Dark* as well as from characters like Sethe and Baby Suggs in *Beloved*. She illumines the otherwise undisclosed and invites us to search for the unseen. Just as our views of freedom are bound up in a misrecognized framework of human bondage, too often our understanding of goodness is predicated on an unstated obsession with evil. Prevailing ideas are negatively defined. Rather than naming what we stand for, our behaviors are animated by the thoughts we stand against. Our quest for freedom is more a fear of bondage, just as our pursuit of the divine is more of a rejection of that which we have been conditioned to fear. Evil is what consumes our attention. So though all religions position goodness as the telos of moral activity and highest aim of one's faith, Morrison was right in her Ingersoll Lecture to assert that it is evil that "hogs the stage." Unfortunately, like America's racialized literary canon, this evil takes the form of the spectral Africanist presence that Morrison examined in *Playing in the Dark*.

I would argue that this specter of the Africanist presence continues to inform the religious identities of a broad swath of American society. Consider the conservative evangelical population who understand themselves as a righteous remnant called to protect and conserve "traditional American values." That these values too often take the form of gender complementarianism that defends male hierarchy, ethnocentric defense of white Protestant hegemony, and xenophobic denunciations against immigration and religious diversity is rarely questioned. The spectral presence of a gendered, religious, and racialized other is what makes a professed freedom in Christ possible for a particular class of people. This is why one might even argue that a contemporary white nationalist imaginary has expanded this constructed Africanist presence to include immigrants from south of the United States border or those who are in any way associated with Islam. The spectral presence now bears the constructed names Malik, Miguel, Maria, or Muhammad. Yet as Morrison identifies in her analysis of the American literary canon, names are too specific for those who are willfully ignorant of the presence of minoritized others. Their identities must be obscured. Their faces must be veiled and names erased. Then, and only then, can those who claim freedom and autonomy maintain their specious claims of innocence in regard to the suffering of

FIG. 9. Janet McKenzie, *The Divine Journey — The Companions of Love and Hope.* (Courtesy of the artist)

those who make their constructed identities possible. Evangelicals who have been washed in the blood of the lamb, freed from sin, and delivered from evil must hold on to the idea that they are embracing a positive vision. They are good because their God is good. That their God happens to hate all of the same people and policies that they do is an inconvenient truth few conservative evangelicals desire to interrogate. Their spiritual freedom is bound up with the natural bondage of others. Their goodness feeds off a constructed evil — the poor, the sexually deviant, the idolatrous religious other, and the barbarians seeking to break through the southern gate.

This is why the primary moral lesson that I take away from Toni Morrison's incredible insights on freedom and goodness is the importance of self-criticism. We, particularly those of us who believe in the saving power of God, must always interrogate our claims of purity. We are all implicated in the willful erasure and marginalization of those who do not fit our ideals of what it means to be American — what it means to be good. Just as American literature is marked by "a dark and abiding presence that moves the hearts and texts of American literature with fear and longing," maybe our innocence, too, is based on the imagined guilt of a constructed evil other.[15] If so, I suspect James Baldwin was right. "It is the innocence," he once wrote, "which constitutes the crime."[16]

NOTES

1. Toni Morrison, *Playing in the Dark: Whiteness and the Literary Imagination,* The William E. Massey Sr. Lectures in the History of American Civilization (Book 6) (Cambridge: Harvard University Press, 1992), 5.
2. Morrison, *Playing in the Dark,* 6.
3. Morrison, *Playing in the Dark,* 64.
4. Morrison, *Playing in the Dark,* 13.
5. Morrison, *Playing in the Dark,* 90.
6. Henry Louis Gates and Cornel West, *The Future of the Race* (New York: Knopf, 1996), 85.
7. Morrison, *Playing in the Dark,* 38.
8. Orlando Patterson, *Freedom in the Making of Western Culture* (New York: Basic, 1991), 319.
9. Toni Morrison, *Beloved* (1987; New York: Vintage International, 2004), 295–96.
10. Morrison, *Beloved,* 296.

11. Frederick Douglass, *My Bondage and My Freedom* (New York: Penguin Classics, 2003), 188.

12. Morrison, *Beloved,* 102.

13. Morrison, *Beloved.*

14. Morrison, *Beloved.*

15. Morrison, *Playing in the Dark,* 46.

16. James Baldwin, *The Fire Next Time* (New York: Vintage, 1992), 6.

Going Backstage

Soaphead Church and the (Religious) Problem of Goodness in *The Bluest Eye*

BIKO MANDELA GRAY

> The power of silence is so unlike the power of words that we have no words to express it.
> —CHARLES LONG, *Significations: Signs, Symbols, and Images in the Interpretation of Religion*

> Evil has a blockbuster audience; Goodness lurks backstage. Evil has vivid speech; Goodness bites its tongue.
> —TONI MORRISON, "Goodness: Altruism and the Literary Imagination," Ingersoll Lecture 2012

STARTING BACKSTAGE, OR SITTING WITH SILENCE

There is something about silence. To sit in silence — to sit *with* silence — one come to grips with oneself. More specifically, sitting with silence is hard because it makes us attend to many things that we've tried to repress. A meditation session or classroom test, for example, opens the space for wary thoughts and unwanted memories; a quiet moment in church might dredge up failed interactions and lost opportunities; a solitary drive in the car might remind us of friends and family members we've lost, or open the space for thinking about long-repressed experiences that have caused us pain. In silence, we are often forced to attend to those things that have long been pushed back, pressed down, subdued and marginalized. To sit with silence is to realize that it contains those things that we've tried to forget; it is to confront those things that we have tried to abandon.

But, if we sit with silence long enough, we realize that it offers us new ways of thinking; by reflecting on what has been forgotten or abandoned, one is given the opportunity to move differently, to think differently, to *act* differently. I think this is, in part, what Toni Morrison was after when she gave her Ingersoll Lecture on goodness. The power of the lecture is that it attempts to think about what has been silenced and forgotten — namely, goodness.

According to Morrison, goodness has been silenced because evil is *loud*. It's dramatic. It crashes in and "hogs the stage" with its "theatricality, its costume, its blood spray." Comic book villains and real-life dictators captivate audiences, demanding that we respond in awe, anger, or indignation. We're enraged by white supremacists who kill in the name of statues, and we're appalled at images of children in cages. Documentaries chronicle evil's actions, alerting us to past genocides or contemporary crises. Evil puts on a show, demanding our attention. And while we're caught up in evil's theatrics, goodness takes its place backstage, behind the scenes. Drowned out by evil's "vivid speech," goodness keeps quiet. It goes silent.

Morrison, however, asks more of us than that we watch evil's loud and dramatic show. Morrison pushes us to go backstage with goodness. She asks us attend to what has been silenced, to what has been forgotten in the face and sounds of evil. And she doesn't simply do this in her lecture; as I will show in this essay, there is a connection between Morrison's attempt to "give language" to silenced goodness and her first novel, *The Bluest Eye*. I think that both the lecture and the novel push us to think about what happens when we *don't* sit with silence. Between *The Bluest Eye* and the Ingersoll Lecture, we are offered the possibility of exploring what happens when we don't pay attention to what is happening backstage.

I want to suggest that our lack of attention to the silent and silenced nature of goodness has devastating consequences for how we understand goodness in the first place. By not sitting with silence, by not paying attention to goodness's silent presence, we open up the possibility for considerable harm to be done *in the name of goodness itself*. By thinking with Morrison's lecture and *The Bluest Eye,* I want to think about how, why, and when goodness *does wrong.*

NARCISSISTIC GOODNESS: PECOLA, SOAPHEAD CHURCH, AND THE BLUEST EYE

The connection between the lecture and *The Bluest Eye* is not arbitrary: Morrison herself actually invokes *The Bluest Eye* as part of her lecture, suggesting that one of the characters — Soaphead Church — embodies a particularly pathological form of goodness: "An example of . . . Goodness as a form of narcissism, perhaps mental disorder[,] occurs in the first

FIG. 10. Ogo J. Johnson, *Untitled* [black girl with prism]. (Courtesy of Pexels)

novel I wrote. Determined to erase his self-loathing, Soaphead Church, a character in *The Bluest Eye,* chooses to 'give' or pretend to give, blue eyes to a little girl in psychotic need of them. In his letter to God, he imagines himself doing the good God refuses. Misunderstood as it is, it has language." Soaphead Church describes himself as a "Spiritualist," which means something between a priest and a magician. I will discuss his life in more detail later in the essay; however, for now, what is important is that

Church is a heinous man who has a history of enacting horrific forms of deceit and sexual violence. Aware that he is both a thief and a predator, Church seeks absolution. He finds it through the "little girl" who shows up at his doorstep in need of blue eyes, and he attempts to "erase his self-loathing" by "giving" her what she cannot have.

As we'll see, Church *thinks* he has done good; his "gift" to the girl was given as a genuine attempt to provide her some relief. But the "goodness" he performed was empty; it was only for him, for his narcissistic desire to make himself feel better. His act of "goodness" contributed to the young girl making a complete psychotic break with reality, which eventually left her on the outskirts of town, alone and talking to herself. Church is "determined to erase his self-loathing," and his narcissism convinced him he was doing good when he was actually doing harm.

The harm of Church's narcissism is directly related to the silence of goodness. He didn't provide healthy relief for the girl because she was rendered silent in the face of his own needs and desires. Until now, I've left her nameless, because her name didn't matter to Church. But she has a name: Pecola Breedlove. And she *does* matter. She's not simply a character in the story; she's the story's protagonist. And Pecola, like goodness, was silenced.

PECOLA'S STORY: BEAUTY, RACE, AND SILENCE

Unlike conventional protagonists, Pecola does not overcome challenges or emerge victorious over her opposition — in fact she succumbs to it. Pecola rarely speaks throughout the novel — instead, the narrator Claudia, a young black girl who both protects and, at times, ignores Pecola, speaks for her. Pecola is present throughout the novel, but she is consistently pushed aside, berated, and ignored. As Morrison herself says, Pecola was "dismissed, trivialized, misread."[1]

Set in Lorain, Ohio, in 1941, *The Bluest Eye* is a novel about how Pecola tries to navigate long-standing conceptions about the relationship between beauty and race. In fact, it could be argued that the whole novel is about how black people navigate standards of beauty. Claudia herself clues us into this by beginning the novel with her disdain for Shirley Temple: "Frieda and [Pecola] had a loving conversation about how cu-ute Shirley Temple was. I couldn't join them in their adoration because I hated Shirley. Not because she was cute, but because she danced with

Bojangles, who was *my* friend, *my* uncle, *my* daddy, and who ought to have been soft-shoeing it and chuckling with me. Instead he was enjoying, sharing, giving a lovely dance thing with one of those little white girls whose socks never slid down under their heels."[2] Bojangles was black, and therefore Bojangles should have been dancing with Claudia, *not* Shirley. Claudia may not have hated Shirley Temple because of her cuteness, but she unconsciously connected Temple's (allegedly "cu-ute") whiteness — which eventually becomes an object of love for Claudia as well — with a man who should have been her relative, *her* friend. Claudia's words announce the inextricable binding between whiteness and the possibility of a valuable and valued existence.

If one wasn't white, then getting as close as one could to whiteness could still suffice. When Maureen Peal came to town, for example, Claudia remarked on how differently she was treated because of her appearance:

> The disrupter of seasons was a new girl in school named Maureen Peal. A high-yellow dream child with long brown hair braided into two lynch ropes that hung down her back. She was rich ... as rich as the richest of the white girls, swaddled in comfort and care. ... She enchanted the entire school. When teachers called on her, they smiled encouragingly. Black boys didn't trip her in the halls; white boys didn't stone her, white girls didn't suck their teeth when she was assigned to be their work partners; black girls stepped aside when she wanted to use the sink in the girls' toilet, and their eyes genuflected under sliding lids.[3]

Maureen Peal, the high-yellow dream child, could still get some of the benefits because of her complexion and presentation. In *The Bluest Eye,* the residents of Lorain were preoccupied with the connection between beauty and whiteness: the closer you were to whiteness, the more beautiful; and the more beautiful you were, the better you were treated.

It only makes sense, then, that the opposite would be the case. If Shirley Temple's "cu-ute" whiteness was valued and offered benefits, and if the Maureen Peals of the world could move freely without harassment or ridicule, then it only makes sense that those who were darker-skinned would receive different treatment. And unfortunately for Pecola, she wasn't simply *darker*-skinned; she was *dark*-skinned. In fact, the townspeople reviled Pecola and her family's presence; they could not get enough of berating Pecola for her (ascribed) "ugliness." Claudia tells us, "Long hours

[Pecola] sat looking in the mirror, trying to discover the secret of the ugliness, the ugliness that made her ignored or despised at school, by teachers and classmates alike." Pecola was despised because she was deemed ugly; and she was deemed ugly because she was *black*.

But this isn't quite right. There were others who were black, who were darker than Maureen Peal, and who didn't receive the maltreatment to the degree that Pecola did. Pecola's alleged ugliness seemed deeper; it came from somewhere far beyond mere skin color. After all, Pecola's whole family was ugly, which made people wonder: did the Breedloves' purported ugliness come from a divine source? Claudia takes this line of thinking from here:

> You looked at them and wondered why they were so ugly; you looked closely and could not find the source. Then you realized that it came from conviction, their conviction. It was as though some mysterious all-knowing master had given each one a cloak of ugliness to wear, and they had each accepted it without question. The master had said, "You are ugly people." They had looked about themselves and saw nothing to contradict the statement; saw, in fact, support for it leaning at them from every billboard, every movie, every glance.[4]

At first glance, this passage seems to be about the Breedloves: they were divinely called to be ugly — this was their lot in life. But there is something curious about the last lines of this passage: seeing "nothing to contradict the statement" that they were ugly, Claudia also raises questions about who the "they" is in this passage. Billboards, movies, and glances speak to something bigger than the Breedloves; in fact, it announces that maybe blackness *itself* is a mark of ugliness — a mark that the residents of Lorain were all too eager to excise from their midst. The "all-knowing master" may have made the statement, but unlike the Breedloves, the black residents of Lorain spent their lives refusing to accept the truthfulness of the claim.

Pecola became the principal site of this refusal. It was *easy* to ridicule and revile her because, as I said above, Pecola was *quiet:* "She hid behind her [alleged ugliness]. Concealed, veiled, eclipsed — peeping out from behind the shroud [of her alleged ugliness] very seldom, and then only to yearn for the return of her mask."[5] Pecola said little. She bit her tongue. She kept to herself — to the point where she could become invisible, even when someone was looking directly at her. Or at least that's what happened when she went to Mr. Yacobowski's Fresh Veg. Meat and Sundries Store: "Somewhere between retina and object, between vision and view, [Yacobowski's] eyes draw back, hesitate, and hover. At some fixed point in time and space he senses that he need not waste the effort of a glance. He does not see her, because for him there is nothing to see. . . . [Pecola] looks up at him and sees the vacuum where curiosity ought to lodge . . . The total absence of human recognition — the glazed separateness. . . . Yet this vacuum is not new to her."[6] Invisible to and despised by the world, Pecola suffered from continual neglect and ridicule. When she wasn't being unseen by white shopkeepers, she was being called "Blackemo" at school. And when she wasn't being bullied at school, she was being invited by little black boys to their houses to bully her; and when the bullying would end, black adults would call her filthy.[7]

No wonder she wanted blue eyes. They became an obsession; she *needed* them. They were her opportunity to rid herself of the neglect and violence inflicted upon her. Blue eyes would be her ticket out, her key to a life where people treated her differently: "It had occurred to Pecola some time ago that if her eyes, those eyes that held the pictures and knew the sights — if those eyes of hers were different, that is to say, beautiful, she herself would be different."[8] Had Pecola had blue eyes — a staple of the whiteness that stopped stonings and let people see you — then "she herself would be different"; she herself would be treated differently, understood differently. "If those eyes of hers were different, that is to say, beautiful," there would be a change at the very ground of Pecola's being. Rendered silent by neglect and abuse, Pecola internalized the town's racialized standards of beauty. And that's why she ended up on Soaphead Church's doorstep.

RELIGION AS BEAUTY: THE RELIGIOUS DIMENSIONS OF
THE BLUEST EYE

Before we get to Church and his encounter with Pecola, it's important to highlight how important beauty and ugliness were for the residents of Lorain. Beauty and ugliness weren't simply aesthetic standards; they had everything to do with one's *value*, with how one understood and navigated one's place in the world. People were treated differently based upon how beautiful — that is, how close to whiteness — they were. And, on top of this, people understood *themselves* in relation to these standards.

Beauty and ugliness were standards for one's *being;* they helped to establish the very meaning of one's existence. In other words, beauty and ugliness were *religious* standards.

Long tells us that religion is "orientation in the ultimate sense."[9] Religion orients us; it is the process whereby we come to grips with the meaning of our existence in this world. This was certainly the case for Pecola and for the residents of Lorain; as Claudia told us earlier, the Breedloves' ugliness felt divinely ordained, as if it came from some ultimate source. And, as I showed above, it wasn't simply the Breedloves; there was something about *blackness* itself that made it feel like a divine curse. When "every billboard, every movie, every glance" confirms your ugliness, it begins to feel ultimate; it begins to feel like something that is inescapable. And when this occurs, it only makes sense to make peace with one's cursed lot in life; it only makes sense to turn one's curse into a way of being in the world. And this is precisely what the Breedloves did.

> No one could have convinced [the Breedloves] that they were not relentlessly and aggressively ugly. . . . And they took the ugliness in their hands, threw it as a mantle over them, and went about the world with it. Dealing with it each according to his way. Mrs. Breedlove handled hers as an actor does a prop: for the articulation of character, for support of a role she frequently imagined was hers. . . . Sammy used his as a weapon to cause others pain. He adjusted his behavior to it, chose his companions on the basis of it: people who could be fascinated, even intimidated by it.

We already know what Pecola did with hers. She "hid behind" it, allowing it to silence her, to render her quiet. Beauty and ugliness operated as norms through which members of the community could orient their lives; and they did.

In *The Bluest Eye,* Toni Morrison's religious imagination is deeply connected to issues of beauty and ugliness. Beauty and ugliness are standards that contribute to how one orients oneself. To be beautiful — again, read as being (close to) white — was to move through the world in a particular way, to receive benefits, goods. In *The Bluest Eye,* to be beautiful is not simply to live into a religious standard; it is also to be valued and valuable. In other words, *to be understood as beautiful is to also be understood as good.* If beauty is, as Morrison tells us, something we "do," then *The Bluest Eye* speaks to the complexities of doing beauty.[10] And in the novel, these complexities are religious.

I guess it only makes sense, then, that Soaphead Church's approach to the world would incorporate beauty, religion, and goodness. He, after all, was also a resident of Lorain and therefore shared some of the same dispositions and convictions. Only some, though; as we'll see, Soaphead Church had his own issues and concerns.

SOAPHEAD CHURCH: A LIFE OF PERVERTED DESPAIR AND FAILURE

Church and his ancestors were descendants of a slave owner who bequeathed his interracial and illegitimate child a small fortune that brought with it a yearning for the sanitized simplicity and purified order of whiteness. Trained in the best (read: white) schools and conversant in the highest (read: European) forms of literature and theology, Church's worldview was characterized by a philosophical and psycho(patho)logical predilection for whiteness; he had fully adopted the maxim that "transparency [is] a metaphor for a theory of knowledge," as Charles Long tells us.[11]

This white predilection for transparency, order, and sterility may have been purely intellectual had it not been for his sadistic father, who brutally and creatively punished him. This combination of brutality and academic seriousness — filtered through an insatiable desire for the cultural and intellectual trappings of whiteness — allowed Church to cultivate "a hatred of, and fascination with, any hint of disorder and decay."[12] For Church, beauty was still white, but it wasn't simply whiteness; it was the *purity* of whiteness. Church relished detached and disinterested observation but could not stand human contact. In fact, he was disgusted — literally "nauseated" — by it, by its messiness, its complexity. There was no place in his life for matted dogs with film-ridden eyes; there was no room in his life for the smells and sounds of human passion. There was only room for a neatness that he cultivated through a life of rejection, violence, and internalized hatred.

This is why Velma left him. He'd met Velma, a "lovely, laughing big-legged girl," and married her, hoping she could "rescue him from the non-life he had learned from the flat side of his father's belt." But Elihue was too gloomy; Velma could deal with his impotence — Claudia tells us "he did not experience sustained erections" — but she couldn't endure his lack of joy, his inability to respond to her beauty and laughter in kind. Church "resisted [Velma] with such skill that she was finally driven out to escape the inevitable boredom produced by such a dainty life."[13] He was too sterile, too serious, too self-deprecating to actually live with; she eventually left him "the way people leave a hotel room."[14]

And if all of this wasn't enough, Elihue couldn't succeed academically. He studied widely, but not deeply; he was a perpetual student but did not finish any of his academic studies. After years of intellectual and academic failure, he found himself moving from job to job, until he settled in Lorain. His theological studies were just good enough to trick others, but he knew, more than anyone else, that he was a failure, that his life had amounted to little to nothing. Beaten by his father, abandoned by Velma, and unsuccessful in his studies, Church was a failure, impotent and powerless.

Maybe this is why he'd resorted to the pedophilia. Claudia doesn't tell us when the molestations started; we don't know whether he started doing this before or after Velma. Claudia only tells us that, due to his impotence and because he "abhorred flesh on flesh," he had "settled" on touching little girls, whose taut bodies and inability to process what was occurring allowed him to satisfy his "rare but keen sexual cravings."[15] The young girls whom he molested were perfect for him because "there wasn't nastiness, and there wasn't any filth, and there wasn't any odor, and there wasn't any groaning — just the light white laughter of those little girls and me. . . . With little girls it is all clean and good and friendly."[16] In what he'd convinced himself was mutually beneficial engagement, he gave these girls candy and ice cream. It was an unspoken exchange for their bodies and minds: bodies that appealed to his thirst for purity and minds that were susceptible to manipulation and deceit.

It should come as no surprise, then, that he'd become the duplicitous "spiritualist" of the town of Lorain. It afforded him a power that was supposed to be reserved for God, a power that, Church was sure, God had abdicated. Claudia tells us that he lived his life accordingly: "He was aware, of course, that something was awry in his life, and all lives, but put the problem where it belonged, at the foot of the Originator of life."[17] Intentionally or not, God had abandoned God's post as source and guarantor of goodness in this world. And in God's absence, Elihue "graciously" (which is to say, *selfishly*) accepted God's mantle. If God wouldn't produce the good God was tasked with creating, then *he*, Soaphead Church, would claim that "I had received Your Powers," taking ownership over the responsibility, power, and certainty that God should have provided, but didn't.[18]

It didn't matter that he was a charlatan. The ineffectiveness of his miracles didn't matter, because the town had already deemed him super-natural — not because he was effective, but because he was celibate. The women of Lorain couldn't seduce him, and "not being able to compre-hend his rejection of them," they "decided that he was supernatural rather than unnatural."[19] He was deemed divine because he was impenetrable; and this "divine" impenetrability — or, in theological terms, this divine impassivity — provided him an unshakable and narcissistic certainty and unwavering self-assuredness in his own goodness and power: "Celibacy was a haven, silence a shield."[20] Cut off from the rest of the world and refusing to let others get close to him, Soaphead Church sanctified him-self through detached engagement and perpetual isolation. The town had deemed him supernatural, and he obliged them by acting as if he were.

Church, therefore, saw himself as above the people he "served" because his (white) training, his (white) blood, and their belief in his supernatural existence allowed him a perspective on goodness that the black people of Lorain could never have. Indeed, how *could* these people, whose (hid-eous) blackness ontologically excluded them from the realm of the "light white" goodness that he himself espoused, attain a good life?[21] After all, the "all-knowing master" had left an entire population of people bereft of the possibility of blessedness through the sinful stain of blackness im-printed on their bodies.[22]

Denied this possibility (but not having the language to articulate why they were denied it), Church's black clients came to him asking for goods that they thought they *could* have: "Make him love me. Tell me what this dream means. Help me get rid of this woman. Stop my left hand from shaking."[23] And although he couldn't provide those to them either, he could lie to them. He could provide the false goods described on his busi-ness cards.

> If you are overcome with trouble and conditions that are not natural, I can remove them; Overcome Spells, Bad Luck, and Evil Influences. Re-member, I am a true Spiritualist and Psychic Reader, born with power, and I will help you. Satisfaction in one visit. During many years of practice I have brought together many in marriage and reunited many who were separated. If you are unhappy, discouraged, or in distress, I can help you.

Does bad luck seem to follow you? Has the one you love changed? I can tell you why. I will tell you who your enemies and friends are, and if the one you love is true or false. If you are sick, I can show you the way to health. I locate lost and stolen articles. Satisfaction guaranteed.[24]

What Church offered was nothing less than a reversal of one's misfortune. He could work miracles; he could "overcome spells" and "bad luck." In short, Church offered the benefits of his (empty) connection to the other world.

Benefits—not curses. Soaphead Church's power was limited to the production of fortune, the manufacturing of blessedness, the elimination — or at least the decreasing — of dread. "People came to him in dread, whispered in dread, wept and pleaded in dread. And dread was what he counseled," Claudia tells us.[25] Benevolence was his trade; goodness was his currency. Church's job was not to "suggest to a party that perhaps the request was unfair, mean, or hopeless" but instead to fulfill the desires of the party who stood before him.[26] "Goodness" was his business, and he always promised results. And nothing — not even God — would stop him from making this happen. *Satisfaction guaranteed,* his card said. And although he knew it wasn't true, the benefits outweighed the harm. He may have been lying to people, but it was not "a complete *lie*"; it was a "*complete* lie," a coherent fabrication of his powers.[27] Though he was lying, this "*complete* lie" became his truth, his understanding of the power of his own goodness — a goodness he fabricated and maintained.

"FOR THE FIRST TIME": PECOLA'S ARRIVAL AS RELIGIOUS EXPERIENCE

Claudia tells us that Church was thinking about his life — about his failures and his shortcomings — when Pecola showed up at his door. And, in her presence, the fleeting and false form of goodness Church offered was exposed for its failure. Not all of it, of course: he still deemed Pecola "pitifully unattractive." But her unattractiveness could not stop Church from being self-assured of the goodness he provided and embodied. He was narcissistic, and she was silent. And her silence, cultivated by a life of neglect and abuse, didn't give him pause but affirmed his own sense of goodness.

Pecola didn't say anything when Church first opened the door. Biting her tongue, remaining silent, all she did was hand him his card. But, of course, the card wasn't enough. Church needed to know what she specifically needed. So she spoke. Quietly, she told him she wanted blue eyes.

The request was damning. He knew he couldn't give her what she wanted. Unlike his other clients, who were merely means to an economic end, Pecola was someone he actually wanted to help: "Of all the wishes people had brought to him — money, love, revenge — this seemed to him the most poignant and the one most deserving of fulfillment. A little black girl who wanted to rise up out of the pit of her blackness and see the world with blue eyes. . . . For the first time he honestly wished he could work miracles."[28] For the first time, Church was confronted with the futility of his trade. For the first time, he had been forced to reckon with the limitations of his deception and the implications of his duplicity. Through Pecola, he was forced to come to grips with the meaning of his own existence.

He wanted to do *good* for Pecola. Never mind that it was impossible, and never mind that the young girl appeared desperate. It didn't matter that the source of Pecola's plea came from how cruelly she had been treated or that she'd internalized the religious standards of white beauty and black ugliness. Church saw neither the impossibility or the desperation of Pecola's wish as a moment to pause. After all, he, too, saw whiteness as beautiful. So instead of inquiring further, Church found Pecola's request simultaneously "fantastic" and "logical." And it called his whole identity into question: "He thought it was at once the most fantastic and the most logical petition he had ever received. Here was an ugly little girl asking for beauty. A surge of love and understanding swept through him, but was quickly replaced by anger. Anger that he was powerless to help her."[29] The encounter that Church has with himself discloses a structure of religious experience. Scholars have many terms for such experience, but one stands out: the *mysterium tremendum et fascinans.*[30] This is the experience of something so "wholly other," novel, and contradictory that it forces us to wrestle with ourselves and imagine a larger world. It is novel in the sense that we haven't encountered it or its effects before (hence "for the first time"), but its novelty stems from its contradictory nature: it is repulsive and attractive, perceptible and imperceptible, amazing and mundane, all at the same time.[31]

Pecola literally embodies contradiction: she is "ugly" but wants "beauty"; her petition is simultaneously "fantastic" and "logical"; and

Church moves from "love and understanding" to anger — in a matter of seconds, it seems. And all of this is operative in service of self-reflection. Pecola forces Soaphead Church to come to grips with the futility of his trade. Pecola's desire to be white both disrupted and confirmed Church's sensibilities; she had become his religious object. His "compassion" for her was matched only by his anger that he couldn't make her wish come true. He was drawn to and disgusted by this piteously ugly black girl, by her wish to have the very whiteness that he had coursing through his veins.

However, Church's certainty of the goodness of (his) whiteness occluded his perception: although he couldn't do what she wanted, he wasn't going to leave her empty-handed; she was getting those blue eyes even if no one else would see them. After telling Pecola to give his landlord's dog a poisonous concoction of old meat, Church tells her, "If the animal behaves strangely, your wish will be granted on the day following this one. . . . Good-by, God bless."[32] A few moments later, the dog writhed, and eventually died. Pecola retched, but she had received the sign that confirmed that she'd gotten what she'd asked for. Her eyes would be blue. The dog's death confirmed it. Church was, indeed, a miracle-worker.

"BUT YOU TOO ARE AMISS HERE, LORD": SOAPHEAD CHURCH'S NARCISSISTIC LETTER

Pecola walked away satisfied. But Church knew that he'd made an empty promise. And it made him continue to reflect on the impotence and failure that his life had become. In the wake of his encounter with Pecola, Church is forced to reflect on his past failures, his past violence, and the futility of his actions. However, the source of his failure and impotence could not, to his mind, be his own. His narcissism couldn't allow for this. He found the source of the problems not in himself, but in God.

After Pecola left, after he had given her what he could not and should not have tried to give her, Church wrote a brutal sermonic letter to God in order to call God to the carpet for God's failures. The entire letter operates as a criticism of God's impotence. It is an indictment along the lines of Job, that patient sufferer who wanted to simply know why such evils had been visited upon him. But unlike Job, Church knows God will not respond to him: Job was the last one for whom God broke God's "long-ago habit" of not responding to the suffering cries of God's people.

Addressed to "HE WHO GREATLY ENNOBLED HUMAN NATURE BY CREATING IT," Church's letter announces — from the start — the potency of human agency to enact great good and horrible evil. Church begins the letter by recounting all of the good and horrible things that had happened to him, letting God know that he is a product of his past.

But Church does not let himself off the hook in a traditional sense. Despite the fact that Velma left him like one leaves a "hotel room," and despite his father's abuse and his academic failures, he owns up to the fact that he did do heinous things. In one of the most chilling sections of the letter, Church admits his pedophilic and incestuous activity, "apologizing" for his actions: "You remember, do you, how and of what we are made? . . . I apologize for the inappropriateness (is that it?), the imbalance of loving [little girls] at awkward times of day, and in awkward places, and the tastelessness of loving those which belonged to members of my family. Do I have to apologize for loving strangers?"[33] Church had done horrible things. But even his own moral failings and violent abuse couldn't be attributed to him. After all, he'd suffered under the hands of a brutal father, a spouse who neglected him, and an inability to succeed academically. He may have been a sexual predator, but this wasn't his fault. It was God's and God's alone. Consider the paragraph that follows:

> But you too are amiss here, Lord. How, why, did you allow it to happen? How is it I could lift my eyes from the contemplation of Your Body and fall deeply into the contemplation of theirs? The buds. The buds on some of these saplings. They were mean, you know, mean and tender. Mean little buds resisting the touch, springing like rubber. But aggressive. Daring me to touch. . . . Have you ever seen them, Lord? I mean, really seen them? One could not see them and not love them. You who made them must have considered them lovely even as an idea. . . . The love of them . . . was not just an easy luxurious human vice; they were, for me, A Thing To Do Instead. Instead of Papa, instead of the Cloth, instead of Velma, and I *chose* not to do without them.[34]

If the letter speaks to where the second form of goodness (narcissism and madness) "has language," then the form that this language takes is a language of self-vindication and a subsequent transference of blame upon God. It wasn't Church's fault that he was a pedophile; it was God's fault for creating the girls in the first place. All he had done was fall prey to what God had given. And he couldn't be blamed for this. After all, "instead of Papa, instead of Velma, instead of the Cloth"—in other words, instead of all the things that reminded him of his own failures—he "*chose*" to do things that were violent, invasive, abusive, and repugnant. Church *could* admit to his moral failings. But he could not be shaken of the idea of his own (white and male) goodness. Pecola may have forced him to acknowledge his past violence, but even her "fantastic and logical" plea could not penetrate the shield of his own narcissism.

Instead, it had the opposite effect: by giving "or [pretending] to give, blue eyes to a little girl in psychotic need of them," Church absolves himself of the guilt of his pedophilic violence. "I gave her those blue eyes she wanted," he writes. "I, I have caused a miracle. I gave her the eyes. I gave her the blue, blue, two blue eyes. Cobalt blue. A streak of it right out of your own blue heaven. No one else will see her blue eyes. But *she* will."[35] Church concludes the sermonic letter by asserting that, despite the violence God "caused" him to enact, his "gift" to Pecola made everything "Quite all right. Quite." Church had done *good;* he'd told himself so.

CONCLUSION: WHEN GOODNESS DOES WRONG

The Bluest Eye's conclusion is haunting. After Pecola leaves Church, she suffers a complete psychotic break. She believed she'd gotten the blue eyes, and one of the largest implications of this belief was that she began speaking wildly to herself, commenting on her own, schizophrenically slipping out of the shared world of Lorain, Ohio. Church's "good" was harmful. It was abusive. It was *wrong.*

Unfortunately, we don't know if Church saw it this way. We don't hear from Church after he writes his letter. What we *do* know is that he thought he was doing good. On its own merits, goodness was an afterthought, if it was even thought about at all. Church, after all, was a broken man, pained by the suffering and failure he'd both endured and caused. As a result, Church did what Morrison cautions us against doing in her lecture: instead of mitigating the theatrical evil he'd experienced, he succumbed to it, allowing it to occupy the entire terrain of his consciousness. Reflecting on the evils and pains visited upon him, Church drew from his own theological reasoning in order to develop a defense against evil; instead of listening to goodness's silent whisper, he instead focused on how God was the source of evil, how God had abandoned this world. And, because the townspeople deemed him supernatural, he began to believe that he actually *could* do the good God refused. In Church's mind, quiet goodness had taken second fiddle to evil's loud and brash presence, lurking backstage. And, like goodness, Pecola's quiet presence took a backseat to the primacy of Church's thoughts and desires.

When Church encountered Pecola, it was her presence, *not* her otherness, that he saw. Through this encounter, Morrison challenges us to see the connection between silence and goodness *through* Pecola. Both goodness and Pecola "lurk backstage" in Church's mind, quietly awaiting their opportunity to be seen and heard clearly. Mistaking her need for blue eyes as "logical" and not symptomatic of a deeper issue, Church heard only himself in Pecola's desire. Like the white shopkeeper who didn't see Pecola, Church only saw *his* wretchedness, *his* desires.[36] The "fantastic" nature of Pecola's plea never forced Church to ask *why* it was "fantastic." Because he'd already and uncritically accepted (his own) whiteness, celibacy, and isolation as given and unshakeable goods, he never stopped to think that the irrational nature of Pecola's supplication could be due to a severe depression and self-hatred that had taken psychotic hold over her consciousness. In other words, he never stopped to think about whether the "good" Pecola desired was *actually* a good in itself.

Goodness (Pecola?) was a mere afterthought, already understood with little to no critical reflection. Church had already been given a sense of the good as the very whiteness and Anglophilia that was passed down to him. Whiteness was understood as the "fortune" that "had smiled on" him and his ancestors through a long-ago enactment of white guilt. There was no need to think about goodness because his family history had dictated what it was. Rendered silent by the loud pain he'd endured, goodness never got a hearing. Church had become too self-interested for this; he already knew what goodness was.

Church couldn't see or hear Pecola herself. He only saw a little girl whose needs mirrored his own desires. He never sat with her silence; her quiet demeanor only became his opportunity for redemption. And, quiet as it's kept, Church wasn't alone.[37] The residents of Lorain were also preoccupied with the beauty of whiteness, and therefore practiced a kind of studied dismissal — if not outright denigration — of Pecola as part of their unacknowledged but nevertheless violent internalized racist standards. Their religion — their orientation in the world — was situated in direct relation to white aesthetic norms; (white) beauty became their God.

As a result, (white) beauty became an assumed good. No one thought about it; no one gave it any consideration. Everyone assumed that this was the case. Therefore, Pecola's presence—her dark skin, her quiet demeanor—became the site of all that was in need of repudiation. What is left except to excoriate this little girl? What else can be done, other than the cleansing of oneself through the public and private decimation of a quiet girl whose silence was a shield of defense for her?

> All of our waste which we dumped on her and which she absorbed. And all of our beauty, which was hers first and which she gave to us. All of us—all who knew her—felt so wholesome after we cleaned ourselves on her. We were so beautiful when we stood astride her ugliness. Her simplicity decorated us, her guilt sanctified us, her pain made us glow with health, her awkwardness made us think we had a sense of humor.[38]

Morrison is not demonizing the townspeople of Lorain. She says as much in the novel's afterword. What she's pointing to is the pervasiveness of this aesthetic predilection. The goodness of the beauty of whiteness is in the air: it's what people breathe; it is orientation without the dynamic possibility of *re*-orientation; it's already given, hardened into an experiential and evaluative given that need no longer be questioned or resisted. The invectives, the blue eyes, are all manifestations of an unthought-adoption of the assumed goodness of whiteness—even if one experiences this norm as repressive, insurmountable, or undesirable. In *The Bluest Eye*, white beauty is so internalized that it is no longer called into question; it is an unthought good, uncritically deployed, unanimously assumed, and maybe even fought against, in the face of purported black ugliness.

Both *The Bluest Eye* and Morrison's lecture are instructive for us as we witness the increasing theatricality of evil in our world. We are attuned to atrocities: mass shootings flood our newsfeeds, and we are held hostage to images of incarcerated children and indiscriminate violence. But unfortunately, it seems that we, like Church and the townspeople of Lorain, have been so attuned to the loudness of evil that we've forgotten to interrogate our own senses of goodness.

This is precisely the issue. As Morrison shows us in her writings, goodness begins to do wrong precisely when it isn't heard, when we fail to hear its message, when we're so preoccupied with evil that we no longer have space to sit with the silence of goodness. Goodness has the capacity for harm when it's already been thought, when we assume that "the exquisite and persuasive language of religions — all of which implore believers to rank goodness as the highest and holiest of human achievement" has already done the thinking for us: Christian sacrifice, Buddhist nothingness, Islamic submission, Jewish holiness. This isn't simply the case for specific religious traditions, either: in the United States, representative democracy, freedom, and equality are ethical norms, "goods" already thought and articulated through the nation's founding documents and sustained through the continued development and occasional rejection of laws.

Failing to critically reflect on these goods, refusing to hear the quiet speech of goodness, we rest easy on our assumptions, and begin to perpetuate harm in the process. Freedom, justice, and equality all sound straightforward until we find ourselves confronted with the Pecolas of the world, whose pleas are as fantastic as they are logical: the black activist, the victim of sexual abuse, the woman of color, the LGBTQ community member. The radical otherness of Pecola disrupts our sensibilities and forces us to confront what has been assumed to be good.[39] As philosopher Emmanuel Levinas teaches us, this experience of otherness places us in an ethical conundrum: Do we allow that otherness to penetrate us and try and see the other as a good unto itself?[40] Or do we try and incorporate the otherness of the other into our predetermined schemes of reference, comprehending them only through our own senses of what is good, thoughtful, and rational?

Too often, the latter happens: too often we, like Church, see the other, but its silenced presence fails to penetrate our ethical, political, and religious sensibilities. In the process, we try to retrofit the other into one-size-fits-all schemes of legitimation and classification: we give them blue eyes when their pleas were far deeper and far more substantial. Standing astride the silenced otherness of goodness, we think ourselves good.

I think this might be why Morrison gives attention to silent and silenced realities like Pecola and goodness itself. By "allowing goodness its own speech," by attempting to show that goodness "has language," by attributing *The Bluest Eye*'s accolades to *Pecola* and not herself, Morrison attunes us to ethical possibilities that are often overlooked and dismissed. If we listen to and for goodness, if we — unlike Church — hear in Pecola's gestures and almost whispered conversations a powerful criticism of the norms we uncritically accept, we open up the possibility of gaining further moral clarity, perpetually reorienting ourselves in the process. Through our attention to the silent nature of goodness, we create possibilities for no longer *silencing* it, encouraging it to speak and no longer "bite its tongue." Maybe it's time that we sit both *in* and *with* the silence of goodness.

Which is to say, maybe it's time we go backstage.

NOTES

1. Toni Morrison, *The Bluest Eye* (New York: Penguin, 1993), 216.
2. Morrison, *The Bluest Eye,* 19.
3. Morrison, *The Bluest Eye,* 62.
4. Morrison, *The Bluest Eye,* 39.
5. Morrison, *The Bluest Eye,* 39.
6. Morrison, *The Bluest Eye,* 48–49.
7. Morrison, *The Bluest Eye,* 82–93.
8. Morrison, *The Bluest Eye,* 46.
9. Charles Long, *Significations: Signs, Symbols, and Images in the Interpretation of Religion* (Aurora, CO: Davies Group, 1995), 7.
10. Morrison, *The Bluest Eye,* 209.
11. Long, *Significations,* 207.
12. Morrison, *The Bluest Eye,* 169.
13. Morrison, *The Bluest Eye,* 170.
14. Morrison, *The Bluest Eye,* 178.
15. Morrison, *The Bluest Eye,* 166.
16. Morrison, *The Bluest Eye,* 181.
17. Morrison, *The Bluest Eye,* 172.
18. Morrison, *The Bluest Eye,* 179.
19. Morrison, *The Bluest Eye,* 171.
20. Morrison, *The Bluest Eye,* 165.
21. Philosopher Calvin Warren has explored blackness not simply as a space of exclusion but as a space of nothingness, structurally and metaphysically excluded from the white world within which it finds itself. For Warren, blackness is the nothingness against which the world militates; blackness has no possibility of licit appearance in the world because it is always and already given as the nothingness, the encroaching nonbeing, that threatens existence itself (see Warren, *Ontological Terror* [Durham, NC: Duke University Press, 2018]).
22. For more on this, see Sylvester Johnson, *The Myth of Ham in Nineteenth-Century American Christianity: Race, Heathens, and the People of God* (New York: Palgrave Macmillan, 2004).
23. Morrison, *The Bluest Eye,* 172.
24. Morrison, *The Bluest Eye,* 173.

25. Morrison, *The Bluest Eye*, 172.

26. Morrison, *The Bluest Eye*, 172.

27. Morrison, *The Bluest Eye*, 179.

28. Morrison, *The Bluest Eye*, 174.

29. Morrison, *The Bluest Eye*, 174.

30. For the first and most in-depth exploration of this structure of religious experience, see Rudolf Otto's *The Idea of the Holy*, trans. John W. Harvey (Oxford: Oxford University Press, 1958). But my analysis of Pecola as a religious object is made possible by Charles Long's analysis of Otto in "Prolegomenon to a Religious Hermeneutic," in *Significations*, 31–42. There are other places where Long analyzes Otto's structure in *Significations*, and in each of these cases, we encounter the possibility that the *mysterium tremendum* can appear *in* human history, through contact and exchange.

31. Otto, *The Idea of the Holy*, 12–40.

32. Otto, *The Idea of the Holy*, 175.

33. Morrison, *The Bluest Eye*, 178.

34. Morrison, *The Bluest Eye*, 178–79.

35. Morrison, *The Bluest Eye*, 182.

36. Morrison, *The Bluest Eye*, 48.

37. Consider Morrison's afterword: "I focused, therefore, on how something as grotesque as the demonization of an entire race could take root inside the most delicate member of society: a child; the most vulnerable member; a female.... In exploring the social and domestic aggression that could cause a child to literally fall apart.... I mounted a series of rejections ... all the while trying hard to avoid complicity in the demonization process Pecola was subjected to. That is, I did not want to dehumanize the characters who trashed Pecola and contributed to her collapse" (*The Bluest Eye*, 210–11).

38. Morrison, *The Bluest Eye*, 205.

39. Emmanuel Levinas, *Totality and Infinity: An Essay on Exteriority*, trans. Alphonso Lingis (Pittsburgh: Duquesne University Press, 1969).

40. Levinas provides a full-scale analysis of this question in *Totality and Infinity*, but see also his essays "Transcendence and Height" and "Is Ontology Fundamental?," in *Emmanuel Levinas: Basic Philosophical Writings*, trans. and ed. Adriaan Peperzak, Simon Critchley, and Robert Bernasconi (Bloomington: Indiana University Press, 1996), 1–32.

Unsung No More

Pilate's Mercy! Eulogy in *Song of Solomon*

GERALD "JAY" WILLIAMS

> Love is strong as death, passion fierce as the grave.
> —CANTICLE OF CANTICLES 8:6

> Allowing goodness its own speech does not annihilate evil, but it does allow me to signify my own understanding of goodness, the acquisition of self-knowledge.
> —TONI MORRISON, "Goodness: Altruism and the Literary Imagination," Ingersoll Lecture 2012

> Surely goodness and mercy shall follow me.
> —PSALM 23

SACRED TIME, SACRED TEXTS

Morrison's arrival at Harvard was well-timed, coming as it did during the first week of Adventus. Although she came to explore immortality,[1] her work had already given life. Years later her speech echoes: To speak of that Ingersoll Lecture is to confess that her voice haunts Harvard and her words possess an afterlife. Such utterance reaffirms Morrison's claim that goodness is an absent presence, of sorts.[2]

Reading Morrison is a spiritual experience because Morrison's novels in/spire. They breathe spirit into lips of clay and animate our mortal bodies. Her voice had long ago helped me find my own, joining the chorus of those who, in conversation with Morrison's novels, learned to sing. While I had been warned not to be *star*-struck upon meeting her, how could I not be? I grew up poring over *The Bluest Eye* and *Beloved,* and in my context Morrison's literary canon has become canonical scripture. She writes against texts that have written violence upon black flesh. Morrison advances the truth-telling tradition of Ida B. Wells-Barnett and protests literature that has lynched black bodies.[3] In the face of daily assaults on black dignity and black life, Morrison writes resistance that disarms death and dying. The honor to speak in the presence of one who had penned such holy writ was to stand on holy ground.

I could hardly contain my excitement. With each passing day she was closer to us. While I resisted at first, finally I succumbed to my initial urge and did what seemed natural for a millennial in the wake of life-changing events: I posted to social media. "She is coming . . . no, now she is here!" The coming present had arrived. Indeed, I had been given a gift.[4]

The moment of her coming is not insignificant. In the Christian tradition, Advent is the beginning of time, signaling the start of a new liturgical year. This season heralds the incarnation of Christ, inviting the adherent into a mode of ritualized reorientation. Each year, one returns to the same place differently. Key themes like home and healing repeat, as in Morrison's corpus, and the scripture readings function as a lens of re/presentation — of beginning again. These repetitions, though familiar, remain full of a mystery that brings us to the limit of knowledge. "This holy mystery"[5] redirects our gaze and focuses our attention to see that which is too often unseen by too many.[6]

My Advent proclamation of Morrison's coming to Harvard, however, betrayed the mixed emotions that filled my body. I had been pondering the question: What might it mean during the season that anticipates the coming of Emmanuel — "God Is With Us" — to deliver a sermon from a text where the author of scripture is literally here *with us?* Fear joined joy. And self-doubt, also one of Morrison's recurring themes, resurfaced — but this time in me.[7] Although I preach on Sundays in the black Methodist congregation of the great abolitionist David Walker, now the appeal "in particular and very expressly" was for me to re-member the life-affirming lessons I had learned in Morrison's school.[8] It was my turn to be reminded of the Advent angel's words to Mary before the star appeared: "Do not be afraid."[9]

Only then would I realize that, in order to reflect on the "mercy sermon" in *Song of Solomon,* the best thing to do — in fact, the *only* thing to do — was to follow the practice[10] already in my bones. Every Sunday morning before approaching that "sacred desk," preachers in the black church tradition must "take a text."

So, to begin my sermonic remarks on the panel preceding Morrison's lecture, using my tattered childhood copy, I offered a reading from *Song of Solomon:*

Two days later, halfway through the service, it seemed as though Ruth was going to be the lone member of the bereaved family there. A female quartet from Linden Baptist Church had already sung, "Abide with Me"; the wife of the mortician had read the condolence cards and the minister had launched into his "Naked came ye into this life and naked shall ye depart" sermon, which he had always believed suitable for the death of a young woman; and the winos in the vestibule who came to pay their respects to "Pilate's girl," but who dared not enter, had begun to sob, when the door swung open and Pilate burst in, shouting, "Mercy!" as though it were a command. A young man stood up and moved toward her. She flung out her right arm and almost knocked him down. "I want mercy!" she shouted, and began walking toward the coffin, shaking her head from side to side as though somebody had asked her a question and her answer was no.

Halfway up the aisle she stopped, lifted a finger, and pointed. Then slowly, although her breathing was fast and shallow, she lowered her hand to her side. It was strange, the languorous, limp hand coming to rest at her side while her breathing was coming so quick and fast. "Mercy," she said again, but she whispered it now. . . .

"Mercy?" Now she was asking a question. "Mercy?"

It was not enough. The word needed a bottom, a frame. She straight-ened up, held her head high, and transformed the plea into a note. In a clear bluebell voice she sang out — the one word held so long it became a sentence — and before the last syllable had died into the corners of the room, she was answered in a sweet soprano: "I hear you."

The people turned around. Reba had entered and was singing too. Pilate neither acknowledged her entrance nor missed a beat. She simply repeated the word "Mercy," and Reba replied. The daughter standing at the back of the chapel, the mother up front, they sang. . . .

Conversationally she spoke, identifying Hagar, selecting her away from everybody else in the world who had died. First she spoke to the ones who had the courage to look at her, shake their heads, and say, "Amen." Then she spoke to those whose nerve failed them, whose glance would climb no higher than the long black fingers at her side. Toward them especially she leaned a little, telling in three words the full story of the stumped life in the coffin behind her. "My baby girl." Words tossed like stones into a silent canyon.

Suddenly, like an elephant who had just found his anger and lifts his trunk over the heads of the little men who want his teeth or his hide or his flesh or his amazing strength, Pilate trumpeted for the sky itself to hear, "And she was *loved!*"

FIG. 11. *Funeral for Last Mass Lynching Victims, Georgia, 1946.*
(Getty Images/Bettman)

It startled one of the sympathetic winos in the vestibule and he dropped
his bottle, spurting emerald glass and jungle-red wine everywhere.[11]

Thus ends the (sacred) reading. And so begins these grace notes on
Pilate's "Mercy!" sermon.

In *Song of Solomon,* Morrison writes a liturgy of "Word and Table"
in which Pilate's eulogy—literally, "good words"—becomes Eucharist,
transforming both Hagar's corpse and the wino's cup into "means of
grace."[12] This reimagined ritual at once marks both a discontinuity and
consonance with a Christian tradition that establishes a memorialized
celebration of the altruistic and emancipatory power of love. Through the
disruptive power of Pilate's voice, Morrison reenvisions the black body as
sacred and mercy as an alternative to suicide.

SACRED DISRUPTIONS, SACRED SONG

At this funeral there is no occasion for a platitudinal eulogy. Hagar, the namesake of the biblical Abraham's deserted concubine, lay dead on the bier.[13] The novel's ambiguity of suicidal flight, which doubles as "magical flight,"[14] is thickest here: it is uncertain whether Hagar dies from a broken heart or by her own hands.[15]

Whatever the case, it is clear that the appointed preacher's prepared message was inadequate. The generic "naked came ye into this life and naked shall ye depart" sermon had no *place*[16] at a young black woman's funeral. Already there has been enough liturgical disrobing of black women's bodies in sacred spaces of the African American church.[17] Who can stand to hear another sermon that, in the face of devastating loss, rather flatly and uncritically rehearses Job's theodical refrain: "The LORD giveth and the LORD taketh away; blessed be the name of the LORD,"[18] and then still ends in a whoop?[19] No, his prepackaged sermon did not fit the "hysteria" of her body. Especially not one rain-soaked in clothes purchased to please a man-cousin who never fully loved her.

The preacher's canned words will not win Pilate's approval, just as Hagar could never win Milkman's. Only Mama could speak of such love, only a mother and daughter can sing of this mercy. There is no space in this place to speak disembodied words that fail to give full account for tragedy. Instead, Pilate foregrounds Hagar, disallowing her granddaughter's body to be the backdrop for just another funeral sermon that barely even speaks of the life of the dead.

Consequently, Pilate preaches a homily of self-love that disrupts the patriarchal status quo and claims interruptive power, thereby instituting a womanist[20] counter-reality through a song that doubles as a Eucharistic prayer. Pilate proclaims a message that Hagar did not receive in life: have mercy on one's self. Such a transgressive feat nonconforms to life's debilitating and destructive conventions. Loving oneself is a queer, radically courageous act—one that resists the eviscerating pain of loneliness and rootlessness. Altruism begins with inward goodness, a love that defies the death of spirit.

Pilate stands in the tradition of Jarena Lee, the nineteenth-century African Methodist Episcopal exhorter who, after being denied a preaching license because of her gender, interrupts the preacher because he lacked spirit, and then proceeds to exegete his text extemporaneously![21] Pilate joins Lee in converting the sermon into a site of subversion and struggle; a place of pain and passion, the very crucible of confrontation. Because perhaps Pilate knew that the minister would attempt to tidy up a life fucked over by love. In so doing, Pilate rebukes the rule of black preaching that stipulates that no matter where the sermon begins, it always ends in joy.

No, there can be no "homegoing celebration" until one encounters Hagar as she really is: Dead. When life has not granted you the privilege of *navel-gazing,* you must confront things as they really are. Like the biblical Hagar, freedom is not free; it comes at great cost. Pilate becomes a "sister of the spirit" who leans on the brea(d)th of God[22] to question patriarchy and authority, all while resisting the disciplinary constraints of race and class.

Pilate interrupts the preacher, just as the Spirit of God disrupts the worship celebration when the biblical King Solomon returns the Ark of the Covenant to the temple. It is written: "The house of the LORD was filled with a cloud, so that the priests could not stand to minister because of the cloud; for the glory of the LORD filled the house of God."[23] Filled with spirit, this sister of subversion, Pilate rejects the priestly performance of ministry. Pilate refuses to join in Solomon's song of praise in worship that would leave Hagar's life unexamined; she must sing her own. Her word from the LORD is more prophetic, because it gives voice to grief while still declaring the fundamental reality that Hagar was loved—a message that could easily be lost in the wake of death from a broken heart.

Pilate had had enough of what she heard, or that which she knew would be said or left unsaid. So she interrupts, and gives voice to the voiceless Hagar. And instead of a traditional sermon, we get a song.[24] The preached word is not the good news here. Rather, it is the gospel music of the lullaby: "Who's been botherin my sweet sugar lumpkin / Somebody's been botherin my sweet sugar lumpkin / I'll find who's botherin my sweet sugar lumpkin."[25] The eulogy and the celebration come not in the conventional preacher's closing salvo but in the "blessed assurance" of being acknowledged and recognized.[26] The aesthetic performance of the priest is overshadowed by Pilate. Then, Reba joins her mother, answering, "I hear you." Mother and daughter claim the interruptive power of women in worship, and together they sing Hagar's muted verse, a remix of Solomon's song.

In this act we hear Morrison giving voice to silenced goodness. Morrison does in fiction what other black women have done in nonfiction: she courageously speaks what has not yet been spoken.[27] A previously quiet resilience declares itself. It is an incarnated celebration of life and love in the pattern of the Canticle of Canticles, the novel's namesake. While Milkman refused Hagar the erotic sonnets found in Song of Songs, Morrison reimagines and retells that type of embodied adoration and devotion. Through the voices of mothers, Morrison praises the divinity of dark skin, coarse hair, brown eyes, and wide noses of black women's bodies.[28] Despite denials of failed lovers and the assaults of a harsh world, Morrison challenges us to delight in the beauty of blackness. To be sure, this is profoundly theological work: even when unnoticed and unnamed — like in the biblical Song of Solomon where "God" is not uttered — still the divine dwells within.[29]

Pilate's "mercy sermon" foreshadows the more famous "clearing sermon" in Morrison's *Beloved,* in which Baby Suggs invites the congregation to love fiercely in a manner that the world does not. In both exhortations, Morrison focuses our gaze on the black body, salvaging it from disposability and scorn. Drawing from the deep well of black mother's wit, these sermons sing a common refrain: black bodies are worthy of love and praise.

Howard Thurman, who delivered the 1947 Ingersoll Lecture, also turns to the body-affirming teachings of a black woman in order to celebrate black life. In his autobiography *With Head and Heart,* Thurman recounts:

> When the slave preacher told the Calvary narrative to my grandmother and the other slaves, it had the same effect on them as it would later have on their descendants. But this preacher, when he had finished, would pause, his eyes scrutinizing every face in the congregation, and then he would tell them, "You are not niggers! You are not slaves! You are God's children!" When my grandmother got to that part of her story, there would be a slight stiffening in her spine as we sucked in our breath. When she had finished, our spirits were restored.[30]

Thurman's grandmother's slave preacher, Morrison's Pilate and Baby Suggs, and Jarena Lee converge. The black church and black preaching in particular — with their origins in slave religion — play an indispensable role in cultivating a sense of black *somebodiness* in white-supremacist America.[31]

Pilate and Reba's song speaks, then, of love and loss just as the "negro spiritual speaks of life and death," the title of Thurman's Ingersoll Lecture. Whereas Morrison blazes trails by mainstreaming the black experience in American literature, Thurman does the same for religion. Thurman, who becomes the first black dean of chapel at a US university, makes the case that spirituals are deeply influenced by the imminent threat of physical death, while not passively resigning to death. Spirituals are sophisticated, though sometimes subtle, existential meditations defined by moods of loneliness and discouragement, as well as moral-ethical imperatives to live well. Death, Thurman argues, "may be inevitable, yes; gruesome, perhaps; releasing, yes, but triumphant, NEVER."[32]

Heard in this light, the funeral song complicates the logic of Hagar's death and the novel's broader theme of suicidal flight. In chapter after long chapter we hear of pain and rejection, heartache and loneliness passed along from generation to generation. Hagar is the silent refrain of *Solomon's Song:* this is to say, Hagar — the great-granddaughter of Sing (who marries Solomon's son, Jake) — is driven to "hysteria" when Milkman leaves, just like her great-great-grandmother Ryna weeps uncontrollably when her husband Solomon flies away to Africa.[33]

The different verses to this song are one and the same; this tragic generational curse remains unbroken.[34] The first generation is torn apart by slavery, as Solomon determines not to die as property and instead flies away to Africa — attempting to take a single child, Jake, and dropping him soon after takeoff.[35] The spiritual "O Freedom" reverberates: "And before I'll be a slave / I'll be buried in my grave / Go home to my Lord / And be free."[36] Liberty comes at a cost, no doubt, because Solomon gains his freedom through the abandonment of his family.[37] Liberation is gained for one, but not for all. This freedom falls short of emancipation, because Solomon's wife and children remained enslaved and the haunt of chattel stalks future generations.

The fallen child, Jake, who is renamed Macon Dead, is killed trying to protect his property from white hustlers who swindle him into signing away the land he earned in slavery's wake, thus capitalizing off his illiteracy. Macon Dead II, spoiled by the drive to procure and preserve property, cannot truly love, and in turn his wife and children seek affirmation outside of the home. Macon Dead III (Milkman) also becomes infected with "gold fever," unwittingly seeking reparations for a lineage eternally marred by chattel. Each new branch in the family tree is covered by this curse; the father's transgression visited unto the fourth generation—just as it is written in the book of Numbers. Rehearsed is this same song of love and loss, of property and pain. What else is there to say but *kyrie eleison*, "Lord, have mercy"?

SACRED BODIES, HOLY COMMUNION

Pilate cries, "Mercy," the novel's refrain—she demands mercy! She takes no written scripture as her text, because upon Hagar's body, her mother Sing's body, and her own body, the story has already been written: "In the nighttime. Mercy. In the darkness. Mercy. In the morning. Mercy. At my bedside. Mercy. On my knees now. Mercy. Mercy. Mercy. Mercy."[38] The repetition of the ancient Taizé plainsong chant reflects the call for mercy that circumscribes Morrison's novel. The text ends the same way it began: when Freddie the janitor spies Ruth nursing the too-old son of Macon Dead II, rechristening him "Milkman," he shouts, "Have mercy. I be damn."[39] Yes, the novel ends the same way it began: when the midwife speaks after the illiterate Macon Dead I plucks the name "Pilate" from the Bible to name his daughter, the midwife cries, "Jesus, have mercy."[40]

The same words end the novel that we find at the beginning, when a desperate and intoxicated Porter sobbingly holds himself hostage by shotgun in an attic window. Morrison writes: "[Porter] would cry great shoulder-heaving sobs, followed by more screams: 'I love ya! I love ya all. Don't act like that. You women. Stop it. Don't act like that. Don't you see I love ya? I'd die for ya, kill for ya. I'm saying I love ya. I'm telling ya. Oh, God have mercy. What I'm gonna do? What in this fuckin world am I gonna dooooo?"[41] Hagar is not the only one enraged because of love lost. The heaviness of love knows no limits. The cavernous feeling of loneliness and emptiness, Morrison suggests, can drive a person to the very brink of life, to death. Humans yearn for intimate communion and contact with others, with those who will call them by name.[42]

Yes, mercy closes the novel just as it opens it: "As it was in the beginning, is now and shall be forever."[43] This lesser doxology is a word of praise in unexpected fashion. Pilate disturbs the sermon with her own sermonic song as she cries, "Mercy." Because, quite simply, there is nothing else that one can say. What else can be uttered when a mother seeks affection by suckling her too-old son? What else can be uttered when a father names his daughter after the killer of Christ? What else can be spoken when one drowns one's sadness in a bottle held in one hand with a shotgun in the other?

When you have reached the margin of what you can bear in life, at the site of death, you can only find three words: "Lord, have mercy." When speech has reached its bound, and yet silence still is unsuitable, these three simple words puncture the void. When the horizon is so close, yet still far away, this refrain signals the limit-experience: the place where otherwise one would only be speechless, but where one refuses to be silenced.[44]

In this scene, Morrison sets the table for communion and transforms a eulogy into Eucharist, one of Christianity's most prominent symbols of *agape.* Pilate's final declaration — And she was *loved!*—affirms in death what Hagar did not fully know in life. Pilate cries out so that this "death does not get the final victory" in a novel stalked by suicide.[45] This mercy sermon presents a countermeasure to (magical) flight and a freedom gained through self-inflicted death. Pilate points to the emancipatory power of kinship, sustaining, albeit in atypical form, the life-affirming function of the black church.

The setting is primed for iconoclasm: sobbing winos bring the "jungle-red" blood of Christ and fill the conspicuous absence of Hagar's family on the mourners' bench. The body of a dis-eased, heartbroken woman becomes the broken bread. And Pilate, the navelless, mythical Christ-figure presides over the memorial. This transubstantiation personifies a transvaluation of values of the highest order.[46]

Morrison's invocation of religious overtones is all but straightforward. The winos who come to pay their respects, and whose very presence upsets the politics of respectability at play, are the only ones grieving. Perhaps they weep for themselves now that the granddaughter of their supplier is dead. Would Hagar's demise bring an end to Pilate's distillery? For everyone knows that a (grand)mother never fully recovers from such loss. Or maybe their lament is sincere,[47] because they too have felt the sting of shame and unacceptance. Thus, the marginalized winos honor Hagar's grandmother, one who challenges social norms of beauty and the good life. Or possibly they are just "drunk with the wine of the world."[48]

Further still, the scene is unconventional because Pilate's message of self-love is a call to communion, which decenters the primacy of the preached word in the African American religious experience.[49] It is Pilate who shifts the ritual performance away from the choir's song and the preacher's sermon. The climax of her message initiates the Eucharist, and therefore the Eucharist becomes the focal point of the funeral. The scene is reframed *in its entirety* and the mercy sermon becomes a "mercy mass." This reversal questions reformed theology's primacy of the preached word through commemoration of love of the body.[50] A different type of incarnation is work: it is not the Word-made-flesh but rather flesh-made-word that shapes this scene.[51] Pilate refuses silence, disallowing Hagar's story to go untold. With Hagar's broken body on full display, Pilate narrates a new chronicle. Solomon's song is unsung no more.

Pilate upsets the problematic of suicide that haunts the novel. Hagar's passion, Solomon's Leap, Robert Smith's flight, and Milkman's ride are not the only alternatives to life's excruciating pain. Suicide is not the necessary condition of experiencing freedom. Rather, one must choose to live as one chosen by love. At the moment of his (and Pilate's) demise, Milkman realizes that "without ever leaving the ground, she could fly" because Pilate believed the promise of love.[52] She loved herself enough to be different and affirmed herself without need of acceptance from a man or society.

Although Hagar did not know Solomon's love ballad — that Song of Songs, "I am black and beautiful"[53] — Pilate did. In her sharing, Pilate helps us re-member the Eucharistic love of God. And in the midst of a funeral, with her granddaughter's beautiful black body in plain view and the weeping wino's shattered bottle spurting out its balm, Pilate offers the words of institution: "Telling in three words the full story of the stumped life in the coffin behind her. 'My baby girl.'"[54] They are clear words that disrupt any remaining ambiguity and birth the new reality of resurrected life. So here lays *her* body, broken. "This is my blood" . . . "jungle-red wine" . . . poured out for you. *Christ, have mercy.*

The eulogy is interrupted by the Eucharist. The words of institution converge with good words of praise. Pilate cries "mercy" as prayer: a plea of intervention that might inaugurate Advent, the coming of a fresh start. *Sing unto the Lord a new song.*[55] It is not an empty phrase or space-filler but rather a *place*holder, until that new day comes and overshadows the lingering tragedy that even though Milkman finally finds roots, he never finds home. Sadly, in order to come to love himself, Milkman too leaves behind those who loved him, especially Hagar, the one who loved him most. And so, we re-member her heartbreaking death, on the night *she* was betrayed.[56]

But we also do this as often as we can: we re-member that she was *loved!*[57] This act of remembrance *begins* to disrupt violence—from within and without—against devalued and disremembered (black) bodies.[58] To be sure, "allowing goodness its own speech does not annihilate evil,"[59] but it is an act of resistance that initiates healing. It composes a "love song" that imagines an-other possibility and beckons us toward the dawning of this new day.

NOTES

1. Toni Morrison, "Goodness: Altruism and the Literary Imagination," Harvard Divinity School Ingersoll Lecture on Immortality, December 6, 2012, in this volume.

2. Cf. Avery F. Gordon's *Ghostly Matters: Haunting and the Sociological Imagination* (1997; Minneapolis: University of Minnesota Press, 2008); and Melanie R. Anderson, *Spectrality in the Novels of Toni Morrison* (Knoxville: University of Tennessee Press, 2013).

3. Toni Morrison reads selections of Wells's memoirs in William Greaves's documentary, *Ida B. Wells: a Passion for Justice* (New York: William Greaves Productions, 1989).

4. As will become clear below, I have in mind the Christian *Eucharist,* meaning "thanksgiving," which is the ritual commemoration of the death and resurrection of Jesus of Nazareth, God's gift of love. See Jean-Luc Marion, *God Without Being,* trans. Thomas A. Carlson (1982; Chicago: University of Chicago Press, 1991), particularly the chapter "The Gift and the Present," where Marion writes: "The eucharistic presence comes to us, at each instant, as the gift of that very instant, and, in it, of the body of the Christ in whom one must be incorporated" (175).

5. See *This Holy Mystery: A United Methodist Understanding of Holy Communion,* which is the denomination's official statement of Eucharistic theology and practice. Copyright © 2003, 2004 The General Board of Discipleship of The United Methodist Church, PO Box 340003, Nashville TN 37203–0003. https://www.umcdiscipleship.org/resources/this-holy-mystery-a-united-methodist-understanding-of-holy-communion.

6. Toni Morrison, *Playing in the Dark: Whiteness and the Literary Imagination* (New York: Vintage, 1993).

7. Marcus Hunter, in "For Colored Scholars Who Consider Suicide When Our Rainbows Are Not Enuf," writes of "the capacity of marginalized and oppressed peoples' actions, attitudes, and histories to produce new knowledge and identify patterns and causes of inequality" (*Berkeley Journal of Sociology,* http://berkeleyjournal.org/2016/02/for-colored-scholars-who-consider-suicide-when-our

-rainbows-are-not-enuf/). The title of this article riffs off of Ntozake Shange's 1975 stage play, *for colored girls who have considered suicide/when the rainbow is enuf.*

8. Union United Methodist Church, previously May Street Methodist Episcopal Church, was the spiritual home of the trailblazing abolitionist David Walker, author of *Appeal, in Four Articles; Together with a Preamble to the Coloured Citizens of the World, but in Particular, and Very Expressly, to Those of the United States of America.* See http://unionboston.org/about/history.

9. Luke 1:30. All Scripture quotations are taken from the New Revised Standard Version Bible, copyright © 1989 the Division of Christian Education of the National Council of the Churches of Christ in the United States of America, and are used by permission. All rights reserved.

10. Michel Foucault writes about the empowering potential of practice: a "major form through which the subject can and must transform himself in order to have access to the truth is a kind of work. This is a work of the self on the self, an elaboration of the self by the self, a progressive transformation of the self by the self from which one takes responsibility in a long labor of ascesis (*askēsis*)" (*The Hermeneutics of the Subject: Lectures at the Collège de France, 1981–1982,* trans. Graham Burchell [New York: Picador, 2005], 16).

11. Toni Morrison, *Song of Solomon* (1977; New York: Plume, 1987), 316–19.

12. John Wesley, the progenitor of Methodism, uses this phrase to describe human practices, such as the Lord's Supper, that convey divine love. See his 1746 sermon "The Means of Grace," as found in *John's Wesley's Sermons: An Anthology,* ed. Albert C. Outler and Richard P. Heitzenrater (Nashville: Abingdon, 1991), 157–71.

13. Genesis 21:8–22 narrates the complicated story of Hagar and Ishmael. In it we encounter a God who sides *not* with the slave, as God does in the Exodus of the Israelites, but rather with the master. Hagar and her son Ishmael, son of Abraham, are sent away to the wilderness with God's approval, because of the legitimate wife Sarah's displeasure. In Morrison's text, Hagar struggles with her own beauty and perceived aesthetic legitimacy in Milkman's eyes, particularly her hair texture and color, complexion, eye color, and nose size (313–16). Delores Williams uses this biblical text as the foundation of *Sisters in the Wilderness: The Challenges of Womanist God-Talk* (Maryknoll, NY: Orbis, 1993), which wrestles with the theodicy of a God who provides sustenance but does not provide complete liberation. Williams's groundbreaking text challenges black liberation theology for its blindness to black women's struggles as surrogates. Williams replaces theological tropes of exodus and substitutionary atonement in black theology for God-talk rooted in survival and sustenance as encountered in the biblical story of Hagar, who gains freedom only in banishment to the wilderness where she must struggle to survive.

14. Davíd Carrasco argues in "Magically Flying with Toni Morrison: Mexico, Gabriel García Márquez, *Song of Solomon,* and *Sula*": "The radical action of a human being

flying through the air reflects the desire to abolish history, or the terror of one's history, and undergo the feeling and experience of freedom" (in *Toni Morrison: Memory and Meaning* [Jackson: University Press of Mississippi, 2014], 150).

15. Suicidal flight is the novel's commencement (insurance agent Robert Smith's plunge), crest (Solomon's Leap), and finale (Milkman's flight). Following this pattern, arguably, Hagar's ambiguous death too is suicidal. Or, is self-hate itself tantamount to suicide?

16. Jacqueline Nassy Brown defines in *Dropping Anchor, Setting Sail: Geographies of Race in Black Liverpool* (Princeton: Princeton University Press, 2005) that place "must be understood first and foremost as an abstraction, not a set of physical properties just there for the eye to see. . . . The very urge to make meaning out of the materiality of places — what they look like, feel like, and where they are, for example, and who occupies them, what social relations define them, and what process unfold within them — is produced through an axis of power and subjectivity that we might call *place*" (9).

17. Patriarchy and sexism have oversubscribed male authority and diminished the centrality of women's experiences within black churches. See, for example, Kelly Brown Douglas, *Sexuality and the Black Church: A Womanist Perspective* (Maryknoll, NY: Orbis, 1999); M. Shawn Copeland, *Enfleshing Freedom: Body, Race, and Being* (Minneapolis: Fortress, 2010); and Cheryl Townsend Gilkes's *If It Wasn't for the Women: Black Women's Experience and Womanist Culture in Church and Community* (Maryknoll, NY: Orbis, 2000).

18. Job 1:21. Cf. William R. Jones, *Is God a White Racist? A Preamble to Black Theology* (Boston: Beacon, 1973); and Anthony Pinn, *Why Lord?: Suffering and Evil in Black Theology* (New York: Continuum, 1995).

19. See *Preaching with Sacred Fire: An Anthology of African American Sermons, 1750 to the Present,* ed. Martha Simmons and Frank A. Thomas (New York: Norton, 2010), esp. Simmons's "Whooping: The Musicality of African American Preaching Past and Present," 864–84.

20. Alice Walker's *In Search of Our Mothers' Gardens: Womanist Prose* (Orlando: Harcourt, 1983) defines: "From *womanish*. (Opp. of "girlish," i.e., frivolous, irresponsible, not serious.) A black feminist or feminist of color. . . . Responsible. In charge. Serious" (xi). Layli Phillips writes that "Womanism is a social change perspective rooted in black women's and other women of color's everyday experiences and everyday methods of problem solving in everyday spaces, extended to the problem of ending all forms of oppression for all people, restoring the balance between people and the environment/nature, and reconciling human life with the spiritual dimension" (*The Womanist Reader,* ed. Phillips [New York, Routledge, 2006], xx).

21. See *Sisters of the Spirit: Three Black Women's Autobiographies of the Nineteenth Century,* ed. William L. Andrews (Bloomington: Indiana University Press, 1986).

In addition to Jarena Lee, Andrews compiles the autobiographies of Zilpha Elaw and Julia Foote, all who committed their lives profoundly to the work of ministry, emerging out of their deeply personal spirituality that confronted patriarchal norms of their time.

22. Luce Irigarary, "The Age of the Breath," in *Luce Irigaray: Key Writings* (New York: Continuum, 2004).

23. 2 Chronicles 5:13b–14.

24. Or perhaps a "sermon as song," which is the title of Charles G. Adams's unpublished lecture at Harvard University, October 1995. See Simmons, "Whooping," 883n4.

25. Morrison, *Song of Solomon*, 318.

26. Fanny J. Crosby's "Blessed Assurance" is a staple in black church hymnody. See *African American Heritage Hymnal: 575 Hymns, Spirituals, and Gospel Songs* (Chicago: GIA, 2001), 508.

27. Mary Burgher, in her essay "Images of Self and Race in the Autobiographies of Black Women," explains: "Black women autobiographers write about experiences more varied, much harsher, and at times more beautiful than most others encounter . . . [Maya Angelou's *I Know Why the Caged Bird Sings*], like other autobiographies by Black women, is a valuable resource because it reveals and symbolizes the Black woman's daring act of remaking her lost innocence into invisible dignity, her never-practiced delicacy into quiet grace, and her forced responsibility into unshouted courage." In *Sturdy Black Bridges: Visions of Black Women in Literature*, ed. Roseann P. Bell, Bettye J. Parker, and Beverly Guy-Sheftall (Garden City, NY: Anchor, 1979), 113.

28. Morrison, *Song of Solomon*, 313–16.

29. Cf. Harvey Cox and Stephanie Paulsell, *Lamentations and the Song of Songs: A Theological Commentary on the Bible* (Louisville: Westminster John Knox, 2012). Paulsell is correct: "The Song makes room for us to respond to its words and images with words and images of our own. Its power to generate new poetry, new thought, new theology is attested over centuries and is still available to us whenever we open its pages. . . . By inviting us into the dialogue of the two lovers, we are encouraged to read as they love — lingering in the presence of the beloved, admiring the beloved's beauty and grace, and adoring both what can be seen and known and spoken of and what is beyond our sight, beyond our ability to know or describe" (292).

30. Thurman, *With Head and Heart: The Autobiography of Howard Thurman* (Boston: Beacon, 1981), 21.

31. See also C. Eric Lincoln's and Lawrence H. Mamiya's description of the importance of affirmative titles in black churches, which counteract denigrating ones

experienced (Lincoln and Mamiya, *The Black Church in the African American Experience* [Durham, NC: Duke University Press, 1990], 206).

32. Thurman, *Deep River* and *The Negro Spiritual Speaks of Life and Death* (Richmond, IN: Friends United Press, 1975), 24, emphasis in original.

33. The Advent-Incarnation biblical story speaks of "a voice is heard in Ramah, weeping and great mourning, Rachel weeping for her children and refusing to be comforted, because they are no more." (Matthew 2:18, Jeremiah 31:15). In *Not Every Spirit: A Dogmatics of Christian Disbelief* (Harrisburg: Trinity International, 1994), Christopher Morse uses "Rachel's refusal" as a linchpin in his systematic theology, forwarding that a constructive assertion must be predicated on an explicit disavowal.

34. "The Lord is slow to anger, and abounding in steadfast love, forgiving iniquity and transgression, but by no means clearing the guilty, visiting the iniquity of the parents upon the children, to the third and the fourth generation" (Numbers 14:18).

35. Solomon's Leap reconfigures the suicide of Robert Smith encountered in the novel's first paragraph: "At 3:00 p.m. on Wednesday the 18th of February 1931, I will take off from Mercy and fly away, on my own wings. Please forgive me. I loved you all" (Morrison, *Song of Solomon*, 3).

36. See James Cone's *The Spirituals and the Blues: An Interpretation* (Maryknoll, NY: Orbis, 1991), especially chapter 2; and Gayraud Wilmore's *Black Religion and Black Radicalism* (1973; Maryknoll, NY: Orbis, 1998), especially chapter 4.

37. The theme of liberative death during slavery will return famously in Morrison's *Beloved* (1987), in which the reader encounters the gruesome "courage" of Sethe, who mimics Margaret Garner's infanticide to spare her children from slavery. As Thurman says in *The Negro Spiritual Speaks of Life and Death*, "there are some things in life that are worse than death" (15) — to live unfree.

38. Morrison, *Song of Solomon*, 317–18.

39. Morrison, *Song of Solomon*, 14.

40. Morrison, *Song of Solomon*, 19.

41. Morrison, *Song of Solomon*, 26.

42. Morrison, *Song of Solomon*, 329–31.

43. *Gloria Patri* ("Glory to the Father and to the Son and to the Holy Spirit, as it was in the beginning, is now, and will be forever. Amen.") is known as the "lesser doxology" in Christian liturgy, in contrast to *Gloria in excelsis Deo*, the "greater doxology" (see Nicholas Ayo, C.S.C., *Gloria Patri: The History and Theology of the Lesser Doxology* [Notre Dame: University of Notre Dame Press, 2007]).

44. See Victor Turner's *The Ritual Process: Structure and Anti-Structure* (New Brunswick, NJ: AldineTransaction, 1969); and Michael Jackson's *The Palm at the End of the Mind: Relatedness, Religiosity, and the Real* (Durham, NC: Duke University Press, 2009).

45. 1 Corinthians 15:54.

46. M. Shawn Copeland writes in *Enfleshing Freedom* that "Eucharist is countersign to the devaluation and violence directed toward the exploited, despised black body. . . . Eucharistic celebration forms our social imagination, transvalues our values, and transforms the meaning of our being human, of embodying Christ" (127). Cf. Friedrich Nietzsche's *On the Genealogy of Morals, The Antichrist, Thus Spoke Zarathustra,* and *The Will to Power.*

47. See John Jackson's *Real Black: Adventures in Racial Sincerity* (Chicago: University of Chicago, 2005), in which he challenges the application of the term "authenticity" to willful subjects. To avoid the deployment of this term, with its essentialist trappings, Jackson instead uses "sincerity" to "add some nuance to contemporary considerations of social solidarity and identity politicking" (13).

48. James Weldon Johnson's "Lift Every Voice and Sing" (1921) is commonly known as the Negro National Anthem (see *African American Heritage Hymnal: 575 Hymns, Spirituals, and Gospel Songs* [Chicago: GIA Publications, 2001], 540).

49. Lincoln and Mamiya write: "The sermon, or more accurately, the *preaching* is the focal point of worship in the Black Church, and all other activities find their place in some subsidiary relationship. In most black churches music, or more precisely, *singing* is second only to preaching as the magnet of attraction and the primary vehicle of spiritual transport for the worshiping congregation" (346).

50. See David Buttrick's "Theology of Preaching," in *The Westminster Handbook of Reformed Theology,* ed. Donald K. McKim (Louisville: Westminster John Knox, 2001), 177–79. Cf. Anthony B. Pinn, *Embodiment and the New Shape of Black Theological Thought* (New York: NYU Press, 2010).

51. John 1:14.

52. Morrison, *Song of Solomon,* 336.

53. Song of Solomon 1:5.

54. Morrison, *Song of Solomon,* 319.

55. Psalm 96:1.

56. See "Eucharistic Prayer C," in *The Book of Common Prayer* of the Episcopal Church (New York: The Church Hymnal Corporation, http://www.bcponline .org); and "The Great Thanksgiving in a Service of Word and Table IV," in *The United Methodist Hymnal: Book of United Methodist Worship* (Nashville: United Methodist Publishing House, 1989).

57. 1 Corinthians 11:23–26. N.B.: One of Milkman's sisters is named "First Corinthians."

58. Cf. Morrison, *Beloved,* (1987; New York: Plume, 1988), particularly the postscript, 274–75.

59. Morrison, "Goodness: Altruism and the Literary Imagination," page 18 in this volume.

Quiet, as It's Kept and Lovingly Disrupted by Baby Suggs, Holy

On the Volume of Goodness in *Beloved*

JOSSLYN LUCKETT

> Expressions of goodness are never trivial or incidental in my
> writing. In fact, I want them to have life-changing properties
> and . . . they are seldom mute.
> —TONI MORRISON, "Goodness: Altruism and the Literary
> Imagination," Ingersoll Lecture 2012

In Toni Morrison's 1987 novel, *Beloved,* Sethe, a young, formerly enslaved mother who recently escaped her torturer's plantation, attempts to kill four children — two boys, two girls, all hers — rather than see them returned to the killing fields of Sweet Home, Kentucky. One daughter dies from a saw to her neck. She is Beloved. In southern Pennsylvania in 2006, Charles Carl Roberts attempts to kill ten Amish schoolgirls. Five die from shotgun blasts to the backs of their heads. Charles then kills himself.

By opening her Ingersoll Lecture on goodness and the literary imagination with a retelling of the story of the massacre of the Amish schoolgirls, Morrison forecasts an important directive of her address: "Thinking about goodness implies, indeed requires, a view of its opposite." In both stories of murdered children, there are still surprising and scene-stealing acts of generosity and mercy. Morrison remarks that the forgiveness of the killer by the Amish community was thought to be as "shocking as the killings themselves" and that the press "quickly ignored the killer and the slaughtered children and began to focus almost exclusively on the shock of forgiveness." The quiet with which the Amish community buried their girls, comforted the killer's widow and children, destroyed the schoolhouse, and built a new one seems "characteristic of genuine goodness" to Morrison. This event triggered for her a fascination with the definition of goodness, a definition that she chases, wrestles, and then illustrates throughout the Ingersoll Lecture by drawing on a dozen or so works of fiction, including four of her own novels, *Beloved* not included.

Not unlike the journalists who raced past the slaughtered children to cover the staggering grace of the forgiving Amish community, when I think about *Beloved,* I think first of the sounding goodness of Baby Suggs, holy, *here,* at the Clearing, *in this here place,* offering her clarifying word, *we flesh.* I lay it down, as instructed, and study war and murdered children no more. I want in on that Suggs-style ring shout. As an unchurched preacher myself, one as "unrobed" and untied to a single tradition as my homiletics mentor, Suggs, holy, I frequently return to her words for their divine and emancipating witness and wisdom. Devout and delighting, I forward as often as I'm able Reverend Baby's charge to laugh, to dance, to cry, and to love our hands, face, mouth, tongue, un-noosed neck, dark liver, womb and lungs and beating heart: "Hear me now, love your heart! For this is the prize."[1]

As Morrison makes clear in the lines from her Ingersoll address excerpted above, goodness in her novels includes "life-changing properties" and is "seldom mute." We feel and hear from Morrison's descriptions of the gatherings at the Clearing in *Beloved* that goodness is expansive and expressive. Goodness moves, makes noise, dances in sunlight, rings from trees, comes in four-part harmonies. Seldom mute, she insists, yet goodness can be "low," as in memories of conversation at Bluestone Road: "Talk was low and to the point,"[2] "healing, ease and real-talk,"[3] and Baby Suggs's voice in particular, "quiet (and) instructive."[4] Literary scholar Kevin Quashie, in *The Sovereignty of Quiet: Beyond Resistance in Black Culture,* considers these quieter expressions of goodness as an underutilized analytical framework for African American identity, culture, expression. The "dominant expectation" we have of black culture is, Quashie argues, resistance. He wonders "what a concept of quiet could mean to how we think about black culture . . . which is often described as expressive, dramatic or loud."[5] Quiet for Quashie is not interchangeable with silence or stillness, though. He considers quiet as a measure for interiority, a metaphor, he writes, "for the full range of one's inner life — one's desires, ambitions, hungers, vulnerabilities, fears." An aesthetic of quiet requires a shift "in how we read, what we look for" and listen for, "even what we remain open to."[6] In the pages ahead I consider the sound and volume of Baby Suggs, holy, listening for the life-changing goodness emanating from her beat and beating heart, even after its collapse. I attempt to highlight the practical wisdom we can and must glean from her message, her movement, her call-and-response with her community, and even her quiet. Finally, I consider the present urgency for communities to protect the great hearts like hers from collapse, so that in our solidarity *and* in our solitude, we won't miss the next dark and coming thing.

"My mother's voice is the reason why sound is so important to me when I write," Morrison recently explained in an interview with Davíd Carrasco, "because I can hear what's underneath the words." Her mother's singing voice, "the most beautiful voice I've ever heard in my life," came to her in multiple genres — opera, blues, and religious music — yet she emphasizes that it was from her mother's singing of hymns that Morrison learned religious language. Because of her deep listening and intimacy with her mother's singing, she could discern emotions — happiness, sadness — beneath the words. Morrison suggests that her mother's ability to communicate in these subtle ways is what "gave me the sense of how to write that way." We learn in this same interview that Morrison became a Catholic at age twelve because she was drawn to its aesthetics, "taken by the liturgy and the beauty." Through deep and intimate listening to the community convened at the Clearing in *Beloved,* we deepen our understanding of how Morrison's attention to sound, to emotion, and to the aesthetic dimensions of liturgy may have impacted her arrangement of the sacred and sonic offerings of Baby Suggs, holy, in that place.

This liturgy begins with a procession. Baby Suggs, holy, followed by "every black man, woman and child who could make it through," takes her "great heart" to the Clearing. She sits separately from the people; her natural, chosen throne is a huge, flat-sided rock. Her Clearing congregation is described as waiting among the trees. With reverence they give her space to prepare, to settle herself on the rock, to bow her head and pray, "silently." She does not stand when she is ready to begin, she simply sets her stick down and they know that she is ready. She ends the silence with a shouting invitation to the children, a call to worship. The first thing she wants them to do is laugh. "Let your mothers hear you laugh," she says. She calls for sound, a sound connecting the children to their mothers, creating joy for all. These days the idea of a preacher remaining seated is unusual to begin with; now, imagine a church where instead of children being forced to "hush," the first act of the service is a call for their audible laughter, a shout for them to make noise. Morrison includes the detail that this laughter within a sacred service invites not scowls but smiles. Everything is flipped in these opening moments, and everything requires full participation: moving, watching, listening. "Let your wives and children see you dance," she tells the men, and, "Cry," she tells the women who previously may have only privately grieved, if at all. Their tears are now "let loose," seen and heard by family and community, so much so they inspire others to cry. Their listening and connection create a space where all feel welcome to weep, laugh, and dance. Ultimately exhausted, the community returns to quiet.

Baby Suggs begins her sermon, much like she began her call to worship, after a period of silence. From that silence, and from her great heart, she offers up a prophetic word on grace. With no judgment, no lies, no directives to "sin no more," Reverend Baby invites her community to imagine, to seek a vision: "She told them that the only grace they could have was the grace they could imagine. That if they could not see it, they would not have it."[7] Then, as if to strengthen them for this radical interior work of imagining grace, she guides them through what these days might be read as an interfaith mash-up of a Black Lives Matter, liberation theology, Thich Nhat Hanh–inspired mindfulness body scan. It's black and loud and equal parts James Brown and James Cone proud (BSH: Love your hands! Raise them up! / BLM: Hands up! Don't shoot!).[8] It is also profoundly interior, drawing attention to the breath, the eyes, all the life-holding, life-giving, love-needing flesh. There is a deep relaxation body scan in Thich Nhat Hanh's *Creating True Peace* that, like Suggs at the Clearing, moves discreetly from hands to eyes to shoulders to the heart. Perhaps the Vietnamese monk and MLK comrade had recently read *Beloved* and stirred in a bit of Suggs, holy, in his section on the heart (TNH: Send your love to your heart . . . smile to your heart . . . get in touch with how wonderful it is to have a heart still beating in your chest . . . a marvelous organ / BSH: . . . the beat and beating heart, love that . . . hear me now, love your heart. For this is the prize.).[9] The inside and outside, the quiet and the shout synthesize then move away from language, from "the word" altogether when Baby Suggs finally stands. She completes the sermon with her body, dancing "with her twisted hip the rest of what her heart had to say."

Morrison does not mention the passing of a hat or any other monetary offering from the community to their celebrant, Suggs. We hear instead that the gathered community gifted her with music, accompanied her dancing with their four-part harmonies delivered perfectly from their deeply loved flesh. Yet, all at once, this order of worship as printed in *Beloved* is followed in the next paragraphs by the most shocking announcement. Baby Suggs, holy, soon after this sermon at the Clearing, dismissed her heart and the wisdom of her homily: "There was no grace — imaginary or real — and no sunlit dance in the Clearing could change that. Her faith, her love, her imagination and her great big old heart began to collapse."[10]

What good is good?

Morrison asks that question in her Ingersoll Lecture, and it could just as easily be a line of dialogue from Baby Suggs, holy, in this moment of heart collapse. Prior to the arrival of the four horsemen and the spilled blood of Sethe's children, Suggs would likely have taken offense to such a question: "What good is good? You askin' me, what good is good?" Then the asker might promptly be invited to the Clearing, a sacred space made possible and power-*full* by the quiet goodness of Baby's son, Halle, who worked five years of Sundays to purchase his mother's freedom, a freedom that allowed his mother to sit, to hear her heart for the first time, then put it to work so righteously. But now that voluptuous heart had collapsed.

This photo of Billie Holiday comes to mind whenever I get to the description of Suggs's great big heart collapsing. "What good is 'Good Morning Heartache'?," Holiday could easily be asking here. "What good is 'God Bless the Child' if there is no grace in my voice, no sun-lit dance slipping from my tongue to this microphone?" The image was photographed by fellow musician Milt Hinton at Holiday's final recording session in March 1959, four months before her death at the age of forty-four. Here Holiday's own collapsed heart makes it look as if she can hardly stand for the absence in her chest. My next thought when I see the photo and consider the great big old heart that produced that voice, so poignantly offered up to us for decades, is how did Holiday's community allow her heart to deflate like that? What could her community have done to bear better witness to its falling/failing and to respectfully work with her to revitalize it? Hinton said of the photos from that session that they were taken when Lady Day was listening to the playback of the tunes they were recording: "Looking at her I could see how disappointed she was about how she sounded. . . . Whenever she listened, her eyes would fill with tears and I had the feeling she was imagining how she had sounded twenty years earlier when she sang the same song."[11] Slight of voice or not, Holiday still attempted to offer up phrase after phrase of love on this recording. *"Do I love you, oh my do I, baby, deed I do,"* and *"If you let me love you, it's for sure I'm going to love you, all the way,"* and *"Give your heart and your love to whomever you love . . ."* and keep virtually anyone

FIG. 12. Milt Hinton, *Billie Holiday, Recording Studio, New York City, 1959.* (Courtesy of the Milton J. Hinton Photographic Collection, www.Milt Hinton.com)

who ever dared to sing this music going forward learning from her genius and generous approach.

Baby Suggs, holy, however, stopped cold. And to hear it from Stamp Paid, she never once looked back at the Clearing. Walking past 124 Bluestone Road, he thought about her "authority in the pulpit, her dance in the Clearing, her powerful Call" but concluded that "all of that had been mocked and rebuked by the bloodspill in her backyard." No matter how hard he pleaded with her, "You can't quit the Word, I don't care what all happen to you," she would not budge. She told him, "If I call them and they come, what on earth I'm going to say?"[12] As often as Baby Suggs asked the women to weep or told Sethe to "lay em down," she could not let this go. Or perhaps, unlike Holiday, was she unwilling to risk the volume of tears that might come upon hearing the sound of her collapsed and broken heart? Stamp Paid much later realized she was suffering from the kind of tired he now understood as "marrow weariness."[13] The horsemen, white people in general, had taken too much. "There was no bad luck in the world but white-people" she told Denver before she died. "They don't know when to stop."[14]

White people, the bad luck that just won't stop, Baby Suggs says at least twice in the novel. Just before the sermon at the Clearing there is a description of the bounty at Baby Suggs's home on 124 Bluestone Road before the horsemen came. It was a house buzzing with love, food, advice, and comfort, "not one but two pots simmered on the stove." But Morrison creates a tension even here between generous hospitality and excess. She writes that Baby Suggs "didn't approve of extra. 'Everything depends on knowing how much,' she said, and 'Good is knowing when to stop.'" After Morrison's Ingersoll Lecture, this last line holds new weight, begs the question, How much good is too good? And following Quashie, what role might quiet play in calibrating a community's capacity for receiving or absorbing goodness?

Grounding these ideas in the examples from the text and imagining a sonic goodness dial or Richter scale, the high-volume moments of goodness at the Clearing are tempered with moments of quiet and inward prayer, of patient observation, of trying on different sets of emotions. In contrast, the characterization of the feast at 124 is more akin to bingeing or eating at full volume rather than enjoying a well-paced and satisfying meal. Both host and guests indulged beyond the place where they could recognize — hear, see, or smell — dangerous excess.

In the final section of *Beloved,* it is once again the youngest child, in this case, Denver, who must go to work to set her mother, Sethe, free. Denver overcomes her fear to leave the yard at 124, to seek help from the community to protect her mother from the increasingly hostile ghost/daughter, Beloved. The Thirty Women, led by Ella, who had previously abandoned the family of women at 124, after the feast and before the horsemen, received Denver's call and responded, because a "rescue was in order."[15] The Thirty Women brought charms and magic, some Christian, some not, but mostly they brought their voices, voices they had been taught to love deeply and use effectively by the woman who had once fed them there. Baby Suggs quit before she died, believing there was no grace. But these Thirty Women pray, then holler, then organize their sounds in a way that cause Sethe to feel as though "the Clearing had come to her."[16] At the Clearing, Baby Suggs, holy, had once compelled these women to cry, *for the living and the dead,* and here they were at 124, doing just that: "The voices of women searched for the right combination, the key, the code, the sound that broke the back of words. Building voice upon voice until they found it, and when they did it was a wave of sound wide enough to sound deep water and knock the pods off chestnut trees. It broke over Sethe and she trembled like the baptized in its wash."[17]

Farah Jasmine Griffin writes about this sonic healing moment in "When Malindy Sings: A Meditation on Black Women's Vocality." She discerns that in a book so overwhelmed with bodies broken, the voice must emerge "as that part of the body and psyche best suited for creating and healing community." The healing harmonies and ghost-banishing hollers of the Thirty Women are within the tradition with which Griffin writes of black singing helping black people to "gather the strength to fight when they had no weapons; it invited and prepared the way for visitations from ancestors and the Holy Ghost."[18] Theologian Roxanne Reed imagines Baby Suggs, holy, as a Holy Ghost figure who returns in this moment of singing as the utterance itself, "in essence, the very embodiment of the word/sound itself that is key to the healing of the fractured community." Reed continues, "The heightened moment when the 'right combination' is found is simultaneous with the sound becoming song, and individual tongues becoming one collective tongue."[19] In a spirit of improvisation and deep listening, the women work together to find the right *life-changing* sound. In working this way, they also pay honor to the woman who taught them the power of this kind of sonic solidarity.

In the last couple of decades there has been an exciting body of work like Griffin's by scholars in jazz studies such as Tammy Kernodle, Karen Chilton, Ruth Feldstein, Franya Berkman, Sherrie Tucker, and Nichole Rustin that insists on looking at the lives of musicians like Holiday in the context of their collaborations with, influence on, mentoring of, support systems around other women musicians, composers, and arrangers. Much in the way that Baby Suggs's story does not end for Morrison with her collapsed heart, the work of these scholars would never tolerate the solo image of Holiday by Hinton, as powerful as it is, as the final word on her life and legacy.[20] There is a sense that the deep listening of these scholars' archival work on women musicians from Billie Holiday and Abbey Lincoln to Nina Simone, Melba Liston, Mary Lou Williams, and Alice Coltrane, which sheds light not only on their public artistry and activism but also their interior lives, provides some modeling about how we might listen closer to the great big hearts alive in our communities today and keep those hearts robust at all cost. Thich Nhat Hanh includes in his mindfulness body scan a line that says: "Breathe out and commit to live in a way that will help your heart to function well." This suggests for me that the healthy hearts of the Baby Suggs–style lovers require a community commitment to keep these hearts functioning well. The sounding goodness of Baby Suggs, holy, was impactful enough even after its collapse to gather the community to save Sethe and Denver. What manner of goodness might have emanated from Suggs's heart in her remaining years if the community had more immediately committed to keeping it healthy? Consider the roll call of the many Bluestone Roads, from urban centers to borderlands, urgently in need of visionaries like Baby Suggs, holy. Imagine their great big hearts kept robust by listening and collaborative communities, offering up the kind of four-part harmonies whose long notes cause murderous horsemen, slave catchers, and other perpetrators of state violence to stand down and to study war no more. Love those hearts. Protect those hearts. Yonder they do not love these hearts. *We* got to.

NOTES

1. Toni Morrison, *Beloved* (New York: Random House, 1987), 88–89.
2. Morrison, *Beloved*, 87.
3. Morrison, *Beloved*, 95.
4. Morrison, *Beloved*, 86.
5. Kevin Quashie, *The Sovereignty of Quiet: Beyond Resistance in Black Culture* (New Brunswick, NJ: Rutgers University Press, 2012), 3.

6. Quashie, *The Sovereignty of Quiet*, 6.

7. Morrison, *Beloved*, 88.

8. I use "BSH" here for Baby Suggs, holy, and "BLM" for Black Lives Matter.

9. Thich Nhat Hanh, "Restoring Body and Mind with Deep Relaxation," in *Creating True Peace: Ending Violence in Yourself, Your Family, Your Community, and the World* (New York: Free Press, 2003), 50–51.

10. Morrison, *Beloved*, 89.

11. This quote accompanies several images from the March 1959 recording session that have been preserved on a webpage devoted to Milt Hinton's music and photography: milthinton.com.

12. Morrison, *Beloved*, 177–78.

13. Morrison, *Beloved*, 180.

14. Morrison, *Beloved*, 104.

15. Morrison, *Beloved*, 256.

16. Morrison, *Beloved*, 261.

17. Morrison, *Beloved*, 261.

18. Farah Jasmine Griffin, "When Malindy Sings: A Meditation on Black Women's Vocality," in *Uptown Conversations: The New Jazz Studies*, ed. Robert G. O'Meally, Brent Hayes Edwards, and Griffin (New York: Columbia University Press, 2004), 110–11.

19. Roxanne R. Reed, "The Restorative Power of Sound: A Case for Communal Catharsis in Toni Morrison's *Beloved*," *Journal of Feminist Studies in Religion* 23, no. 1 (2007): 70.

20. See, for example, Farah Jasmine Griffin, *In Search of Billie Holiday: If You Can't Be Free, Be a Mystery* (New York: Ballantine, 2001); Tammy Kernodle, *Soul on Soul: The Life and Music of Mary Lou Williams* (Boston: Northeastern University Press, 2004); and see also Kernodle's work as part of the Melba Liston Research Collective at Columbia College in Chicago; Karen Chilton, *Hazel Scott: The Pioneering Journey of a Jazz Pianist from Café Society to Hollywood to HUAC* (Ann Arbor: University of Michigan Press, 2008); Ruth Feldstein, *How It Feels to Be Free: Black Women Entertainers and the Civil Rights Movement* (New York: Oxford University Press, 2013); Franya Berkman, *Monument Eternal: The Music of Alice Coltrane* (Middletown, CT: Wesleyan University Press, 2010); and Nichole T. Rustin and Sherrie Tucker, eds., *Big Ears: Listening for Gender in Jazz Studies* (Durham, NC: Duke University Press, 2008). Two images that come to mind that remind us of Holiday's own collaborations/friendship/mentoring relationships with other women musicians are one by William "Popsie" Randolph of Ella Fitzgerald with Holiday, found on the cover of his book, *Popsie: American Popular Music through the Camera Lens of William "Popsie" Randolph* (Milwaukee, WI: Hal Leonard, 2007) and also Roy de Carava's breathtaking 1957 image of Holiday with Hazel Scott, printed in *Roy De Carava: A Retrospective* (New York: Museum of Modern Art, 1996).

Writing Goodness and Mercy

A 2017 Interview with Toni Morrison

In August 2017, Davíd Carrasco interviewed Toni Morrison at her home on the Hudson River to explore further her thoughts about "Goodness: Altruism and the Literary Imagination," her Ingersoll Lecture at Harvard presented in 2012.

DAVÍD CARRASCO: Toni Morrison, your 2012 Ingersoll Lecture for the Harvard Divinity School was entitled "Goodness: Altruism and the Literary Imagination." In the first half of the lecture you also spoke feelingly about both good and evil. You asked why is evil, "so worshiped, especially in literature. Is it its theatricality, its costume, its blood spray?"

TONI MORRISON: I always thought the Nazis gained followers because of their uniforms.

CARRASCO: Uniforms?

MORRISON: Yes, the high boots, those pants. During that period in Germany many people were very poor. It was a lower-middle-class country and people were wearing the clothes from World War I. But the Nazis had this design, and those uniforms were fabulous. People are still playing off the fashion of those caps and those high, shiny leather boots. The people felt they had to respect, almost worship the Nazis because of that. That's the nature of evil, it's theatrical, and people admire theatrical violence and try to get on the best side, the winning side, in part because it has a handsome costume, it has panache.

CARRASCO: In your lecture, you juxtapose this theatrical evil with how goodness appears and is valued in literature. You say, "Evil has a blockbuster audience: Goodness lurks backstage."

MORRISON: In a lot of literature, goodness is like this big bore. It doesn't do anything; it just doesn't hurt you! It might step out and help you, but, who cares? So, I thought, rather than just having an attitude about goodness and its portrayal and feeling bothered by how backstage goodness is, I wanted to really talk about the nature of it and to explore

FIG. 13. Justin Knight, *Morrison in Motion.* (Courtesy of Harvard University)

examples, extreme examples of goodness even, like the Amish who after the murder of those five girls at the Nickel Mines School refused to seek vengeance. Rather, they went and helped the murderer's widow and her children, and asked, "What do you need?" That attitude, that response moved me to explore the nature of goodness, of altruism.

CARRASCO: You said once about black folks responding to slavery, "the story is that the people who were treated like beasts did not become beastly." A big part of the African American response to centuries of brutality was new cultural forms in music, dance, church life, nonviolence, and social criticism.

MORRISON: They chose creation.

We have generation after generation of enslaved people, and they do their work, and they sing, and they create things — jazz, the blues, schools, ideas — and they become a culture that this country could not do without. Can you imagine America without black people in it, or the residue of their lives? You ask any European about America without blacks, and to them it's unimaginable.

CARRASCO: What you say reminds me of what the French philosopher Paul Ricoeur said he learned after he came to teach at US universities. For him the history of America is a "strange history." The immigrants came to a land that was already inhabited by Native Americans whom they exterminated or pushed onto reservations. The immigrants brought along other immigrants by force, the Africans who were the slaves and helped build American wealth. He claims that "it is a singular history that has no equivalent in Europe."

MORRISON: It's an American thing. Erase the native peoples to get their land and put the slaves to work to build the country.

CARRASCO: In your lecture, you explore three definitions of goodness, of altruism. The first definition is "goodness taught and learned"—the habit of helping strangers or taking risks for neighbors. My question is, Where in the African American community, and in your novels, is the socialization for goodness most expressive?

MORRISON: Some of this socialization for goodness was in the church and the community itself. My mother was an avid churchgoer, and I became a Catholic when I was twelve, not for any sane reason but because my best friend was a Catholic. I liked the aesthetics of being in the Catholic church, and so my mother agreed. I was taken by the liturgy and the beauty. That church setting taught me a social closeness, and I learned black people's assumptions of the ways people should treat each other.

CARRASCO: Where did you learn the religious language that sometimes appears in your writing?

MORRISON: I learned religious language through the hymns and the sermons. My mother was a serious singer. She had the most beautiful voice I've ever heard in my life, better than everybody else. She sang opera, the blues, and religious music. She not only sang in the church, she sang all the time, when she was cooking, sweeping, hanging out clothes. The religious content, the stories of her songs came to me in beauty.

CARRASCO: Did growing up around that voice, that inspiring language with religious meanings, influence your writing?

MORRISON: My mother's voice is the reason why sound is so important to me when I write, because I can hear what's underneath the words.

When she sang, I could hear if she was sad, I could hear if she was happy, and her ability to communicate that way gave me a sense of how to write that way. I know how I feel when I get something right in my writing, and now I wonder if my interior feeling is like hers when she sang in very satisfying ways, in ways that lifted her and us up in our little lower-middle-class lives. I grew up hearing those hymns and sermons in church, full of uplifting language, eloquence, and meaning,

CARRASCO: So, in Lorain, Ohio, where you grew up, the church was a social force for goodness?

MORRISON: I learned that there are different kinds of Christianity, and in each kind the communication between people and their churches was very important. There were many churches in my hometown, mainly because it was such a mixture of immigrants from Europe, black folks from Canada, and families like ours from the South. There were, I think, three Protestant churches including Episcopal, Methodist, and a bunch of Catholic churches including eastern European. There were three black churches, AME Zion, AME, and what we called "Holy Roller." There was a lot of churchgoing. You know what? There was only one high school, where we were all mixed together. We shared in our learning experiences — black, white, Italian, Polish, Mexican, and more. But the only time that you were separate culturally was Sunday, when everybody went to their different church. Very little separation in school, but on Sundays, we all went to our own churches to hear different sermons and sing different hymns.

CARRASCO: Beyond church, what did the black community in Lorain teach you about good and evil?

MORRISON: I learned the ways black people treated even their masters with some respect — I mean the white folks they worked for in and around my hometown. I saw how black people worked with great skill and attention. When I was young I didn't give it all a lot of credit. But I realized over time, they knew how to survive, teach each other love, and they also knew who the villains were.

CARRASCO: In your first novel, *The Bluest Eye,* we see an extraordinary example of this kind of dedicated African American worker in the character of Pauline Breedlove. She's known to the white family she cooks and cleans for as Polly. She works hard and with skill for that white family, and they refer to her as the "ideal servant" they will never let go. Of course, they do let her go once a bit of the reality of the struggle of her family shows itself.

MORRISON: Yes, it becomes clearer to her who the villains are.

CARRASCO: Would you say that in your church and community, one of the forms of goodness was to speak out against the evil that was also going on?

MORRISON: I was recently talking with a colleague about children who had been molested by their parents, by their fathers. I recalled that I had a friend, a girlfriend who had been raped by her father. I didn't know it at the time, when I was a kid, but learned about it later. There were six or seven children in that family, and they were all molested by the father except the last one. The youngest one mentioned it to a teacher, and that man, that father, ended up in jail. I remember during that time, the women in the community, including my mother, hated his wife for not protecting her children, but him. They didn't expect much from him, but she knew.

CARRASCO: She knew and stood by—

MORRISON: And didn't do anything! Their contempt for her and their rage was unbelievable. They knew where the problem was. And I learned as time went on through these expressions about dissent and love and justice. There were confrontations, and they were often driven by a striving for goodness.

CARRASCO: Your comments about goodness versus evil take me to the end of your novel *Love,* where two elderly women, violated by a man when they were best friends as children, are locked in a life-and-death struggle.

MORRISON: I wanted to discover and write about the best lovers. I thought, Who are the people who really love?, and it occurred to me, it was children. When one child falls in love with another, it doesn't care if the other has any money, what the other looks like. It's pure. It's goodness before socialization. In *Love,* I wanted to show the destruction of that love in order to show how wonderful it was. At the end of the story, the two old women—Heed and Christine—are comforting each other as one of them is dying. They are talking about their childhood and what was taken from them, and one says about the domineering character, Bill Cosey, "He took all my childhood away from me, girl." And the other answers, "He took all of you away from me." Soon after that, the word "love" is mentioned for the *only time* in the book — at the very end. What I wanted to do in writing that way was show what happens when love is corrupted by other people. Show its corruption and then show its purity at the end. I think that scene is a good definition of goodness.

CARRASCO: There is a religious tinge to what Heed and Christine share because in the novel you called that passion between the children "a holy feeling." A holy feeling that they expressed in their private language of reversal that reappears at the end:

"Love, I really do.
Ush-hidagay. Ush-hidagay."

MORRISON: Their private language was one way they expressed their closeness and deep caring. That phrase translates to a tender "Hush. Hush."

CARRASCO: Following up on this holy love between Heed and Christine as expressions of an almost primal goodness, I want to ask whether one gender, the female gender, is more the source of good than evil in your novels. Men and women are both well-rounded characters in your writing, but do women, in fact, bring more goodness along the way?

MORRISON: Women do good *and* evil in my novels, but it's true that in *Home* the women of Lotus, Georgia, save the life of Cee, who had never paid those kinds of women, neighbors of hers, any mind earlier in her life. When her brother, Frank Money, rescues her from that mad eugenicist, Doctor Scott, the women take over, and they treat her with their folk medicine and tell her something very important — it's a nice little sermon in there. They tell her life ain't good, but . . . and she listens. It's a learning process for both of them, Frank and Cee, against all kinds of resistance. Frank didn't want to go back to Lotus. He hates that town in the beginning, and he goes off to the Korean War, where he experiences some terrible things. Then he has to go rescue his sister. When he returns to Lotus, the description of the town is full of flowers, and beauty, and women gardening. It's like it's an entirely different place. So, there is goodness in the women and in the place itself.

CARRASCO: While we're discussing *Home,* I'd like to ask you about a figure who appears to Frank throughout the novel and reappears again in your novel *Love.* The zoot suiter relates to my tradition as a Mexican American and yours as an African American. A zoot suiter appears at the wedding in *Love,* just once, and he's a real person. Then, in *Home,* he appears as a kind of spirit three times: on the train, in the room at the preacher's house, and at the end when they bury the bones.

MORRISON: He watches.

CARRASCO: So, what does he represent for you? Is he a devil? Is he a cool guy? Where does the zoot suiter come from in *Home?* What does he mean?

MORRISON: He just inserted himself when I was writing the novel. That's the second time that happened to me. It's true. The zoot suiter, for me, when I was a teenager, was hip, knowledgeable, cool, all those things. And he wore these outrageous suits with those big shoulders. Soon, even white guys began to put on those clothes with those big shoulders and hats. When the zoot suiters appeared, it was so startling and sudden, it was right after World War II. I just thought, "Where did that come from?" I knew it started in California, but it was such a shocking thing, because they were black men who just changed the fashion all by themselves.

CARRASCO: And the Mexicans picked it up.

MORRISON: Right. So, this zoot suiter is a guy who appears as a kind of stable and unstable figure when there's something troubling Frank. The zoot suiter, at least for the reader, if not for Frank, who doesn't see him at the end, expresses that quality of revolution, and evolution.

CARRASCO: Which Frank is going through in the novel.

MORRISON: Yes, and that is what the appearances mean. Even at the end when Frank and his sister Cee finally bury the bones of the murdered black man. Remember at the start of the novel they are kids hiding on their stomach in the tall grass when the white men throw the black man's body in the ground. At the end they are standing up together, and the zoot suiter is there to watch because he approves of it.

CARRASCO: Can you talk more about the males and their struggle to do some good in their world?

MORRISON: Well, I had to finish two books before I was able to write a book with men as major characters, in *Song of Solomon*. I was a little afraid to write about men because I didn't know the masculine world as an insider. Then my father died, and before I began writing it, I remembered thinking, "I wonder what my father knew about men." He'd said nothing to me about that world. Yet I felt an avenue would open up for me and that he would let me know in his own way. As I started to write the novel, I felt strong enough to write with men as central characters and get it right.

CARRASCO: Did your father, your memory of him, help you?

MORRISON: You know I didn't know any of my father's friends' real names. I knew their nicknames and some of them were negative, some of them were very positive. There is a kind of teaching about the history of black people in these names. Names like Duke, Lover, Cool Breeze, and I remember one man who was called Jim the Devil.

CARRASCO: Jim the Devil?

MORRISON: And they said all of it. "Hey, Jim the Devil." We didn't have a straight line of names. There were slave names and masters' names and all that. My maiden name is Wofford. There is Wofford College, there is a Senator Wofford.

CARRASCO: So, powerful Woffords?

MORRISON: Yes, it's a big deal. Every black person's name that's "legitimate," in quotes, is probably a name that's imbued with slavery. I reflected this in the names I gave the men in *Song of Solomon*: Milkman Dead, Guitar Bains, and others. What I'm trying to say is, in the community, in the church, even by using these names, like Jim the Devil, they made you face the worst, but with love!

CARRASCO: Fascinating that these names were also a kind of socialization, a way of teaching and knowing the villains in one's slave history and its aftermath. Like, who made Jim into the devil, and by calling him that it took some of the danger out of him and put some humor in the name.

MORRISON: You know, men are very good to each other. Women are good to *both* women and men. The men will take a bullet for each other, but not for a woman like me.

CARRASCO: That's so true. Women are good to women *and* men.

MORRISON: That's right. Men are good to each other. They think about women that "If you come along, it's all right," but the woman is not the point. The point is to stand up with, for, another man, to be buddies, to be comrades, someone they'll die for. In a war, they're killing, killing, killing, but the stories are not about who they kill, it's about who they loved and died for. The war story is about who you fought with, who you rescued or dragged to some place.

CARRASCO: Do you have an example in your writing?

MORRISON: I have a character, a soldier in this book I'm currently writing. He's really an awful husband, he drinks a lot, and is violent. I was trying to write about his war experiences and his closeness to the other men in his unit. They know each other well, and they love each other. At some point, his buddy, his best friend, gets killed, and he crawls over to him on the battlefield. Mind you, I had to study some pictures of blasted bodies. To write about it you've got to know what that looks like. Horrible.

He crawled over to his buddy who was split and blown up, but sometimes, despite great physical trauma, the heart doesn't stop right away. The heart might keep pumping for some time.

When my character reaches the body of his dead friend he embraces him and hears his heartbeat, and it stays beating. Afterwards, when he goes home, every night, he hears that heartbeat.

CARRASCO: He hears it every night?

MORRISON: And every day. And the only thing that makes it quiet is when he drinks; then it gets a little softer. That heartbeat is the physicality, as well as the emotion, as well as the residue of these veterans. Only other veterans understand what he's been through. Only they understand each other.

CARRASCO: I've known vets like that who return home, and they're with their families in their houses, but they're still thinking about, obsessing over their buddies, and they talk about reenlisting so they can go over and be with the other guys in their unit, in the danger.

MORRISON: These expressions of violence—it's a man thing. Well, I shouldn't say that, because women can be very violent, particularly in romantic situations.

CARRASCO: I want to reverse my question about the socialization of goodness and ask about the socialization of evil in the African American community. From your first novel, *The Bluest Eye,* and through your latest, *God Help the Child,* you write about black people who have been taught and then internalized negative and sometimes destructive views of themselves.

MORRISON: When I was eight or nine I had a girlfriend, and walking down the street one day, we had this semi-quarrel about whether God existed—the way you would at eight years of age. And I said, yes, God exists, and she said, no, he doesn't, and we went back and forth, and she said she had proof. I said, "What is it?" And she said, "I have been praying for blue eyes for two years and he didn't give them to me. So, he doesn't exist, right?"

I looked at her, and I tell you, for the very first time, David, you don't think of beauty when you're eight, you think maybe cute or something, and I looked at this girl who was pitch black, exquisitely beautiful, big eyes, high cheekbones, beautiful lips, she was just gorgeous, and that's the first time I saw that evil we call racism. At the same time, I thought, well, if she had blue eyes she'd look horrible. I mean, I knew that would ruin the way she looked. So, when I was writing *The Bluest Eye,* I was thinking about the protagonist Pecola Breedlove living with that horror, the yearning to be white. You know what I mean? I felt that this yearning is truly destructive, it still is. And so, *The Bluest Eye* is about that kind of evil, about who might rescue her, but told from the child's point of view. We didn't hug her, we didn't embrace her, we didn't, in the book, not that girl. In the book, Claudia MacTeer says about Pecola, "We tried to see her without looking at her, and never, never went near." It's venom, it's a form of poison. As I write toward the end, "The damage done was total."

CARRASCO: This example of Pecola being socialized into self-hatred by imbibing lessons of white supremacy reminds me of a powerful paragraph in *The Bluest Eye* about black ugliness. Here it is:

It was as though some mysterious all-knowing master had given each one a cloak of ugliness to wear, and they each accepted it without question. The master had said, "You are ugly people." They had looked about themselves and saw nothing to contradict the statement; saw, in fact, support for it leaning at them from every billboard, every movie, every glance. "Yes," they had said. "You are right." And they took ugliness in their hands, threw it as a mantle over them and went about the world with it.

It's a "conviction" as you say. But it becomes more than a social conviction, Toni. It's a cosmological conviction; it's how beliefs that have a religious power are constructed. And the white master, or any master, is like God.

MORRISON: Yes, this is the depth of the destructive power, how blacks get their view of themselves.

CARRASCO: And that view of themselves is so overpowering, it overpowers empirical reality.

MORRISON: Look at these girls now who walk around with unstraightened hair. They already look good, really good. So, I guess if you live long enough, maybe you see some real changes, and I do think that this contempt for the self, because you're black, is really moving away, melting a little bit.

CARRASCO: We come to the second definition of goodness that you were exploring in the Ingersoll Lecture, which is very different from the first. It isn't goodness at all but rather a "form of narcissism, ego enhancement, or even a mental disorder." Your example in the lecture is the character Soaphead Church, alias Elihue Micah Whitcomb, in *The Bluest Eye*. Soaphead is an avid reader of the classics, and you signal his narcissism and ego enhancement when you write, "For all his exposure to the best minds of the Western world, he allowed only the narrowest interpretation to touch him." In Soaphead Church, we gain insight into your concern for the religious orientations of African American people. Soaphead has failed at everything — career, marriage, sex — but he's got a charisma in his voice and ability to con people when he advertises that he can "Overcome Spells, Bad Luck, and Evil Influences." Discovering his celibacy, the women of Lorain, Ohio, "decided that he was supernatural rather than unnatural." Toward the end of the novel Soaphead writes a letter to God. Pecola has prayed for blue eyes, wishes for it as a miracle, and goes to Soaphead Church in search of his strange magic. He cons her into unknowingly killing a bothersome neighbor's dog, further damaging her crippled mind. Soon after that he writes his "Dear God" letter in the form of a critique of the Almighty and a sermon of self-justification for the damage he has done.

MORRISON: Soaphead is a deeply disappointed, disturbed man.

CARRASCO: He's disappointed, and some of his critique about the suffering of little girls and how God has forgotten them makes his letter like a sermon, maybe the first sermon you wrote in novels.

MORRISON: It may be the first real sermon in my novels. It must be taken seriously, and his letter shows one of the ways in which we define God. In Soaphead's letter, I wrote his vision of what he thinks God *ought* to be like. There should be no suffering. He implores, How can you, God, do this to small children, leave them sitting by the "shoulders of the road, crying next to their dead mothers. I've seen them charred, lame, halt. You forgot, Lord. You forgot how and when to be God." He's not blaming other people, and he's not taking responsibility for his abuse of little girls and others who come to him for help. Who put these children on the side of the road to starve? You saw those little kids during the Vietnam War burned by military napalm. That isn't God, that's us.

CARRASCO: There are several sermons in your books where God is invoked. I want to ask about the art of writing those sermons. Is writing a sermon like writing a novel?

MORRISON: Yes. Sermons were mainly songs for me. It's the same sort of thing as writing a novel. Sermonizing is an art; it's artful. It may look like somebody just standing up there rapping, but it's more than that.

CARRASCO: Which of the sermons you've written most closely reflects your own beliefs or theology?

MORRISON: In *Paradise,* I had those two preachers: the older, more conservative Reverend Pulliam of the Methodist Church in the all-black town of Ruby, Oklahoma, and the younger, more progressive Reverend Misner at Mount Calvary Baptist Church. When Reverend Pulliam preaches, he is cussing everybody out: "If you say God loves you, he doesn't. You have to earn God. God isn't just out here for you." He says at one point: "You have to earn God. You have to practice God. You have to think God — carefully." And then Reverend Misner, the other, more modern preacher, just stands up and holds the cross. He preaches silently that not only is God interested in you; He *is* you."

I sort of agree with Reverend Pulliam's sermon in *Paradise*. God isn't interested in you.

CARRASCO: He's too powerful to be interested in you.

MORRISON: You have to be interested *in him*.

CARRASCO: People think of you as a writer of black life and the legacy of slavery. But your novels are full of paragraphs about nature, the ocean, the forest, flowers, and plants. And their connection to human life, struggle, pleasure.

MORRISON: Yes, they're connected. Human beings can fail us, hurt us, like they do in *Paradise*. Nature, I suppose you can have a volcano or something, but generally speaking, it's restorative and it's accessible, and it's not just there for the aesthetics, which help, but it's also what it does for us. I have a greenhouse in my home, and I used to spend hours down there with the radio on, repotting and tending my plants. There I found solitude and belonging, the sense of belonging in this place. A sense that you control a bit of life, because you care for plants. That sense of control is not easily come by in the regular world.

CARRASCO: What about the ways you write the "supernatural" into the natural world in your novels? What you called "all the strange stuff" in your writing. You've got those storm clouds and "Police-heads" just off-shore rearing up out of the ocean to drown people in *Love*. Here's how you refer to them: "creatures called Police-heads — dirty things with police hats who shoot up out of the ocean to harm loose women and eat disobedient children." The marigolds don't come up in the Ohio town the year of Pecola's rape by her father in *The Bluest Eye*. You write, "Quiet as its kept, there were no marigolds in the fall of 1941. . . . [W]e could think of nothing but our own magic, if we planted the seeds, and said the right words over them, they would blossom, and everything would be all right." Magical flight is a theme that runs through *Song of Solomon*, and Guitar and Milkman are flying in the last scene. Again, in *Love*, the ghost narrator known only as "L" says, "*The ocean is my man, now . . . and he's a tenor*," signaling a spiritual and sexual tie to the water. This kind of writing reminds me of the great Colombian writer Gabriel García Márquez.

MORRISON: Oh, yes, he taught me.

CARRASCO: What did he teach you about this way of writing?

MORRISON: When I read his book *One Hundred Years of Solitude*, I literally said, "Oh, my God, you can do this"—meaning magic, strange stuff—and be deadly serious. So, that freed me up in my writing. I realized that I could have somebody flying, or a version of it, or have people burn each other up, and more. I felt for the first time that I could follow the emotional train and close it with something that's not in nature, something outside of that. I became aware of a freedom in writing. Reading him unlocked something important for me.

CARRASCO: Can you say more about this freedom?

MORRISON: Yes. The first line of *One Hundred Years of Solitude*. You read it and marvel.

CARRASCO: The first line goes, "Many years later, while facing the firing squad, Colonel Aureliano Buendía was to remember that distant afternoon when his father took him to discover ice."

MORRISON: Right. I mean, everything's there, everything.

Nobody was writing like that at the time, nobody was. I didn't see anybody in modern writing doing that way. It was just some version of Milton or something. But to write a contemporary novel and say that and mean it!

CARRASCO: Like García Márquez, you don't marginalize spirits, ghosts, phantoms. They aren't foolishness or foreign to everyday life. In *Beloved,* the ghost of the murdered baby becomes flesh. In *Love,* the dead hotel owner Bill Cosey haunts his mansion and its occupants, his widow Heed and his granddaughter Christine carry on a dialogue forever after Heed's death, farmer Vaark comes out of his grave and walks around the big house. And so, how did that fit with what you grew up with in the black community?

MORRISON: There were lots of ghost stories, which were a kind of early-afternoon pleasure with the children and the grown-ups. We would say to the grown-ups, Tell that story about . . . , and it'd be the same story, but you could edit it and change it, and most of them were ghost stories. A man cuts his wife's head off, and then she comes back with her head in her arms. And she says, "It's cold out here, it's cold out here." And the husband says, "Go on some place and warm yourself." In these fairy tales, there were no happy children's stories. "Hansel and Gretel,"

"Jack and the Beanstalk," they were all about death and destruction. And in the black community we had these other stories that were not written down, but were told, and we children repeated them. Tell that story about . . . , and you felt you had to hear it and you could modify it a little bit. And then, they would say, go on upstairs and go to bed, and we did, scared to death.

CARRASCO: Did García Márquez contribute to your writing in other ways?
MORRISON: Oh, he was so funny. He came to Princeton and visited my class for a week. He taught in the class about writing stories. One of the class requirements was you must be bilingual and speak good Spanish and good English. But neither one of us was bilingual! The students were, and I learned something I didn't know about the varieties of Spanish. There was not only a difference between those Spanish speakers from Spain versus the Spanish speakers from Mexico. There was also tension among Spanish as spoken throughout Latin America including the Caribbean. Not only is the language different in the writing, you can hear it in the speaking.

FIG. 14. Mauricio Chavez, *Morrison as Storyteller with Friends* (Gabriel García Márquez and Carlos Fuentes). (Courtesy of the photographer)

CARRASCO: You and García Márquez met at least three times, twice in Mexico and once for that week in Princeton.

MORRISON: He was fantastic. What a joy he was.

CARRASCO: There is a wonderful photo of you, García Márquez, and Carlos Fuentes on a couch together at Fuentes's home the first time you met. Gabo, as García Márquez is known, is gazing at you as though in a swoon. Fuentes has wide open eyes in amazement, and you are animated while telling a story.

MORRISON: Oh, I love that photograph.

CARRASCO: I'm interested in the powerful role that places play in your writing. You wrote a novel entitled *Home.* In *Sula* you open with, "In that place ... called the Bottom." *Beloved* opens with 124 Bluestone Road, and the little girls in *Love* create a playhouse out of a boat on the beach which they name "Celestial's Palace." What does "home" mean to you across your novels? After all, Toni, as you write in *The Bluest Eye,* "Outdoors, we knew, was the real terror of life."

MORRISON: Home is shelter, but it's also comfort. It's where you really belong. It's like skin, almost. It's where you really are at your best, and you do your best. It doesn't mean some extraordinary thing, but you are the best human being you can be when you're at home. Now, for me, it has another meaning, I think, because we moved so much. My son tells me I'm doing the same thing because I must've lived in seven houses. Anyway, where I live now on the Hudson River, where we are now *is* home, I finally found home. For me it's not things. It's place. You know when you've arrived, a person knows when he's arrived. Home can be anywhere; it can even be outside, on a beach. It's where the comfort is, and the knowledge of belonging. This place is mine, mine, and will always be, that's all.

CARRASCO: Returning to the Ingersoll Lecture, you explore a third definition of goodness. You explore whether goodness is "an embedded gene automatically firing to enable the sacrifice of one's self for the benefit of others, a kind of brother or sister to Darwin's 'survival of the fittest.'"

MORRISON: It was a realization that people will endanger themselves to protect other people or children. You don't have to think about it; you just do it. It is as though you don't have to teach anybody that kind of sacrifice.

CARRASCO: In your view, then, this capacity for sacrifice is deeply located in life.

MORRISON: It's the same for birds and many animals, one sacrifices so the others can get away.

CARRASCO: Given this observation, would you say your moral imagination is focused primarily on the human-to-human relationships, or does it include a wider view of the moral universe to include human and nonhuman, human and nature?

MORRISON: It's a wide worldview. As you quoted earlier, L says in *Love,* "Now the ocean is my man . . . he's a tenor." I don't know why other people don't feel that about nature. They want to conquer it, use it up for profit; people want to ski through it without noticing, and they want to shoot it. In the theater, in movies, and on television, the relationship between humans and nature is more often about conquest, not seduction. For me, the moral imagination of nature in my writings is about recognition, revelation, and somehow, love. It's true that there are awful accidents in nature, but they result in combinations of survival, death, and sometimes triumph. It's all in there.

CARRASCO: Your comments about goodness, sacrifice, and evil lead me to ask you about what can be called your "moral imagination" as a writer. In *A Mercy,* for example, what we refer to as religiosity is used to both protect and harm people. One character has a reaction against slavery that the narrator connects to religious formation. A passage reads, "The dregs of his kind of Protestantism recoiled at the whips, chains, and armed overseers." We also learn that a Native American character, orphaned by the violence of white settlers, was raised by "kindly Presbyterians." So, the reader might get the impression that religious ethics are a resource for goodness. But that's not always the case. In the same novel, a young woman thinks, watching her mistress, "she will whip me too as she believes her piety demands." Are you showing us something about the ways in which religion can serve multiple ends? Given this paradox, do you lean toward a voice of goodness at the end of your novels?

MORRISON: I do strive to give goodness its own speech in my novels. I know this won't annihilate evil, but it shows my understanding of goodness, which is the acquisition of self-knowledge. The protagonist really does learn something morally insightful that she or he did not know earlier on. That's what I call a happy ending. The characters go through things as we all do, but they learn something they would not have ever learned. It's a real acquisition of knowledge.

CARRASCO: Thank you, Toni, for the knowledge you share with us.

CONTRIBUTORS

DAVÍD CARRASCO is a Mexican American historian of religion, and Mesoamericanist scholar. He holds the inaugural Neil L. Rudenstine Professor of the Study of Latin America with a joint appointment at Harvard Divinity School and in the Department of Anthropology in the Faculty of Arts and Sciences, and is the author of *City of Sacrifice: The Aztec Empire and the Role of Violence in Civilization.*

BIKO MANDELA GRAY is an Assistant Professor of Religion at Syracuse University College of Arts and Sciences. His research is at the intersection between continental philosophy of religion and theories and methods in African American religion.

WALTER JOHNSON is an American historian who teaches history and directs the Charles Warren Center at Harvard University as Winthrop Professor of History and Professor of African American Studies.

CHARLES H. LONG is the preeminent historian of religion in the United States. He has served on the faculties at the University of Chicago, the University of North Carolina at Chapel Hill, Syracuse University, and, most recently, the University of California at Santa Barbara, where he is a Professor Emeritus.

JOSSLYN JEANINE LUCKETT is an Assistant Professor in the Department of Cinema Studies at NYU's Tisch School of the Arts. Her research interests include and combine media studies, jazz and improvisation studies, and comparative and relational ethnic studies, with special attention to the intersection of race, media, and social justice.

TIYA ALICIA MILES is a Professor of History at Harvard University and Radcliffe Alumnae Professor at the Radcliffe Institute for Advanced Study. She is a public historian, academic historian, and creative writer whose work explores the intersections of African American, Native American, and women's histories.

JACOB K. OLUPONA, a scholar of African religions, is a Professor of African Religious Traditions, Harvard Divinity School, with a joint appointment as a Professor of African and African American Studies in the Faculty of Arts and Sciences at Harvard University.

STEPHANIE PAULSELL is the Susan Shallcross Swartz Professor of the Practice of Christian Studies at Harvard Divinity School. She is the author of *Religion around Virginia Woolf* and *Honoring the Body: Meditations on a Christian Practice;* coauthor, with Harvey Cox, of *Lamentations and the Song of Songs;* and coeditor of *The Scope of Our Art: The Vocation of the Theological Teacher.*

MATTHEW POTTS, an Associate Professor of Religion and Literature at Harvard Divinity School, studies the thought and practice of contemporary Christian communities through attention to diverse literary, theological, and liturgical texts.

JONATHAN L. WALTON is the Plummer Professor of Christian Morals and the Pusey Minister in the Memorial Church of Harvard University. He is the author of *A Lens of Love: Reading the Bible in Its World for Our World.*

MARA WILLARD, a Visiting Assistant Professor at Boston College's Morrissey College of Arts and Sciences, serves their International Studies Program in the area of religion, theology, and ethics. Her research focuses on the intersection of religion, ethics, and politics in the twentieth century.

GERALD "JAY" WILLIAMS is lead pastor at Union United Methodist Church in Boston's South End. An ordained Elder in The United Methodist Church, Jay has also served congregations in New York City and San Francisco. His research explores the meaning of "Spirit" in black cultural discourse at the intersection of race, class, gender, and sexuality, particularly how spirit-talk has been a marginalizing language of power. Through his pastoral and academic work, Jay strives to help more disinherited folk find their voices.

INDEX

Italicized page numbers refer to illustrations.

meaning of, 1, 81–82, 93–94, 242; personal experience of, 85. *See also* return to homeland

Home, 81–98; as bildungsroman of pilgrimage, 9, 87–90; choice of character names in, 84–85; coming home in, 93–96; *communitas* (space and time in pilgrimage journey) in, 89, 92; compassion in support of community members in, 18; difference between the given and the possible in, 90–93; disjunctive structure of, 83; dread and caring in, 87; epigraph's role in, 84–87, 90, 91; "have mercy" in, 2; horses in combat in, 86–87, 88–89, 92; human capacity to exceed in, 5; human orientation and knowledge of belonging in, 85–86, 93–94, 96–97; initiatory ritual structure in, 88, 92; Korean War service of Frank in, 82, 83, 87, 90, 94, 96; place, understanding of, 242; possible influences on Morrison while writing, 123; religious motifs in, 3–4, 5, 88, 162; secret burial of black man in, 86–87, 88–89, 92, 96, 234; women as source of goodness in, 232–33; zoot suiter as spirit in, 233

Hooker, Dr. Olivia, 157

Horne, Gerald, 25

Hughes, Jennifer Scheper, "Cradling the Sacred," 108, 114n37

human belonging, 85–86, 93–94, 96–97, 116–17, 127–29, 131–32, 242

human capacity to exceed, 5, 7

human dignity and humanity, 1, 31, 49, 58n17, 87

humor and laughter, 16, 18, 30, 31, 143, 144, 186, 217–19, 234, 241

Hunter, Marcus, 210n7

Hurston, Zora Neale, 168

hymns, 101, 218, 229–30. *See also* "Stabat Mater" (poem and hymn)

identity: of African Americans, 37, 40; dual identity, 37, 48–49; of the other, 53–54. *See also* Africanity; other, the, and othering

imagery and literary devices: "Africa," use of word, 48–49; America's large spaces in black experience, 86; animals used for human characters, 121; birth metaphors in *Sula*, 110; in *The Bluest Eye*, 50; choice of character names in *Home*, 84–85; clear-cutting metaphor, 28, 31–32; for colonial America's capitalism in *Mercy*, 142–44; cross and Christian religion, 49, 162–63; lock symbolism, 84; physical and natural sources in Morrison's imagery, 37, 47–49; pilgrimage as departure from home, 89; power of, 53; religious motifs in *Home*, 3–4, 5, 88; roots and branches metaphor, 44; Song of Songs and Christian metaphors, 105, 205, 213n29; symbiotic relationships of slavery and freedom, darkness and light, flesh and Spirit, 170–73. *See also* landscapes; pietà

imagination: black religious imagination, 6; humanist imagination of Morrison, 117; "imagination of otherness," 118; moral imagination, 243–44; opening of religious imagination, 115n48; spiritual imaginary and, 118, 121, 123

Imbrie, Ann E., 101

immigration: Europeans' effect on American history, 94, 143, 229; of free Africans to America, 37, 42, 55; pietà-like photo of paramilitary police officer carrying Syrian child's dead body (2015), 104; slave ships coming to America as form of, 94, 229; white Protestant hegemony's denunciations of, 174

in-betweenness of black experience in America, 37, 42–44, 48–49

Indian Removal Act (1830), 73

indigenous Americans. *See* Native Americans

individualism, 41